570

NONFICTION February 26, 1977

ACPL ITEM DISCARDED

Captains & Kings

By the same authors

A Guide To Aircraft Ownership
The Tiger Moth Story
Flight Briefing for Pilots (in four volumes)

Neville Birch and Alan Bramson

CAPTAINS & KINGS

Pitman Publishing

First Published 1972

SIR ISAAC PITMAN AND SONS LTD
Pitman House, Parker Street, Kingsway, London WC2B 5PB
PO Box 46038, Portal Street, Nairobi, Kenya

SIR ISAAC PITMAN (AUST) PTY LTD
Pitman House, 158 Bouverie Street, Carlton, Victoria 3053, Australia

PITMAN PUBLISHING COMPANY SA LTD
PO Box 11231, Johannesburg, South Africa

PITMAN PUBLISHING CORPORATION
6 East 43rd Street, New York, NY 10017, USA

SIR ISAAC PITMAN (CANADA) LTD
495 Wellington Street West, Toronto 135, Canada

THE COPP CLARK PUBLISHING COMPANY
517 Wellington Street West, Toronto 135, Canada

© Neville Birch and Alan Bramson 1972

ISBN: 0 273 31569 2

Text set in 12/14 pt Monotype Bembo, printed by photolithography,
and bound in Great Britain at The Pitman Press, Bath
G2—(G.3370:11)

Preface

At one time the journey from London to Edinburgh by coach and horses was an ordeal lasting perhaps several weeks. The railway reduced this to half a day of relative comfort and a modern subsonic jet will devour the route in rather less than one solitary hour. Progress in all endeavours is cumulative and technologically human progress this past fifty years has exceeded all that achieved by mankind over the previous centuries of recorded history.

Aviation has been a leader in this progress and it is perhaps not surprising to find that Royalty throughout the world has taken an active part in its spectacular development. The true value of this contribution to the art may be argued about endlessly but this is beside the point. We are primarily concerned with recording the activities of a wide cross-section of international Royalty, we hope without bias and with a minimum of personal opinion.

Heads of State have many calls on their time and so do Princes and Princesses. Yet once the nature of the book had been explained an interview was granted us at the first available opportunity, for Royal pilots are no different to any other— they like to talk flying. We are under no illusion that but for the common interest of aviation it would not have been possible for us to interview five Kings, nine Princes, two Princesses and many Generals, court officials and other distinguished persons, all within a period of less than fourteen months. The discussions involved some ten thousand miles of travel to palaces as far apart as London and Teheran.

It has been a fascinating experience meeting these royal flyers. Some have made valuable contributions to the world of aviation, some are old with memories like the pages of history, while others are involved in matters of vital consideration to their people. Then there are the young Kings and Princes who have grown up in an age of supersonic aircraft. We thought it was a story that had to be told.

NEVILLE BIRCH
ALAN BRAMSON

The equatorial sun at midday pushed up great banks of cumulus and massive towers of cumulo nimbus.

A day at leisure cloudgazing at castles in the air.

A lone bird soaring and wheeling took me on a flight of fantasy—wings and flight—birds and castles—castles and kings.

Kings and Princes who for adventure, royal duty or force of arms have found themselves captains of aircraft, their stories yet untold.

A line from Rudyard Kipling's 'Recessional' ran through my mind . . . . the Captains and the Kings . . . the birth and inspiration of this book.

NEVILLE BIRCH

Contents

Preface	page v
List of Illustrations	ix
1 PRELUDE · Early Royal Interest	1
The Spanish Royal Houses 2 SPAIN · Sixty Years a Pilot Prince	14
The Royal Family of Belgium 3 BELGIUM · The Adventurous Kings	42
The Shahs of Persia 4 IRAN · Absolute Monarch and Jet Pilot	66
The House of Orange-Nassau 5 HOLLAND · Fighter Pilot to Inspector-General	90
The Chakri Dynasty 6 THAILAND · Pilot Princes and the Flying Princess	116
The Hohenzollerns 7 GERMANY · The Kaiser's Flying Family	140
The Hashemite Kingdoms 8 JORDAN · King in the Desert Sky	162
The Kings of the Hellenes 9 GREECE · In the Path of Daedalus	180
The House of Windsor 10 BRITAIN · Flying Heirs of the Sailor King	196
The Duke of Edinburgh 11 BRITAIN · Like Father, Like Son	228
Index	253

List of Illustrations

The Death of Icarus	*page*	xvi
King Bladud, mythical pioneer aviator		3
Wilbur Wright explains his 'flier' to King Alfonso XIII of Spain		9
The Infante Alfonso of Orleans and Bourbon		13
At the controls of an Antoinette		15
The simulator		18
The airship *España*		20
King Alfonso XIII flying in the *España*		21
Lohner biplane purchased by the Infante for the Spanish-Moroccan War		23
Sophisticated bomb-release on the Lohner		23
King Alfonso XIII at Cuatro Vientos airfield		24
Pilot's brevet of the Spanish Air Force		26
The Royal Palace, Madrid		29
Savoia Marchetti bomber		33
The Infante with his grandson, Prince Alonso		36
With pilots of the U.S. Air Force, flying an A3D jet aircraft from Rota base		38
King Baudouin, jet fighter pilot		42
With one of his personal aircraft		43
Signing the certificate of serviceability before flying the F104 Starfighter		44
Making final adjustments to his 'G' suit		45
Entering the Starfighter		47
Prince Leopold on the occasion of his first flight, with Jean Stampe		49

	page
In the rear cockpit of a Fairey Fox	49
King Leopold in his study	50
King Albert in a Farman F40	53
The Air Gunner King	55
Queen Elizabeth about to join King Albert in an Italian Caproni CA42 bomber	57
King Albert looks on while Queen Elizabeth talks to Belgian pilots after flying over the Front	58
With his personal pilot, Lt. Crombez	59
Queen Elizabeth about to fly over the Western Front	59
King Albert in the Bristol Fighter presented to him by the British Government	61
The Shah of Iran on the flight deck	65
Receiving his pilot's wings from Iran's first pilot	70
Visiting the McDonnell factory in the U.S.A.	73
At the controls of a Phantom jet	75
Preparing to fly an F5 jet at the Northrop factory, California, U.S.A.	76
With Queen Farah in one of the royal helicopters	77
The Shahanshah and Queen Farah with the Crown Prince	78
The Royal Jetstar	80
Entrance to the Golestan Palace, Teheran	82
Throne Room at the Golestan Palace	83
The Shah's coronation: he places the crown on the head of his Queen while Crown Prince Reza looks on	85
The Prince of the Netherlands	89
Soestdijk Palace	91
Prince Bernhard flying a Tiger Moth	93
At General Montgomery's desert caravan	95
The end of a Tiger Moth	97
Preparing for flight	98
With his dog 'Pilot Officer Martin'	99
King Peter of Yugoslavia prepares for his first solo flight	101
Prince Bernhard and King Peter with their flying instructors	101

Leaving the cockpit of a Canadian Hawker Hurricane *page*	103
Undercarriage failure	103
With Air Chief Marshal Sir Sholto Douglas	104
322 Squadron Badge, showing 'Polly Grey'	105
Prince Bernhard with 'Polly Grey'	106
Final briefing in an F104 Starfighter	109
On the flight deck	110
Pilot's wings awarded to Prince Bernhard	111
Prince Birabongse	115
The first aeroplane to fly in Thailand, 1911	117
Prince Birabongse in the famous E.R.A., with Prince Chula Chakrabongse	118
Prince Bira after winning the 1936 International Trophy Race	119
The Gemini at Beirut en route for Bangkok	123
Prince Varanand	127
The end of a Mosquito	130
Prince Varanand in R.A.F. uniform	131
Fighter Combat Leader certificate	132
Princess Galyani learning to fly in a Tiger Moth	135
After gaining her pilot's wings	135
Flying a Chipmunk	135
Jet Pilot Princess	135
Prince Varanand and Princess Galyani arriving at Don Muang Airport, Bangkok	136
Prince Louis Ferdinand of Prussia	139
Prince Louis Ferdinand and Princess Kira with Kaiser Wilhelm II	144
Prince Louis Ferdinand, with his son, admiring 'Preussenadler'	147
Prince Louis Ferdinand Jr at the controls	149
Ex-King Michael of Rumania	150
Prince Henry of Prussia at Brooklands, 1911	155
At the Rhone sailplane competitions of 1924	157
King Hussein of Jordan	161

The Royal Dove	page 165
With Colonel 'Jock' Dalgleish	166
Flying a Vampire jet fighter	167
At the controls of a Jordanian Army helicopter	171
Preparing for a helicopter visit to the outlying settlements	173
King Hussein, airline pilot	175
King Constantine of the Hellenes	179
King Paul	181
The Royal Palace, Athens	182
King Constantine and Queen Anne-Marie in their wedding carriage	185
On a private visit to London	187
King Constantine flying the Royal Gulfstream	188
Prince Don Juan Carlos of Spain in close formation	191
After the flight	191
King Edward VIII and his brother The Duke of York arriving at R.A.F. Mildenhall, 1936	195
Edward, as Prince of Wales, in a Bristol Fighter with Captain Barker	199
About to leave Marseilles aerodrome, 1930	199
The Duke of York, with his flying instructor, Lt. Coryton	200
Settling into the rear cockpit of an Avro 504	200
The Prince of Wales with the 1929 British Schneider Trophy Team	202
After flying over the Schneider Trophy course	203
The Prince's Vickers Viastra	205
Inspecting Handley Page Heyford bombers at Mildenhall	207
The Duke of Windsor standing with his portrait	209
The Duke of Gloucester with the Prince of the Netherlands	211
The Duke of Kent with his children, 1940	213
King George VI	214
Visiting R.A.F. College, Cranwell, 1938	217

Prince William of Gloucester	page 218
With a Chipmunk at Cambridge	221
Alighting from a Gnat advanced jet trainer	221
With a Tiger Moth at Redhill aerodrome	224
Marshal of the Royal Air Force, The Duke of Edinburgh	227
In a Harvard shortly before receiving his wings	230
The Queen and the Duke, with other members of the Royal Family, watching an R.A.F. fly-past at Odiham	231
The Duke of Edinburgh looking over a VC10 airliner with Sir George Edwards	232
In a Turbulent single-seater being started by his equerry	233
With his helicopter	234
Entering a Condor at R.A.F. Benson	235
In Army uniform at the controls	237
Charles, Prince of Wales	239
At the controls of a twin-engined Basset	241
Discussing the Phantom jet fighter	242
After flying the Nimrod at R.A.F. Kinloss	243
Preparing for his parachute jump	244
Moment of departure	245
Receiving his wings at R.A.F. Cranwell	247
Flight Lieutenant the Prince of Wales, qualified R.A.F. pilot	249
Prince Charles with his father after the wings ceremony	250

Acknowledgements

We are grateful to the Kings, Princes and Princesses who most graciously agreed to see us.

We would like to express our appreciation to the Ambassadors, members of their staff, Court Officials and Equerries who made these interviews possible.

We are indebted to Mr. Charles H. Gibbs-Smith, the aviation historian and Air Vice-Marshal Arthur Gould Lee, for their advice. Mr. Andrew Fyall of the *Daily Express* for assisting us with research, Miss Ann C. Tilbury, Photographic Librarian at *Flight International* and Mr. John Blake of the Royal Aero Club for suggesting so many valuable sources of information.

For their help and encouragement, our gratitude to our wives, Patricia and Miriam.

To Tina, Karen & Brian

CHAPTER 1

PRELUDE

Early Royal Interest

Man's quest for the secrets of flight has been a long-drawn-out struggle. His centuries-old ambition to emulate the birds was only satisfied after passing several blind alleys which at the time appeared to offer tantalising prospects for aerial navigation. Early successes brought with them the inevitable protesters who advanced the usual line of argument: 'If God had wanted man to fly he would have been born with wings.' While the rightness of man's desire to fly may be argued about indefinitely, aviation has now been with us for more than fifty years, a permanent feature of modern life. It has developed within living memory from the frail oversized box kite to the supersonic airliner, thanks to the industry and ingenuity of those who followed the pioneers.

Fortunately for the aviation historian, considerable documentary evidence has been left behind by the early aspirants and much has been written about their first attempts to fly. Yet, so far, little has been said of royal patronage or participation; this is rather strange, because during the early experiments emperors, kings and princes were all-powerful and often the prime movers in progress, or its restriction, according to whether or not the activity met with their approval. However, from authoritative papers and works of reference emerges a distinct pattern of royal interest in aviation which may be traced back to the dawn of history, for even then the urge to fly was apparent among men.

The story must commence in Greek mythology with the tale of Daedalus and his son Icarus. Daedalus, a prince of royal Athenian birth, was from all accounts an engineer of some merit. He is said to have invented the wedge, the sail and the saw. It appears that King Minos of Crete commissioned Daedalus and his son to construct a labyrinth for the imprisonment of the Minotaur, his monstrous stepson. But the King of Crete was a man of uncertain temperament, unable to display gratitude towards his architect and builder, who on completion were thrown into the very labyrinth they had created. To effect his escape, Daedalus made two sets of wings from goose feathers, attaching them with wax to the shoulders and arms of himself

LEFT Icarus plunges to disaster while his grief-stricken father Daedalus flies on to freedom. *Reproduced from the Air B.P. Magazine.*

and his son. During the pre-flight briefing, Icarus was warned by his father to avoid flying too near the sun but, like so much parental advice, it went unheeded. During the flight to Turkey, no doubt in a fit of exuberance with the joys of flying, the boy climbed higher and higher, the wax melted in the Mediterranean sun and a grief-stricken Daedalus watched the first-ever recorded air accident as his son plunged into the waters of what is now the Icarian Sea.

Early reports of royal aviators are by no means confined to Greek mythology. Some are of the opinion that the first man to 'fly' was the Emperor Shun of China, said to have lived in the period 2258–2208 B.C. Shun is also credited with the first parachute descent, which happened when his father endeavoured to kill him by setting fire to a granary where he had taken refuge. Legend tells us that with great presence of mind Shun tied together a number of large conical hats made of straw, using them as a parachute for his unscheduled departure from the top of the blazing building.

Kao Yang, a Chinese Emperor in the years A.D. 550–559, became interested in aviation, using prisoners for a series of experiments. The unhappy 'pilots,' fitted with bamboo and paper wings, were made to jump from the hundred-foot-high Tower of the Golden Phoenix which overlooked the old town of Yeh near the Yellow River. According to the records all but one of the prisoners died, very much to the amusement of the Emperor. The exception, a young Prince named Juan Huang-Thou, succeeded in drifting from the tower in a semi-controlled glide before landing near 'The Purple Way.' He was rewarded for his achievement by being starved to death.

Anticipating these events by some four hundred years was the flying meeting arranged by the Emperor Wang Mang. Hard pressed by nomadic warriors on his north-western frontier, and in need of a secret weapon to help keep down the Huns and restore confidence among his people, Wang Mang gathered together all those in his land who professed an ability to fly. One of the participants claimed he could 'fly a distance of one thousand li in a day' and thus spy out the movements of the Huns. For the flying test he took the pinions of a large bird, covered head and body with feathers, and interconnected the contraption with a complicated system of rings and strings. It is claimed that he flew a distance of several hundred paces before falling to the ground, a report that must surely be exaggerated. Although the tests were a practical failure the Emperor sought to gain prestige from the trials and ordered the 'pilots' to be issued with chariots and given senior places in his army.

Another early royal flier was said to be Bladud, mythical tenth King of Britain, founder of the city of Bath and father of the equally mythical King Lear. It appears that King Bladud was something of a magician. Indeed, it became his practice to travel the length and breadth of his kingdom, teaching the art. This culminated in a spectacular flying attempt with the disastrous results so inevitable in the early days of flying experiments. The 1516 edition of Fabyan's *Concordance of Histories* describes the incident thus:

> This Bladud as affermeth y foresayd Auctor Gaufride [a reference to Geoffrey of Monmouth who wrote on the subject in 1147] taught this lore of Negromancy [magic] through his Realme. And fynally take in it suche pryde and presumpcion that he take upon hym to flie into y ayer but he fyll upon the temple of his god Appoly and thereon was all to torne when he had ruled Brytayne by the space of XX yeres leaynge after hym a sone named Leyre.

This very early flight is said to have occurred in the year 852 B.C.

Another reference to King Bladud appears in Taylor's *Memoriall of English Monarchs* (1622), where a simple head-and-shoulders portrait shows him as a man of character, adorned with a remarkably modern service-type moustache. The portrait is accompanied by this verse:

> Bathe was by Bladud to perfection brought
> By Necromanticke Arts, to flye he fought:
> As from a Towre he thought to ſcale the Sky
> He brake his necke becauſe he ſoar'd too high.

The early clergy did much to advance aviation in its formative days. Often they invoked the wrath of the church and had of necessity to continue their experiments in secrecy. Some were killed while attempting to fly. Others had narrow escapes,

King Bladud, mythical pioneer aviator, father of King Lear and founder of the City of Bath.

like Oliver of Malmesbury who, it is recorded, succeeded in gliding from the top of a tower a distance of more than a furlong, whereupon he

> came fluttering down, to the maiming of all his Limbs: yet so conceited of his Art, that he attributed the cause of his fall to the want of a Tail, as birds have, which he forgot to make to his hinder parts.

Thus wrote Milton in his *History of Britain* (1670). The incident is believed to have occurred in A.D. 1020 and the reference to the need of a tail may be regarded as a remarkable appreciation of the vital part this surface must play in the stability of an aircraft.

Another man of the church was Roger Bacon, the first Englishman to write seriously on aeronautics. Bacon was a great believer in experimental science with a strong contempt for 'magic arts.' In A.D. 1250 he wrote:

> It is possible to make Engines for flying, a man sitting in the midst thereof, by turning onely about an Instrument, which moves artificall Wings made to beat the Aire, much after the fashion of a Bird's flight.

He also wrote of hot air for lifting—500 years before the Montgolfier balloon enabled man to fly for the first time.

In the year 1507 King James IV of Scotland sent an embassy to France. John Damian, an Italian by birth and companion to the King, suggested that he could fly to France and so arrive before the embassy. It is hard to credit that Damian really believed himself capable of this feat and equally incredible that the King should share his optimism. Yet Damian made himself wings from the feathers of many hens, and one autumn day hurled himself from the top of Stirling Castle, only to crash into a dung-heap directly below. Surprisingly, he survived the enterprise with only a few broken bones. Writing of the attempt at a later date John Lesley, Bishop of Ross, accused Damian of trying to outdo King Bladud and attributed failure of the project to the fact that 'Hen's feathers had a more natural affinity to return to the dunghill than to support flight.'

It is one thing to design and construct an aeroplane, but quite another matter to fly the machine successfully, a problem anticipated by John Wilkins, Bishop of Chester (1614–72), who attributed lack of success with previous experiments to 'want of Experience and too much Fear.' Until the latter half of the eighteenth century, most attempts at practical flight were based upon bird-like flapping wings. But without an engine the ornithopter was bound to fail, because weight for weight, man is a weakling compared to a bird. When he finally broke the lift barrier and for the first time in history climbed into the air it was in a device without parallel in nature—the balloon—and in the event destined to do little to advance aviation as we know it.

The balloon was born out of the failure of flapping wings, and at a time when experimental science was becoming more acceptable to the peoples of the western world, for the early pioneers worked in the shadow of ridicule most of the time. Often this was earned by the futility of the enterprise, or in some cases a downright lack of commonsense, like that of the early French philosopher who, when told his theory did not accord with the facts retorted, 'Then so much the worse for the facts.'

By the year 1767, Dr. Black, of Edinburgh, was able to suggest that thin bladders filled with 'inflammable air' [hydrogen] would rise. While he was never able to achieve success, some years later one Tiberius Cavallo demonstrated the principle by filling soap bubbles with the gas. In the event it was the non-professional mind which first put man in the air. Two paper makers from Annonay in France, the brothers Stephen and Joseph Montgolfier, drew inspiration from the fire in their grate, driving smoke and burned paper up the chimney. Experiments with a paper balloon held over a flame met with little initial success until one day a woman servant, watching the proceedings with much apprehension and little understanding, came out with one of those profound suggestions which so often elude those more closely involved. 'Why not attach the fire to the balloon?' she asked. Why not indeed, for such an arrangement may now be seen at any hot-air balloon meeting of modern times in this reviving sport.

The first successful prelude to putting man into the air after centuries of failure occurred on 19 September 1783. After rapid progress from little paper globes to larger and still larger balloons, a royal invitation saw the brothers at Versailles with their most ambitious aerostat, a seventy-foot-high balloon elaborately painted with scrolls and heads. A pit had been built for the fire which would pre-heat the balloon, then immediately before the launch a separate heater attached to the neck of the balloon was to be ignited. Around the neck was provided a wicker basket for the passengers, on this occasion a sheep, a duck and a cock.

Before King Louis XVI, Marie Antoinette and a large crowd, the balloon rose to a height of some 1,500 ft., landing eight minutes later, having drifted a distance of just under two miles. It is reported that after the flight, the sheep was feeding undisturbed and the duck was quacking lustily, but the cock had a broken leg, believed to have been caused inadvertently by the sheep. By now an enthusiastic France was counting the days before the first human passenger made an ascent—but who should be the first to fly? Opinion was sharply divided, with the King in favour of sending up prisoners awaiting execution. If they landed safely then they would be pardoned: should they die in the attempt, sentence would have been carried out. Others argued strongly that the opportunity of becoming first man to fly was a great honour, not to be conferred upon prisoners awaiting the guillotine. This reasoning found popular acceptance and in the event Jean François Pilâtre de Rozier, a respected citizen of Metz, became the first pilot in history when, with Giroud de Villette as crew, he ascended to the end of an 80 ft. restraining rope from the Jardin Reveillon in Faubourg St. Antoine on 15 October 1783. This flight, lasting 4 minutes and 25 seconds, must be regarded as the turning point in man's struggle to conquer the air. On the occasion of the first free flight carrying a human crew, the Dauphin placed at the disposal of the Montgolfiers his garden in the Bois de Boulogne. The hot-air balloon was some 74 ft. high, nearly 50 ft. in circumference and equipped with a 15 ft. wicker gallery around the neck, so arranged that Pilâtre de Rozier and his second pilot, the Marquis d'Arlandes, were able to stoke the fire and control the rate of ascent or descent. Thus equipped, they arose on 21 November 1783 to a height of 300 ft. and were airborne for some 25 minutes, extinguishing several minor fires in the envelope before descending. Flying had arrived.

Looking back on these events, it is perhaps surprising that the Montgolfier brothers apparently failed to understand why their balloons were capable of flight. To them it was not because the heated air within the balloon was less dense than the colder surrounding atmosphere. Instead it was the lifting powers of 'buoyant smoke,' the product of a particular type of fuel used both in the heating pit and the balloon fire itself. So convinced were they of this that at the time the smoke was named 'Montgolfier Gas.'

It was not long before the sport of sending up small balloons, usually of the hot-air type, caused a minor boom in the umbrella industry, which had been quick to turn its hand to producing miniature envelopes as a sideline. Royal interest developed early, resulting in various private demonstrations, some not without moments of drama. One such occasion was the unsuccessful attempt by a Brazilian priest named Friar Jusmão to fly a model Montgolfier balloon before the King of Portugal and his distinguished guests. The demonstration culminated in the priest setting fire to the royal curtains.

Ten days after the first ascent of a hot-air balloon, Professor J. A. Charles and the brothers Roberts began a series of flights using the buoyancy of hydrogen instead of hot air, thus avoiding the risk of uncontained fire always present in the early Montgolfier machines. Their first flight, on 1 December 1783, ended in a landing at Nesles, witnessed by the Duc de Chartres, eldest son of the Duc d'Orleans. So impressed was he with the performance of the balloon that Charles was commissioned to build for him a cylindrical machine in which he flew at St-Cloud on 15 July 1784. While in flight the Duc became convinced that his balloon was about to burst and so, displaying more practical ability than pilot skill, he took hold of a flagpole (flags were usually in evidence in balloon flights of this period) and thrust it into the underside of the envelope, making a safe if premature landing at Chalais-Meudon.

At one time there existed considerable rivalry between the two schools of thought, hot-air and hydrogen, but the Montgolfier type of balloon is generally regarded to have gone out of favour after the failure of Godard's massive attempt with an envelope of half a million cubic feet and a heating stove said to have weighed no less than 980 lb.

In an otherwise apathetic Britain, King George III wrote early in October 1783 to Sir Joseph Banks, then President of the Royal Society, offering financial support for experiments with air balloons. The council of that august body declined the royal offer on the grounds that 'no good whatever could result.' However, King George arranged for himself a private demonstration at Windsor Castle on 26 November 1783, when the eminent Swiss scientist Aimé Argand inflated a 30-inch balloon with hydrogen, whereupon the King amused himself by raising and lowering it on the end of a length of string, allowing the balloon to ascend to the Queen and Princesses who were watching from upper windows of the castle. The string was then cut and for some ten minutes the King watched while the balloon climbed out of sight. Such was the King's enthusiasm for balloons that he invited Argand to remain at Windsor Castle for a further two days in order to repeat the demonstration.

One of the first balloonists in Britain was the young Vincent Lunardi, only 22 years old and on the staff of the Neapolitan Ambassador to the Court of St. James. His first flight, on 15 September 1784, drew a large crowd to the Artillery Grounds at Moorfields. The Prince of Wales attended, along with many famous personalities of the day, among them Pitt, Fox, Burke and Lord North. Around 10 a.m. young Lunardi shook hands with the Prince, entered the balloon car with his cat and his dog, then cast off. Very slowly the balloon rose, to the acclamation of the crowd to which he answered by throwing down his flag. Dr. John Sheldon followed the balloon on horseback, first westerly, then northwards, the balloon descending at North Mimms, where Lunardi put his cat in the care of a woman spectator before ascending again. The flight, lasting two hours fifteen minutes and covering a distance of some 24 miles, ended at Standon, Hertfordshire. Many were the demonstrations given by this and other balloonists both in Britain and abroad, and it was a feature common to all countries that almost invariably when a balloon failed to ascend, the crowd became violent and tore it apart. Some of these flights were of scientific merit (for instance the collection by Dr. Jeffries of upper air samples for the great Lord Cavendish during an October flight in 1784); others were more frivolous. There were ascents at night with lighted fireworks (and one or two appropriate accidents); balloons used for advertising; a balloon for the coronation of King George IV, which was the first to use coal gas instead of the more expensive hydrogen; other balloons for the coronation, early in 1814, of King Louis XVIII and on the occasion of the opening of London Bridge by King William IV (1 August 1831).

Ballooning had become something of a sport, too, and it was by no means confined to the heroic males of the day. One intrepid lady achieved a degree of notoriety by knocking down, with her balloon, a number of chimney pots from some of the more fashionable residential areas of London. But the early promise of the balloon soon turned to disappointment. Apart from its limited military use for the purpose of observation during the Franco-Austrian war and a partly successful balloon post, organised to maintain contact with Paris during the Siege of 1870, there was little that could be claimed of the balloon other than its power to rise and descend under limited control, while at the mercy of every wind. All attempts to row, paddle or sail the balloon having failed, it was soon realised that as a means of travelling to a particular destination the aerostat had no future.

While the balloon was earning its brief moments of glory, the supporters of heavier-than-air flight had not been idle and by the mid-eighteen hundreds some antagonism had developed between the two schools of thought. The Duke of Argyll, first president of the Aeronautical Society (now the Royal Aeronautical Society) came down decisively on the side of heavier-than-air flying when he described the balloon as a 'mere toy with no analogy in nature.' Nevertheless, lighter-than-air technology was to die hard, for after many attempts to propel and navigate a balloon had failed, on 24 September 1852 Gifford ascended from the Hippodrome, Paris in an aerostat 144 ft. long, achieving moderate success on the 3 h.p. available from its steam engine. Thus was born the airship, a vehicle destined to attain mammoth proportions and to provide an awe-struck public with some of the most spectacular disasters on record.

Aviation history has been marked by successes and failures of all kinds; hot-air balloons, hydrogen balloons, a combination of both methods; flapping wings, wings that rotated in the horizontal plane and wings designed to gyrate vertically. But the fundamental soundness of a simple fixed wing was bound to prevail, and on 17 December 1903 Orville Wright flew across the windswept sand dunes of Kitty Hawk, North Carolina, U.S.A. It was not much of a flight, no longer in fact than the wing-span of a large modern aircraft. But it had far-reaching effects that in years to come would influence the life of every man on earth. Fortunately for aviation historians the Wright brothers kept adequate records of their experiments, and these, together with various exchanges of correspondence, have been edited by McFarland and published in two volumes entitled *The Wright Papers*. From these it seems clear that it was some years before the outside world fully appreciated the implications of the 'Wright Flyer.'

One of the earliest records of royal interest in their achievements formed the subject of a letter written on 14 February 1906 by Wilbur Wright to the veteran pioneer aviator Octave Chanute. In this he referred to the enquiries made about their 'flyer' by the Kaiser, expressing the opinion that German interest was for the purpose of making war on France. Either by accident or design a section of the French press mistranslated or misquoted a statement attributed to one of the Wright brothers, claiming he had described the Kaiser as 'a disturber of the peace.' The original words were 'The German Emperor is in a truculent mood,' a fair enough comment, for at the time officials close to the Kaiser went in constant fear of losing their jobs. As a result, such was the antagonism of the Kaiser towards the Wrights that it was made clear to them during a visit to Berlin on 5 August 1907 that even if they performed everything claimed of the 'flyer,' Germany would do no business with them. At one

Wilbur Wright explaining the 'flier' to H.M. King Alfonso XIII of Spain. (Pont Long—Saturday, 20 February 1909.)
Royal Aeronautical Society Photo.

stage it was generally believed that the Kaiser had lent his patronage to a German firm which was to manufacture aircraft for war purposes.

In 1907 it was proposed that the Wrights should put on an exhibition before the Czar of Russia for a guaranteed payment of $50,000. The Wrights were to receive 90 per cent of the proceeds from whatever business might follow, but the demonstration never materialised.

On Friday 17 September 1909, before an audience including the Empress of Germany, Prince August Wilhelm and Prince Adalbert, a demonstration flight between two tethered balloons was made by Orville Wright. To Frederick William of Prussia, Crown Prince of Germany, must go the distinction of being the first member of royalty to fly in an aeroplane. A fortnight later, on Saturday 2 October 1909, he accompanied Orville Wright on a ten-minute flight from a field near Potsdam. So impressed with his new experience was the Crown Prince that he presented Orville with a diamond and ruby tie pin incorporating a crown and the letter 'W.'

It is one thing to be a passenger but such an experience can never equal the satisfaction of handling an aircraft and very soon members of the royal houses began to take flying lessons. They were among the earliest of 'Those Magnificent Men in their Flying Machines,' for even in 1911 the qualified pilot was still a rarity, as this list of certificate holders will confirm:

France	353	(First certificate issued to L. Blériot)
Britain	51	(First certificate issued to L. Moore-Brabazon)
Germany	46	
Italy	32	
Belgium	27	
America	26	(First certificate issued to Glenn Curtiss)
Austria	19	
Holland	6	
Switzerland	6	
Denmark	3	
Spain	2	
Sweden	1	

The tradition of royal interest in flying has continued to the point where some of today's kings and princes have as much flying experience as many an airline captain. They were born to the blood royal, yet they were impelled to fly by the same reasons that prompt the humblest pilot—a passionate interest in aircraft and a consuming love of the air.

The Spanish Royal Houses

The Visigoths, a resourceful people from Southern Russia, had by the fifth century established the Royal House in Spain. Their rule continued until the invasion of the Moors, who were eventually driven back to North Africa. Two great Spanish kingdoms emerged, Aragon and Castile. In the fifteenth century King Ferdinand of Aragon married Isabella, heir to the throne of Castile. United Spain prospered and reached a position of growing power under their grandson Charles I, a Habsburg who in 1519 became the Holy Roman Emperor Charles V.

When the Habsburg line died out in 1700 there followed the War of the Spanish Succession. The French House of Bourbon emerged victorious and Louis XIV's younger grandson became Philip V of Spain. Bourbon rule was briefly interrupted by Joseph Bonaparte. In 1833 King Ferdinand VII died, leaving his daughter Isabella as successor, but in 1870 there was a revolt leading to the first Spanish republic and the Queen's exile.

After only four years Isabella's son Don Alfonso, at the time a cadet at Sandhurst, was recalled to Spain and crowned King Alfonso XII. From his marriage to Maria Christina of Habsburg there were two daughters. When the King died in 1885 another child was expected, a boy later to be proclaimed King Alfonso XIII. His mother remained Queen Regent until he reached the age of sixteen.

King Alfonso XIII married the English Princess Victoria Eugénie of Battenberg and while the union cemented relations between Britain and Spain his was nevertheless a turbulent reign. On his Coronation Day, in 1902, he narrowly missed assassination. Then there was trouble with Cuba, insurgence in Catalonia and a long-drawn-out war in Morocco. Political instability in Spain reached such proportions that in 1931 King Alfonso went into exile, leaving a vacuum that led to the civil war. Parliamentary government began a rapid decline and, according to Winston Churchill in Volume 1 of The Second World War, 'Murders began on both sides and the Communist pestilence had reached a point where it could take political opponents in the streets or from their beds and kill them.'

Sotelo, the Conservative leader, was murdered, then General Franco struck against the Communist-infiltrated government, eventually assuming control. He has named Prince Don Juan Carlos, grandson of Alfonso XIII, as the next King of Spain.

This chapter deals with another Alfonso, a cousin of the late King. He is the Infante Don Alfonso of Orleans and Bourbon, a Royal Prince born in Madrid in 1886. In Spain the title 'Infante' is usually confined to children of the reigning monarch but it may be extended by Royal Decree to grandchildren before they are born. Don Alfonso was thus endowed by the Queen Regent, Donna Maria Christina.

RIGHT H.R.H. The Infante Don Alfonso of Orleans and Bourbon, General of the Spanish Air Force and his country's first military pilot.

CHAPTER 2

SPAIN

Sixty Years a Pilot Prince

A tall figure in a white flying overall may often be seen at the Base Aerea Jerez. There is always an admiring group of officers and men nearby and this is hardly surprising because he is the Infante Don Alfonso of Orleans and Bourbon, cousin of the late King Alfonso XIII and still flying his own aeroplane at the age of 85.

When the Infante was first approached in the hope that he would provide material for this book his reply was very much in character:

Many thanks for your letter...

Your proposal to put into a book reminiscences of people who flew at different times seems to me an excellent idea, but there are many sides to flying, from serious facts to funny episodes. I fear I am just an old fossil who likes flying and can contribute very little. I am 83 and have been in our military aviation since it began, but took my ticket before that in France in 1910 on an Antoinette... You could come for a swim and walk on the beach with me and talk. There is lunch here when I am not out and I usually fly Mondays, Wednesdays and Fridays, so no beach on those days.

I only eat a little, at 20.00 hrs. and am in bed at 21.30 hrs. Lunch is at 14.00 hrs. I only wear shorts unless I have a formal lunch or serious visitors.

I write all this to save you wasting your valuable time if the programme does not suit you. It is better than your making the journey and going back sadly saying 'What a crashing bore.'

Clearly here was the promise of a fascinating interview, so on Monday 11 May 1970 there occurred the first of a number of meetings which were to continue over a period of five days.

At home the Infante spends most of his time dressed in shorts and open-neck shirt. He is very active both physically and mentally, and he will give a detailed account of events that occurred sixty or more years ago, often with touches of humour accompanied by a pseudo-wicked twinkle of the eye.

He talks with absolute frankness about his relatives within the great royal houses of Europe and will compare the international character of royalty with 'gipsies, who belong nowhere. My Greek relatives are not Greek at all' he said, again with that twinkle of the eye. 'They're Danes—and that really means Germans.' By this time you have given up trying to follow the family tree! His wife, the Infanta Beatrice, died in 1966 and the Palace in Sanlucar, a large red building with green shutters, has been vacated in favour of a much smaller but nevertheless very beautiful residence called 'Botanico.' It stands in fine gardens some 5 kilometres from the centre of town. Next to the house is an old water-tower now converted to a retreat where the Infante can escape the telephone and attend Mass. Most of the interviews took place in this room, while some half dozen assorted mongrel dogs, all with name tags, waited at the foot of the stairs for their master to appear.

A man in his mid-eighties, sound in mind and limb, is a potent human being, particularly when experience in years has been matched with acute intelligence. Here is a prince who can remember, as a young boy, meeting Gladstone, who has witnessed the transition from horse and carriage to jet travel, who played a leading part in the birth and development of an air force and who is a living part of Spanish history, yet still forward-looking and enthusiastic about life.

The Infante seated at the controls of an Antoinette at Mourmelon, near Paris (23 October 1910.)

One of his great gifts is an outstanding talent for languages. So perfect is his English that a stranger meeting the Infante in London would imagine him to be a retired British army officer. He can put on a Dorset accent and change immediately to convincing Lancashire. He will converse with equal facility in French, Italian and German, so that, with Spanish, the Infante is entirely at home in five languages. When a linguist speaks five languages with native perfection it is hard to imagine what goes on in his mind. Does he think in English, French or his own tongue? Apparently thought is related to shapes; the circular table standing in the window is 'a round object on legs,' the dog occupying too much room by his feet is 'a familiar brown and white friend' and so forth.

In most countries it is considered exceptional to continue flying after the age of 70. Certainly the medical authorities are reluctant even to renew a private pilot's licence when the holder has reached his 'three score years and ten' and no doubt the Spanish authorities are just as careful as those of other countries. Tell anyone that you know an 85-year-old man who continues flying, usually on his own, and you can see their look of disbelief. But there are always exceptions to the general rule, and the Infante is a remarkable exception. Every six months he is required to pass a stringent medical examination, as indeed must all professional pilots. He has the blood pressure of a 25-year-old, his heart and lungs are good and during the five days of the interviews he never wore glasses either for reading or flying.

In between flying he likes to swim from the beach running along the edge of his estate, some few kilometres from Botanico. The house is nearly always filled with visiting relatives, sons, grandsons, granddaughters and great-grandchildren. Lunch is served in the long, narrow dining room. With soup the Infante is handed an instrument best described as three silver-plated metal discs threaded one above the other on a rod passing through their centres. It comes to the table covered in a thin layer of frost, and the gadget is quite baffling to the uninitiated until H.R.H. lowers the three discs into his soup. 'Much better manners than blowing,' he will tell you and certainly the 'Orleans soup cooler Mk. 1' (it is his own idea) works well.

In the Infante's boyhood the horse was still the prime means of private transport. Sail was fighting a losing battle with steam and a heavier-than-air flying machine was yet to lift successfully off the ground when, in 1899, he became a pupil at Beaumont College, Old Windsor, the beginning of five years at a British public school which have left their mark.

Don Alfonso's schooldays in Britain were followed by two years at Heidelberg University reading philosophy, a brief interlude before determining upon a military career which was to continue almost without interruption to the present day. The Infante's introduction to the Army was through the famous academy at Toledo, where he spent two years as an infantry cadet. In 1909 he married the beautiful Princess Beatrice of Great Britain and Ireland, Princess of Saxe-Coburg Gotha (daughter of Queen Victoria's second son, the first Duke of Edinburgh). Almost immediately he became involved in the Spanish–Moroccan war, a long campaign which lasted from 1909 until 1926.

Repeated successful flights by the Wright Brothers and others, many with responsible passengers, had by now convinced even the sceptics of the world that the aeroplane, for all its limitations at the time, had arrived. Foreign governments became interested. In Spain, King Alfonso XIII had meetings with Wilbur Wright and Henry Farman, although he could do no more than sit in the aircraft. Such was the protection exercised over the King by his parliament that there was great opposition, even to his driving a car.

That the King of Spain should in 1909 have been prevented from flying by his senior subjects is, of course, hardly surprising. Airframes were designed by guesswork and engines ran when it was convenient for them and not by request of the pilot, who in any case was regarded as a lunatic, if admittedly an interesting lunatic. What is perhaps surprising is that the King was allowed to fly in the airship *España*, because in the opinion of the Infante it was highly dangerous. The frail craft was propelled by a particularly uncouth petrol engine which belched flames from exhausts situated uncomfortably close to the hydrogen-filled gas-bags. It also had a disenchanting tendency to 'lock on full rudder, despite all opposition from the pilot, when it would fly around in ever decreasing circles.

If the King was not to fly in an aeroplane this did not mean that the potential of the heavier-than-air machine was lost on the Spanish government. At a time when aviation was in its infancy, the young Prince Alfonso went to a flying school. Though America was the birthplace of the modern aeroplane, France was its cradle, for aviation in that country had developed with incredible rapidity. The French fitted wheels to their aeroplanes long before the Wrights discarded their cumbersome skids, with their dependence upon assisted take-off. They constructed engines and airframes with great ingenuity and opened flying schools which found patrons from all over the world. It was to the school at Mourmelon (near Châlons) that the young royal lieutenant reported in 1910.

The modern airline pilot is the end-product of a carefully phased training programme starting with basic flying on a light aeroplane, continuing with multi-engined experience on a small twin, followed by conversion to large transport aircraft where he is allowed to amass experience in the right-hand or second pilot's seat. With operating costs in the region of £800 per hour, it is understandable that where possible radio navigation and procedure training is effected on a simulator

The simulator.

which, although unable to leave the ground, nevertheless represents the flight deck of a real aircraft down to the minutest detail. We tend to regard these simulators, some of which may cost in excess of £500,000, as a modern aid to flying training. It is, therefore, a revelation to learn that in 1910 at Mourmelon they used a simulator out of necessity, because dual control could not be fitted to their training aircraft, the graceful and in its day very advanced Antoinette monoplane.

Pupils were given a demonstration flight in the Antoinette, sitting in a passenger cockpit devoid of controls. Then came the simulator, a barrel-shaped affair bearing a superficial resemblance to the real aeroplane and capable of rocking on its concrete base in the rolling and pitching plane. The pupil sat in the simulator and handled controls similar to those in the Antoinette, their movement being translated into near reality by two *professeurs* (flying instructors) who tilted the contraption appropriately with the aid of long levers. For level flight, pupils were told to position the dummy exhaust pipes so that they appeared 'four fingers' width below the horizon.' Everything was taught on the simulator, including landing. Then came the introduction to the real thing. Engine starting, something of a procedure in those days, had to be mastered first. The Antoinette had a V8 engine of 50 h.p. designed by M. Leon Levavasseur which even today may be regarded as an engineering masterpiece. It was light enough for one man to carry. It had fuel injection, which has only recently been introduced on family cars. It was steam cooled, anticipating the Rolls-Royce Buzzard engine by twenty-five years. The inlet valves opened automatically and the cylinders were encased in copper jackets. Pilots in those days needed an extra pair of hands, for there was a little wheel to control the eight separate fuel pumps and another one for the ignition. In effect there were occasions when it was necessary to use both hands on the engine controls, manipulating them according to the colour of the exhaust smoke and the r.p.m. required. At such times the pilot had to leave the flying controls unattended, so they were made irreversible, remaining in whatever position had been selected by the pilot on his two large wheels, one for 'wing warping' (there were no ailerons) and the other for the elevators. For some reason, chocks were absent from the flying scene in those days and since brakes had yet to be fitted to aircraft it was necessary during starting and engine tests for two men to lie on the ground, each holding a wheel, while awaiting the pilot's signal to 'let go.'

There followed a series of demonstration take-offs and landings by the instructor while the pupil sat in the other cockpit without communication or controls. Then he was let loose on the airfield to try his luck at taxiing, a procedure in those days called 'Rolling.'

The great day finally came when the pupil was considered fit for solo; the engine was started, adjusted to provide the correct smoke, and flying controls set for take-off. Then it happened. A man who had to be both fit and brave lifted the tail of the Antoinette and rested it upon his shoulder, using a cushion to insulate himself from the jolting to come. At a given signal, the two human chocks released the wheels, the pilot opened up the engine to full power and the man holding up the tail ran at full speed until he fell down—this was always part of the take-off! It was necessary to give two forward turns on the elevator wheel, otherwise the tail would sink to the ground. By now the speed would be increasing and it was time to wind back the big elevator wheel until the bumping stopped, indicating that you were off the ground. Pupils were told to climb to the height of the hangars and practise at that level. This, of course, was quite the most dangerous advice imaginable.

'The 'planes were O.K. but we didn't know how to fly them' is the view now expressed by the Infante. For instance, pupils were taught that no bank must be allowed during turns. This he never accepted, for did not the birds bank? And was it not essential to lean to the centre while cycling around a corner? Had he not seen his instructor, none other than the great Latham, repeatedly bank whenever he made a turn? So it was that on his first solo young Lieutenant Orleans banked on every turn.

Then there were the usual 'old wives tales.' Biplanes were believed incapable of turning correctly to the right and various highly complex theories canvassed at the time explained rather unconvincingly why a monoplane could turn both left and right with equal ease. Air disturbances were considered to be fixed: 'There is rough air stationed over that house or those trees' and so forth.

The Antoinette was a big monoplane and beautifully stable, which was quite fortuitous. No instruments of any kind were fitted and the pilot was entirely dependent upon what is now described as the 'Mark I eyeball method'—i.e. he used his natural senses and formed the best assessment he could. The procedure for landing the Antoinette went as follows: having lined up with the field, several turns on the little wheel retarded the ignition and reduced power. When the aircraft descended near the ground five backward turns were given to the large elevator wheel. As the ground came up, a further half turn was added and the ignition still further retarded. Then, just before touchdown, the magnetos were cut by a large switch of the type usually associated with power stations. With luck the great monoplane sank gently and rolled to a halt but the narrow undercarriage made it all too easy to hit the ground with a wing tip. Earlier Antoinettes had a metal propeller and a single large hydraulic shock absorber for the undercarriage. On later examples these were replaced by a wooden propeller and simple elastic cord for the landing gear. On the ground the great wings, each some 8 metres long, were supported by bracing wires. While these were adequate enough for the task they proved quite incapable of withstanding any downdraughts in the air, a condition of flight not understood at the time. On such occasions, the wings invariably parted company with the aircraft, a misfortune which occurred to Laffont, the Chief Flying Instructor, who was killed while the Infante was under training at Mourmelon.

The airship *España*, an unpredictable aerostat, 197 feet long and with its 100 h.p. Panhard engine unable to achieve more than 29 m.p.h. (Cuatro Vientos aerodrome 7 November 1913.)

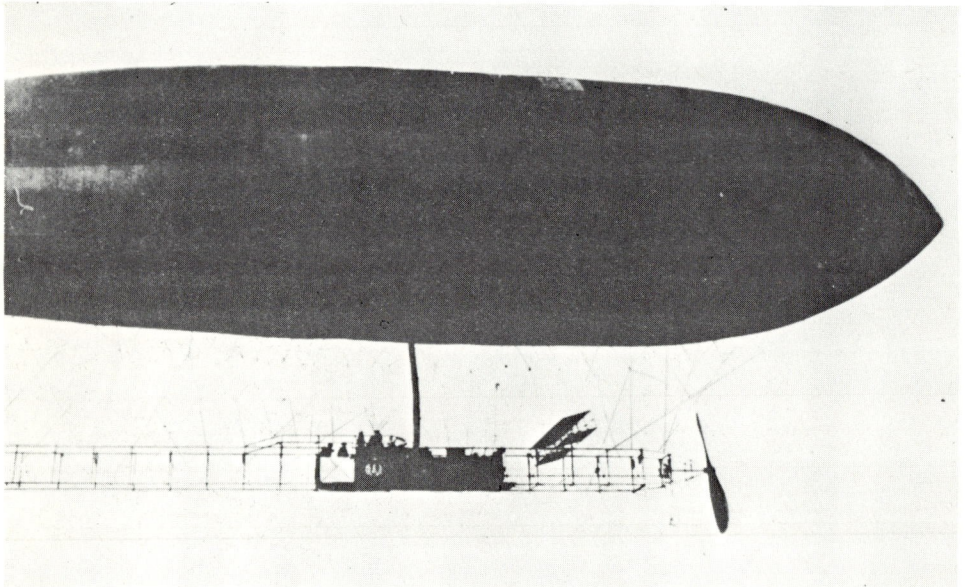

There were no registration letters on aeroplanes in 1910, a period now described by the Infante as 'before the days of passports and slavery.' He did, however, accept one piece of paper with enthusiasm, his aviator's certificate, dated 23 October 1910, which was later transferred by the French to the Spanish Royal Aero Club. Having now returned to Spain, the Infante had become the second of his countrymen to hold a civil pilot's certificate and the first military pilot in Spain. There must be very few men alive today who can claim to have been a founder-member of an air force.

For some years past the Spanish Army had been developing a balloon corps within the engineers branch. It was under the command of a Colonel whose pride and joy was the airship *España* previously mentioned. But now the aeroplane had arrived and Spain, still immersed in the Moroccan war, needed an air force. To whom should they turn for advice other than to the Infante Don Alfonso of Orleans and Bourbon?

In 1912 he had the advantage of two years' flying experience, at a time when pilots were few in number. He went to Vienna, there to purchase on behalf of his country a number of Lohner aircraft, biplanes with swept wings in the modern style with oval steel tube interplane struts, powered by a very reliable 90 h.p. Austro-Daimler straight-six engine. (The manufacturers were long established in the business of making horse-drawn ambulances for the Imperial Austro-Hungarian Army.) By now Spain was training its own pilots with the help of foreign instructors, among

King Alfonso XIII (*left*) flying in the airship *España* accompanied by Captain Kindelan (7 November 1913.)

them two excellent ones, a Frenchman with the unfortunate name of Mauvais and in contrast an Englishman called Truelove.

For the purpose of selecting a suitable training aircraft the Spanish Army conducted a series of tests during December 1912 from Cuatros Vientos, a rough little airfield not far from Madrid that stood baking in the sun at a height of some 3,000 ft. above sea level. King Alfonso was present for the tests, which included a last-minute requirement, the ability to operate into and out of a ploughed field. When this was announced the German entrant said it was impossible to comply and withdrew, but Howard Pixton, flying Bristol-Prier monoplane No. 73, and another demonstration pilot named Busteed, in Bristol Boxkite No. 60, went through the tests without incident. As a result of these tests the Spanish Army purchased three Bristol monoplanes and two Boxkites for the training of its military pilots. The Spanish Treasury department, like those of other nations, regarded the new breed of aviators with the utmost reserve. Although junior in rank, the Infante was able by virtue of his royal status to exert some influence in favour of the fledgling air force, which might otherwise have failed to develop for want of finance.

The Moroccan campaign was now in its third year and the Spanish High Command became interested in the possibility of providing air support for its army in the field. The Lohner aircraft purchased in Austria by the Infante were unarmed and therefore incapable of taking an offensive role. He visited Gotha for discussions with the German General Staff and purchased for the Morocco campaign what must have been among the first bombs designed specifically for delivery by aeroplane. Surprisingly, they had been firmly rejected by the German Army.

By 1913 the Spanish Air Force was ready for operations and the first squadron left Spain for Morocco with twelve machines; four Lohners, four Nieuport monoplanes with rotary engines and four Maurice Farman aircraft powered by 70 h.p. Renault motors. Curiously, the aircraft at the Moroccan war front were under the command of an Irishman, named Captain Kindelan (later General Kindelan and a principal advisor of General Franco during the Civil War). The Infante, now a Lieutenant, had charge of the section of Lohners which gave extremely reliable service, there being no reported cases of engine failure. Nevertheless the Lohner had its limitations. With pilot and one crew it could lift only two 10-kilo bombs or alternatively six of the small $3\frac{1}{2}$-kilo bombs, provided the observer was prepared to carry some of them on his lap! They had a very fine German bomb-sight of advanced design, incorporating

ON FACING PAGE One of the Lohner biplanes purchased by the Infante for the Spanish–Moroccan war. The tall figure in the long greatcoat is Captain Kindelan, the civilian is Colonel Seeley, at the time British Minister of War. Behind him, helmet removed, is the Infante. (Cuatro Vientos aerodrome, 1913.)

BELOW Sophisticated bomb release on the Lohner biplanes used during the Spanish–Moroccan war.

King Alfonso XIII with his Minister of War at Cuatro Vientos military airfield 5 June 1914. Lt. Mayne of the British Royal Flying Corps is explaining the Handley Page bomber to the Spanish King.

a ground glass screen reflecting through a small telescope. An adjustment was provided to compensate for wind effect and, to keep it stable, the entire bomb-sight was mounted in oil-filled shock absorbers. The observer would peer through his highly sophisticated bomb-sight, making corrections for airspeed and drift while guiding his tensed-up pilot into the final bombing run, until the target appeared in the centre of the glass screen. At this point the entire precision performance became nonsense, as the bomb was hastily thrown out of the cockpit—by hand.

A major problem with these early military aircraft was their inability to climb. On occasions the Moors, positioned high in the mountains, were able to look down on the machines flying below and take aim accordingly. One Spanish airman wounded in this way had a bullet enter his shoulder and depart from his backside, incredibly enough without fatal results.

The introduction of a terrible weapon in 1925 hastened the end of this long conflict. Bombs were filled with mustard gas in powdered form and while the Infante describes this part of the campaign as 'very cruel work' he is convinced that the frightful nature of these bombs shortened the war and was thereby instrumental in saving many lives on both sides.

With his command of five languages, it is hardly surprising that in 1921 the Infante was appointed by the King to be president of an important international Congress of Civil Aviation held that year in Madrid. During the same year he became chief instructor of the Spanish Air Force and in this capacity embarked on a tour of England, France and Italy to study the various training methods adopted by their air forces. Although the Germans were prevented from having an air force under the Versailles treaty, the Spanish were helping them to develop a military air arm in secret. With great good humour the Infante explains that his country has suffered at the hands of the English, French and Americans. They like the Germans, however, because although many years ago Spain caused severe damage to their country, Germany has never invaded Spain.

While in Britain Don Alfonso spent some time at Cranwell, Netheravon and Upavon, then the home of the Royal Air Force Central Flying School. He found this to be a stimulating experience, for even at that time the C.F.S. had attained standards which were the envy of the world. In the limited time available, the Infante completed part of the exacting flying instructor's course, coming away deeply impressed with the various training techniques in use at the school. Above all there was the concept of a separate air arm, which to this day moves the Infante to expressions of admiration tinged perhaps with a little envy:

'I had a great friend—he was called Sammy Hoare—and he became Ambassador to Spain later. He was then Minister for Air and I think you ought to put up a statue to him. Sir Samuel Hoare backed one of the greatest geniuses in aviation there had ever been, the great Trenchard. They were the ones who saw aviation as an independent arm of great importance and therefore England was the first country in the world to have an independent Air Force, the first country in the world to have an Air Staff College, and the first country in the world ever to launch a campaign in which the Army and Navy were put under the command of an Air Force. Air Marshal Salmond very kindly lent me many of his papers on the Kirkuk campaign and I tried to persuade the people to do the same thing in Morocco, but failed miserably.'

Although the Spanish Air Force was to remain a branch of the Army until 1936, it did at least have its own aircrew badge, designed by Princess Beatrice, an accomplished painter. Her design for the Air Force brevet was based upon the Egyptian god Osiris, the winged Sun. The original emblem incorporated a pair of hooded

Pilot's brevet of the Spanish Air Force designed by the late Infanta Beatrice.

snakes, but these were replaced by various symbols according to aircrew category: a four-bladed propeller for a pilot, a star for an observer, an anchor for balloon crew and a ship's wheel for airship pilots.

The 'twenties were formative days for air forces all over the world and not unnaturally the lay public was often at a loss to understand some of the mystique inherent in aircraft operation. Spain was no exception. Engines were inclined to stop at inopportune moments and the Spanish Air Force, showing great enterprise, decided to establish a chain of emergency landing grounds. An approach was made to the Mayors of many towns large and small, asking them to assist the air force by marking suitable fields with a large white 'T.' So good was the response that soon the enthusiastic first citizens of Spain were competing with one another in their efforts to provide hospitality for their valiant flying men. One mayor excelled himself by building the 'T' out of rock, the edifice standing some 4 ft. high and guaranteed to wreck a tank, let alone some frail aircraft landing in distress!

It became the practice in many countries to send two or three service aircraft on a flag-showing visit to the more remote towns. Often there were no aerodromes at these towns, but this mattered little because the aircraft of the day were able to land in quite modest fields. At one Spanish town the Mayor himself decided to take charge at the temporary airfield chosen for the visit. Whirling propellers and excited crowds are not compatible, and it had therefore been impressed upon the mayor that on no account was he to allow any spectators on to the field until all three aircraft had completed their landings and were at rest in identical positions. The first machine approached the field, landed and ran across a large rut concealed in the grass.

It promptly nosed over and settled gently on its back. The second aircraft repeated the performance but the third pilot managed to avoid the hazard, coming to rest in a dignified manner, the 'plane on its wheels with the engine ticking over. The crowd was eager to assist the pilots, now scrambling out of the overturned machines, and a few men of action had already started to run across the field. 'Come back' yelled the Mayor, pointing to the one intact aircraft. 'Not yet—wait until he is upside down!'

Hilarious incidents were by no means confined to the spectators. In the air anything could happen, sometimes with tragic results but more often than not without any injury other than a painful loss of dignity. The Infante had his share of emergencies although at no time in his long career as a pilot has he suffered other than superficial injury as a result of a flying accident. Near misses were in abundance, such as the time when a petrol tank burst in the air, leaving a mile long trail of vapour across the sky which by some miracle failed to ignite, in spite of the flames issuing from the engine exhaust.

Some years later, he nearly came to grief while acting as co-pilot in a large Italian seaplane being flown by the Duke of Aosta, a prince of the Italian Royal Family and related to the Infante. They were making for the island of Brioni (once Austrian, then Italian and now part of Yugoslavia) where the Duke had a palace. It was a large seaplane and they had on board quite a party of relations, including several ladies. Suddenly the Infante detected a smell of burning rubber. 'Something smells nasty here' he announced. 'I'm going to go and investigate.' The Infante recalls that none of the royal passengers seemed very upset at his rather laconic announcement 'Look, I'm sorry—we're on fire—don't move!'

The source of the smell was traced to an aluminium battery cover. Flames shot out as it was opened, but the Infante put out the fire with his jacket.

In 1926 the Infante was in command of the air gunnery and combat school at Los Alcazares. For some reason or other grass would not grow at this particular station. They sent for an expert from the Ministry of Agriculture who duly arrived and evolved many theories on the various possible causes of the bald patches around the airfield. During the course of conversation, the Man from the Ministry let it be known that he had, in fact, never been up in aeroplane. All offers to remedy this deficiency met with a firm refusal, until he suddenly spotted a large Dornier Super Wal flying boat moored just off shore, whereupon he announced that as it looked so large and safe he would rather like a ride in it. Ramon Franco, the famous pilot, and brother of General Franco, took the controls. The Infante climbed into the second pilot's seat and the bewildered Man from the Ministry was strapped into the rear gun turret, right in the tail of the aircraft and many yards away from his two pilots.

The Dorner Super Wal had four engines mounted above the wing in tandem pairs.

Shortly after it became airborne, one of the engines decided to catch fire and this rapidly spread to the wing. The Infante remembers the next few moments with great clarity:

> 'The aluminium sheet covering of one wing burned like paper—a wonderful sight! We were a couple of hundred metres high and it seemed to me a half an hour until we reached the water and, thank God, the crash-boat came and put the fire out.'

These were anxious moments, for the fire could have got out of hand all too easily, and a petrol explosion would surely have followed. Right in the bow of the flying boat was an opening used for mooring and the tension was eased by the unexpected appearance of the grass expert, who popped up in the mooring hatch and looked back in horror while they put out the fire. Such is the power of self-preservation that this man, who had never been in an aircraft before, had contrived to run the length of the hull, then dive through a small tunnel leading under the pilots' seats, to emerge out of the foremost hatch rather like the Demon King in a pantomime. The unfortunate man happened to be a pipe smoker, and the Infante jokingly accused him of setting fire to the flying boat. He never flew again!

World affairs in the 1930's were remarkable for their change and instability, and were to culminate in the world conflict which was to break out in 1939. Spain had her share of unrest. Governments were overthrown as early as 1931, but the pattern of events to follow, leading to the Civil War of 1936, meant that the country became a proving-ground, not only for political beliefs, with Communists, Anarchists, Fascists and Falangists joining, but for the use of weapons of war. It was in many ways a rehearsal of the World War to come, a war in which Spain, the earlier victim, was not destined to participate.

King Alfonso had been accepted as ruler until 1931, and the Monarchist party was still a valid force. But, in some of the larger towns, the anti-monarchist parties showed an adverse swing. There were calls for his abdication. This course Alfonso refused to follow, though he agreed to quit the country if this would avoid bloodshed.

On 14 April 1931 the Infante and his wife had joined the King and Queen for lunch at the Madrid Palace. Also present was the Queen's sister-in-law, married to Prince Alexander of Battenberg. Subsequent events which were to change the course of European history are best described by the Infante:

> 'It was a beautiful day and we thought so little of any revolution that we walked about in the garden of the palace till nearly half past four. Then my wife and I drove back home to our house in Madrid. As we went in, the porter said "Your A.D.C. has telephoned and begs you not to waste time going up to any other room or even talking in the hall. You should come straight to the porter's lodge

and telephone him from there immediately." So I rang him and my A.D.C. said "My barber, who lives in the Puerta del Sol (you might call it the Spanish Piccadilly Circus) has told me that the revolution has already started in Spain, with red flags being hoisted on the Ministry of the Interior." So we got into a car and drove back to the palace. I have a full account of this written down, for I accompanied the King on the final journey. We took a ship and went to Marseilles.'

Uppermost in the mind of King Alfonso was revulsion at the thought of having to use his loyal army to subdue the people of Spain. The advice of his ministers and civic leaders must at the time have weighed greatly upon the King. He left Spain, never to return. Was this the correct decision to have taken, and did it prove in the best interest of the very people he so passionately wanted to protect? The Infante feels strongly, looking back over the years, that the King's exile was a mistake. Even if a revolt had commenced on 14 April the use of the troops to maintain order would very likely have caused the loss of perhaps no more than a few hundred lives. As it was, only a few years were to pass before Spain was afflicted by a total civil war,

The Royal Palace, Madrid, viewed from the gardens, where King Alfonso spent his last hours before exile.
London Express Photo.

which cost her a million of her population. The Infante qualifies this opinion with the remark 'You can always prove things later.'

He accompanied his cousin the King into exile. His mother, H.R.H. The Infanta Doña Eulalia of Bourbon and Bourbon, was already in France and the old lady greeted her son with the words 'For you it is the first Republic. I was thrown out with my mamma in 1868!'

Cut off from private sources of income, it was imperative that he should find a job. His three sons, all qualified engineers, were soon in well-paid positions, but he was a man of 46, with only military experience and too old to train as a civil pilot. In more fortunate days, as a Spanish Prince, he had represented his country on a visit to the United States of America. In the course of a conducted tour of the Ford empire he had been introduced to Henry Ford, its founder, so without delay he sent the following telegram from Paris: 'Would like to join your outfit under any conditions.' A reply came advising him to apply to the Asnières factory, situated outside Paris.

Speaking to the staff controller in impeccable French and giving his name as M. Orleans, he got himself on the payroll as a cleaner. His first job was to sweep 110 tarpaulins used for covering tractors awaiting delivery.

At the factory he was moved from one job to another, until one day he was made a salesman. He toured the country at a time when the commercial traveller was regarded as something of a social leper. In his own words:

> 'You will never know what a horrible thing life is until you become a common or garden man-on-the-road. Especially if it is in trucks, because trucks are the lowest class. I started first with tractors, then with spare parts, then trucks and finally, the aristocracy of cars. And then you have sad moments too. I was once picked out with another colleague of mine and we were told to go to the town of Lyons, which in those days was the second largest town in France. They were in trouble with surplus stock and they were trying to sell last year's model with a 20 per cent reduction, when the new one was already on the road. My friend took the odd numbers and I took the even numbers. You went to a house and banged on the door. The servants were extremely rude to you. So you went round to the back door and talked to the cook and tried to get in. After a few weeks of this you felt rather tired!'

One day he was requested by the local sales manager to drive an Englishman named Smith on a tour of the Paris museums and sights. The man asked hundreds of questions on the way round the capital. The Infante returned the visitor to his hotel, thinking little more of the occasion, for he was unaware that Mr. Smith (later Sir Roland Smith) was General Manager of Ford's of Dagenham, the plant near London which even then covered an area of many acres.

Without reason (Ford never gave a reason) he was moved from Paris to Dagenham, where he immediately came to the notice of Sir Percival Perry, Chairman of some fourteen Ford companies, in as many separate countries, all with their own treaties and trade barriers. They moved him in quick succession from one occupation to another: stock checker, foundryman, tallyman, shakeout man, and so on. Then one day he was sent for by Sir Percival. 'Mr. Orleans,' he announced, 'we are very pleased with you. You now need no longer clock in. You may lunch with the departmental heads and you are coming into my office.'

After going through the mill, putting his hand to almost every facet of the industry, and despite a complete absence of business training, less than five years after joining Ford the Infante became Head of the European department, a position of responsibility which he discharged with great dedication. On his eventual return to Spain, he left behind him many friends at Ford, having acquired among other things, a reputation for a phenomenal memory. 'You know what is said of the Bourbon family? They've learned nothing and forgotten nothing' was his comment when reminded of this.

Meanwhile, the Infante contrived to fly a little whenever time and finances allowed. He resented paying £2 an hour for the privilege of handling a Moth when only a few years previously the Spanish Air Force had been paying him to fly the most advanced military aircraft of the period. But now he was in senior management and the work proved of absorbing interest, like the day he received a memo from Sir Percival, written in green ink (only Sir Percival used green ink at Ford's):

> ATTENTION MR. ORLEANS
> No hurry. 8 days to answer.
> 1. Will there be a war in Abyssinia?
> 2. If there is a war in Abyssinia when will it start?
> 3. How long will it last?
> 4. Which side will win?

These were not simple questions to answer. There were many factors to consider, and 'Mr. Orleans' quickly realised that to form an accurate assessment would entail many private talks in high places and of course a lot of travel. So, having persuaded his chairman to give him two weeks to answer, he made off to the Air Ministry, there to study the rainfalls of Abyssinia and the Upper Nile. A royal title and his many influential friends from better days opened doors for the Infante that would have been closed even to the Chairman of Ford's. He had private discussions with Count Grandi, the Italian Ambassador to Britain. He flew to Rome and met General Balbo, head of the Italian Air Force. He made numerous visits to people of importance, working eighteen hours a day and then sent his chairman this reply:

  1. Yes.
  2. After rains.
  3. Until next rains.
  4. Italy.

What was the purpose of this exercise? It arose from the fact that Henry Ford was an ardent pacifist, and Sir Percival knew that the moment war broke out no Ford company would be allowed to sell trucks to either Italy or Abyssinia. However, thousands of trucks and their spare parts were meanwhile being delivered to Egypt and Abyssinia and since the Italians had been buying the same trucks as the Abyssinians, advantage was common to both sides—they could capture one another's trucks in the certain knowledge that spares were available!

Henry Ford was also teetotal—the executives had to obtain special permission before providing the Prince of Wales with a whisky and soda during a royal visit to Dagenham. It is even said as a joke that he took a lease on Ford aerodrome (near Arundel, Sussex) because it was a private airfield unlicensed for drinking. Life at Ford's for Mr. Orleans came to an end when, in 1936, the seeds of disaster planted some five years previously broke through the soil of Spain and erupted into civil war.

Much has been written about this terrible conflict, and in a book of this kind, primarily concerned with the personal stories of royal pilots, it would be inappropriate to engage in deep political controversy. Therefore, at risk of oversimplification, the Spanish Civil War may be described as a conflict between the extreme Left and the fervid Right. On the one hand were the Socialists, Communists and Anarchists endeavouring to maintain control of the country by the Negrin Government. Opposing them was the Army insurrection led by senior officers (some with political affiliations so far to the right that they did not believe in Parliament as an instrument of government) and later the Falange.

The near-Communist Blum government of France shipped anti-aircraft guns to the Left-wing forces and the Russians sent aircraft and tanks. They also posted Marshal Malinovski (later chief of all the Russian armed forces) to the Palace Hotel, Madrid where he took up residence under the assumed name of Manolito. One of his senior colleagues was destined to become a brilliant tank commander—Marshal Koniev, who distinguished himself in the battles around Stalingrad during World War II. The Communist high command in Spain was predominantly Russian, but there was also an International Brigade from many countries.

The anti-Communist forces led by General Franco were supported by aircraft, trained aircrew and naval forces from the Axis powers, Germany and Italy. The

Irish, too, sent men to fight, while Portugal provided the Right with possibly more help than any other nation, since her men were prepared to serve in any unit of the Franco forces. She refused to be a party to the Non-intervention Committee because it was considered primarily to the advantage of the Communist countries and their supporters. She opened her ports to the flow of arms and supplies for the Franco army. So determined was Portugal to thwart the Non-intervention Committee that from time to time her frontier with Spain was moved by up to 20 kilometres. In Britain there were supporters of both sides and such was the depth of emotion created by the conflict that volunteers left to fight in Spain, some for Franco, others in the International Brigade. Some 600,000 men were killed, 300,000 on each side. It was a great tragedy for Spain. It was a great tragedy for humanity.

On 1 August 1936 Don Juan, heir to King Alfonso XIII, entered Spain and made for the front line in the hope of joining the anti-Communist forces. He made contact with the army in an hotel at Avanda de Duero only to be told by an embarrassed Captain of the Civil Guard that on the instructions of General Mola, G.O.C. Northern Army, it was his painful duty to prevent him reaching the front. Don Juan returned to exile. At the same time the Infante was making his way to the nearest flying unit. He arrived in Biarritz and on 2 August went by car to Burgos where he asked to see General Mola. Back came a message to the effect that the General was in bed and could be seen by no-one. Many years previously the Infante and Mola had been brother officers while serving in Morocco. They had also been cadets together at Toledo and the Infante felt moved to protest that he had seen the General in bed often enough in the past. Why couldn't he see him now?

Banned from his country in its struggle against self destruction, the Infante came back to England and rejoined Ford's. It was to be a brief association this time, because very soon he became involved in the Civil War, running an intelligence office in London, at first from the Dorchester Hotel but later at a less conspicuous address. Although he continued to call himself Mr. Orleans, confidential dispatches went to

A Savoia Marchetti bomber used in General Franco's Air Battalions during the Spanish Civil War.

Spain under an assumed Arabic name. Fund raising was an important part of his activities and some of the big sherry importers in London could always be relied upon to donate £20,000 or so when needed.

Most of the arms destined for the Left-wing forces went through Antwerp, and the run to Spain provided some of the Greek shipping lines with lucrative charters (half-payment on loading and the remainder when the arms arrived at the Communist-held Spanish port). A relatively modest sum of money and some convincing talking by the Infante's agents soon persuaded the Greeks that they should allow their ships to be captured by the Franco forces, thus denying arms to the Reds while at the same time ensuring extra business for the shipping companies, for when the arms failed to arrive, the Leftists had to re-order, and the ships had to be chartered again.

During 1937 the Infante was able to return to Spain and command one of the two Franco Air Brigades. Some of his squadrons were equipped with the Savoia 79, a three-engined bomber of Italian origin which in its day was a potent weapon. It had a maximum speed of 320 m.p.h. (520 km/hr) and would cruise over quite long distances at 220 m.p.h. (360 km/hr). The crew of eight had an assortment of defensive armaments at its disposal, including three small cannon which could produce devastating results on another aircraft. The Communists' pilots developed a healthy respect for these cannon and it was therefore possible for the Savoia to go on long reconnaissance or bombing missions without fighter escort. By now the Infante was a Colonel and he applied himself to the leadership of his squadrons with the same sense of purpose that had got him to the top at Ford's. Not content with being a pilot, he flew in every crew position on the Savoia 79 and other 'planes of his brigade. At one time he took part in a bombing raid on Left-wing units of the Spanish fleet lying off Cartagena.

His three sons had also been allowed to return to Spain. The family talent for languages fitted them for liaison duties, the older princes with the Italian Air Force, the youngest being attached to the Germans. It was during an air patrol that Prince Alonso, second son of the Infante, was killed.

When the war ended, Spain was a nation drained of all but a will to live. Hardly a family remained untouched by this terrible conflict, and royalty was no exception. The Infante lost his Madrid home and with it many irreplaceable possessions. But he had returned to Spain, to his air force career and his beloved flying.

During the brief interlude before the commencement of World War II, the Infante was invited to fly in the *Graf Zeppelin* on an experimental cruise from Seville to Rio de Janeiro, returning via Lakenhurst.

Towards the close of 1939 time had expired for Europe, and Franco was resisting pressure from Hitler, whose aim it was to bring Spain into the war on the side of the

Axis powers. While vast areas of the world were aflame the Spanish Air Force went about its daily routine on a peace-time basis and the Infante climbed up the promotion ladder, eventually reaching the rank of Lieutenant-General, the highest attainable in his branch of the Spanish Armed Forces. Generals in Spain are never retired but having reached the mandatory age of 66 during 1952, the Infante transferred to the reserve list. This was merely another milestone in a long career and certainly not the end of his flying.

He often flew a Bucker Jungmeister, a little biplane used by the Germans in great numbers as an elementary trainer. It occupied a similar position in Germany to that of the Tiger Moth in Britain and the Stearman in the U.S.A. The Jungmeister, considered by the Infante to be the most delightful aircraft he has ever flown, was a highly aerobatic little biplane and in it he would often fly upside-down over the circuit of various airfields even in his late seventies.

Some hundred or so kilometres from Jerez are the famous Rio Tinto mines, huge circular man-made holes perhaps a mile and a half in diameter. Started by the Phoenicians and continued by the Romans, these mines have been made deeper and deeper by successive generations. A helter-skelter road and rail track winds its way down from the surface into the depths. The Infante was fascinated by these mines. He would take his Jungmeister down and down in a steep turn, never daring to descend more than half way for fear of being unable to climb out again. One day during 1964 he was discussing the mines with a U.S. Navy pilot who obligingly offered to go down with the Infante in a helicopter. They had descended past some five road levels before the Infante became aware that all was not well: 'Like a fool,' he reports, 'I never noticed there was no traffic on those roads. Then suddenly they started blasting and lumps of minerals and rock twice the size of a large settee came bursting out from all sides. You ought to have seen that chap open up his throttle and pull the stick back.'

While other men in their advancing years (it would be quite incorrect to apply the term 'declining years') devote their every day to reading, stamp-collecting or other worthy but nevertheless inactive hobbies, the Infante maintains his passion for aviation. He is always ready to fly a new type of 'plane and it was not so many years ago that in the company of Chuck Yeager, the famous American test pilot, he tried his hand at a jet fighter. His early flying records were lost during the civil war, but since 1937 he has logged over 4,000 hours as a pilot. Allowing for the years in exile and assuming that he flew only an average of one hundred hours per annum between 1910 and 1937, this brings his total time to well over 6,000 hours—a lot of flying by any standards. At the present time he is totalling between 150–200 hours per year but he will tell you, 'My flying is no use to anyone. My flying is just pure pleasure for myself. If I could find anyone who had invented an underground "worm" I'd immediately go and try that, because I think you must try something new! I like seeing how things work.'

By 1960 the Infante had completed half a century as an active pilot and under the auspices of the Spanish Royal Aero Club, all the flying clubs throughout Spain contributed towards a presentation that was almost as remarkable as the recipient. They gave him an aeroplane! It was a Spanish designed and built light aircraft with two seats called an Aisa 1-11B. The engine is a 90 h.p. Continental and the Aisa will cruise at up to 110 m.p.h. (177 km/hr). It is registered EC-AKL and affectionately referred to by the Infante as 'my private air-pram.' Although he will describe events of sixty years ago with crystal clarity, all the Infante can recall of the presentation at Seville Airport is his acute embarrassment when, in front of a large crowd gathered for the occasion, he broke the canopy lock while entering the aircraft.

Alan Bramson was privileged to go flying with the Infante. Here is the first-hand account of his experience:

It had been arranged that I should meet the Infante at 9 a.m. on a Wednesday morning. Driving through the narrow climbing streets of Sanlucar it was only a few minutes before the green gates of Botanico appeared straight ahead. A long, tree-lined avenue leads to the house, a stone dwelling with walls covered by

The Infante with his grandson Prince Alonso standing before the aeroplane presented to him by the Royal Aero Club of Spain.

multi-coloured climbing foliage and topped by a castellated roof. As I parked the car near the old water-tower the usual little group of servants received me, one accompanying me into the house. The Infante was waiting for me in his study. He was dressed in spotless white flying overalls. Above the left-hand breast pocket were his Spanish air force wings and below them the insignia of a General. As I entered the room he rose from his desk with the agility of a person in active middle age. Donning an air force forage cap he opened the door, insisting that I leave the room first. During five days with the Infante I was never able to persuade him to enter or leave a room before me, as befitted his title, rank and age. 'We have lost everything except our good manners' he used to say.

As we entered a black staff car which carried a general's baton on the right-hand mudguard, a diminutive air force driver came smartly to the salute. Then we were off to the airfield. During the drive the Infante spoke of his days with Ford's. This is a topic which repeatedly entered the conversation during my discussions with him. The Ford organisation has obviously left its mark on the Infante. His non-stop conversation is never boring and at times he delights in poking fun at his royal relatives. He recalls that before the first World War, it was their practice to hold large gatherings when they would be frank to the point of rudeness about each other's countries. According to the Infante, who was often at these parties, they were 'perfectly loyal [to their countries] at the time, just as the General Motors man is perfectly loyal to Ford—if he joins Ford!'

We reached the gate to the Base Aerea Jerez and the Guards came to attention as the barrier was lifted to allow us through. With its dazzling white buildings framed in palm trees, the little air base makes a typically Spanish scene. We drove to a hangar where a small group of Air Force officers and men stood in the shade of the open doors. As the car stopped they sprang to the salute, then came forward and shook the Infante by the hand. A sergeant mechanic busily polished the windscreen of the Aisa, standing checked and ready for flight. It is painted in air force grey, with fluorescent red wing tips and a matching band around the rear fuselage.

The Infante handed me a jockey cap (protection from the Spanish sun). 'How long shall we go for, two hours—three hours? She runs out of fuel after four,' he added with a grin. We started up, taxied out, got a 'green' from the tower (the Infante will not have radio at any price) then took off. Ahead in the distance was a small mountain. 'Have you been to Rio?' my pilot enquired. 'If this were Brazil they would have it moved.'

The Infante believes in the slogan often quoted by old pilots to youngsters under training: 'Fly low and slow!' Most of the time we cruised at 500 to 1,000 ft.,

Flying an A3D jet aircraft from Rota base on 8 August 1961. The Infante with pilots of the U.S. Air Force.

throttled back to 2,000 r.p.m. with the little aeroplane purring along at 76 m.p.h. Arcos appeared to the right of our track, a fairy-tale city built on top of a little mountain, its sheer walls dropping vertically from the very edges of the town. The Infante circled around at rooftop level while I took pictures. Below, stretching for miles in all directions, were olive trees and ahead lay the sea. 'I'm hungry' announced the Infante, unzipping a pocket of his flying suit and removing a small tin of wrapped chocolate bars.

We flew over Cadiz, gleaming white in the sun. The town juts out into the sea on a slender finger of land—in years gone by Nelson divided his fleet so that it could bombard the ancient town from both sides. Just a few minutes' flying distance from Cadiz, at Rota, the Americans have built a combined naval and air base and it was not long before the Infante was providing me with an intimate view of the nuclear submarines in their newly constructed harbour and the assorted collection of jet fighters and long range transport aircraft lined up on the adjacent airfield. I must confess to having felt uneasy when the Infante commenced a series of turns only a few hundred feet above the duty runway. 'Don't they mind you doing this in their circuit?' I asked. 'No,' I was assured, 'they know all about me.'

The Infante pointed to a row of bungalows built on the edge of some cliffs which dropped down to a fine beach perhaps 40 or 50 ft. below. 'When I had the Jungmeister I used to fly upside down over there. Of course I was cheating because I flew just over the edge of the cliffs and there was another 40 or 50 ft. of space below.' Even so, flying inverted at 50 ft. demands a lot of skill and confidence and the Infante was talking of events in his 78th year.

We flew north towards Sanlucar de Barrameda while the Infante allowed himself another bar of chocolate. 'Anti-radar' he said with a grin, as he disposed of the silver paper out of the window (a reference to the World War II practice of releasing vast quantities of silver foil strip for the purpose of confusing enemy radar). Below lay some cotton fields belonging to the Infante and we made one or two low runs while a group of workers waved exuberantly. His estate extends down to the sea where he has the use of an inviting stretch of golden sand. 'I think my grandchildren are there—let's go and have a look,' he announced, turning on one wing tip and descending to below cliff-top level.

At no time was there an anxious moment with the Infante. His judgement of height and distance is perfect, his co-ordination on the controls without fault.

He decided to show me Sanlucar and we flew across the town, passing near my fourteen-storey hotel at about eleventh-floor level. We returned to Jerez air base, announced our presence by flying low over the tower, then my 83-year-old pilot throttled back, lowered the flaps and executed a classic three point landing. As we taxied up to the hangar the officers and men came out to greet us. Their old General climbed down from his little aeroplane, sure of foot and full of energy. There was much saluting and handshaking—a demonstration of real affection that was wonderful to see. But this is hardly surprising, for the Infante is no ordinary man. To know him is to love and admire—and to banish all fear of growing old.

Ask him to-day if he intends to continue flying and you will receive the firm reply 'I go on—I like it.' He looks upon flying as a relaxation, an activity that takes his mind off matters that are to him a source of worry, such as the future of Europe, the management of his estate and the smooth running of a maternity home of which he is patron.

'When I fly I don't have to think about anything. I look at the water catchments, I look at the trains out of sheer habit to see how many trucks there are; I look at the traffic on the roads; I look at the crops; I look at other aeroplanes; I go and look at the various air bases and see what they are playing at.'

There he is—a man in his aeroplane, flying for the sake of the art and, after sixty years, still enjoying the fulfilment of applying his skill to the wings about him.

The Royal Family of Belgium

Throughout its history Belgium has been the battleground for so many major wars that it has aptly been named the 'cockpit of Europe.' Little Belgium, only one-eighth the size of England, so ably defended itself against the Romans that Caesar himself remarked on the courage and fortitude of its people. It was on the banks of the Meuse that the mighty Roman Army came near to defeat before winning a narrow victory and establishing the Roman province of Belgica.

When Rome fell, Belgium became part of the Frankish Empire, then in the twelfth century French influence began and during the next two hundred years Flemish art reached its pinnacle.

During the sixteenth century Belgium suffered at the hand of King Philip of Spain, who set up the Inquisition. After the decline in Spanish power Habsburg rule followed, until the eighteenth century when Belgium was absorbed into the Napoleonic Empire.

The Congress of Vienna united Belgium to Holland as an independent kingdom within the Netherlands but in 1830 there was a revolt when Belgium regained its independence. The ruling Prince Leopold of Saxe-Coburg was then acclaimed King Leopold I of the Belgians, although the new kingdom was not recognised by Holland until nine years later. On his death in 1865 he was succeeded by his son Leopold II who later acquired the Belgian Congo as a personal gift which he presented to his country. His cousin Albert married Queen Victoria of Britain. At the time of his death King Leopold II had no children and in 1909 the Belgian throne went to his nephew Albert, son of Philippe, Count of Flanders.

Albert was a magnificent King, loved by his people, and a colourful character admired by most nations. As a young man living at a time when Europe was engaged in the Industrial Revolution, he was fascinated by the invention and scientific discoveries of the day. He was a keen mountaineer so it is perhaps not surprising that these two interests should have led him to aviation as it then existed, ballooning, for the heavier-than-air machine was yet to arrive in Europe. When he died in 1934 his eldest son became King Leopold III.

Like his father, King Leopold III enjoyed but a few years of peaceful reign before the Belgian tragedy was again enacted. For the second time in twenty-five years the German Army swept through the countryside. After World War II it was some time before the King returned to Belgium, then within ten days he asked Parliament to delegate sovereign powers to his eldest son, King Baudouin, the reigning Monarch.

RIGHT King Baudouin, jet fighter pilot. Note the two squadron badges.

CHAPTER 3

BELGIUM

The Adventurous Kings

The Royal Palace in Brussels is a somewhat dark and formidable edifice, typical of the imposing palaces built during the eighteenth and nineteenth centuries. Entrance is through a grand doorway flanked with pillars in the classic style. The corridors are lined with marble busts of the great of bygone years. Adjacent to the Royal apartment is an ante-room of predominantly gilt and marble decor, the walls hung with paintings: a former king, a famous battle, an historic event. The King's Equerry enters, wearing the uniform of a Commander in the Belgian Navy. There is barely time to exchange a few words of greeting before the double doors of the royal apartment open, and there is King Baudouin of the Belgians, a tall, good-looking young man in his early forties, coming forward with an outstretched hand and a friendly smile. His expression bears little resemblance to the rather solemn portrait of him on the Belgian postage stamps and currency. Some of his good looks, no doubt, have come from his parents: his mother, former Princess Astrid of Sweden, was a notable royal beauty of her day.

After the death of King Albert and the accession to the throne of his father, Prince Baudouin became 'Duc de Brabant,' a title reserved for the Heir to the Throne. He has a sister, Princess Josephine-Charlotte, and a younger brother, Prince Albert. They all lived with their parents in Brussels at the Castle of Stuyvenberg until 1935 when Queen Astrid was killed in a car accident and his father moved with his family to the Castle of Laeken. During the invasion of Belgium in 1940 the royal children were sent out of danger to France and from there to Spain, but soon after the fighting in Belgium was over King Leopold sent for his sons and daughter. They returned early in August of that year.

By the middle of 1944, with Germany rapidly swinging to the defensive, King Leopold III, his second wife Princess Liliane and the royal children were moved on Hitler's orders, first to Hitschtein in Germany and then on to Strobl in the Austrian Tyrol. On 7 May 1945, the day before the end of the War in Europe, they were liberated by the American 7th Army.

RIGHT H.M. King Baudouin with one of his personal aircraft.

This was obviously a turbulent childhood for Baudouin and it was followed by a period of uncertainty in yet another foreign country. In the immediate post-war years, the position of the monarchy in Belgium was a delicate one. In fact King Leopold remained with his family in Switzerland for five years before returning to his country with Prince Baudouin on 22 July 1950. The retirement of the King in favour of his son took place on 17 July 1951, and not many weeks before his 21st birthday Baudouin became King of the Belgians.

It was not the intention, however, to dwell on the past, or on politics, but on flying and the future. The King's first taste of excitement in the air occurred in March 1959, when he was a passenger in a Sikorsky helicopter, flying over the Ardennes. There was a sudden engine failure, at which the pilot instantly went through his emergency drills, putting the Sikorsky into 'autorotation' and descending, like a giant sycamore leaf, to make a heavier than usual landing near Rochefort. With remarkable composure King Baudouin got out, checked that no-one was injured, then took stock of the stricken craft. What must have been an alarming incident, likely if anything to discourage further flying, had the reverse effect. Within a few weeks the King had put into practice his desire to become a pilot, completing his training on a Cessna

Signing the certificate of serviceability before flying the F104G Starfighter.

light aircraft operated by Sabena, the Belgian national airline, at Grimbergen Airport, near Brussels.

Here, one realised, was a man equally at home in the splendour of palaces or the cockpit of a complex modern aircraft. He spoke with enthusiasm of his aviation interest, which although limited to little more than 300 hours as a pilot, has included flying in widely contrasting types of aircraft ranging from the familiar Cessna trainer to the F104G Starfighter, front-line aircraft of the Belgian fighter squadrons, with whom King Baudouin had recently flown at twice the speed of sound. This was at the Belgian Air Force base, Beauvechain, and the occasion was well recorded in photographs of the pre-flight briefing, the signing of the certificate of serviceability or 'form 700' (which owes its title and origin to the British Royal Air Force) and so forth. In them he wears the usual bright fluorescent orange flying suit, decorated with the famous badges of 349 and 350 squadrons. They are typical R.A.F. squadron badges because '349' and '350' were formed in England during the last war and flew on operations with the British. 349 Squadron badge embodies two crossed maces and 350 Squadron features the head of L'Ambiorix, a Belgian warrior reputed to have fought against Julius Caesar. Spur-like objects are attached to the King's

King Baudouin making final adjustments to his 'G' suit, with his ejection 'spurs' for all the world like a modern knight in armour.

flying boots for the purpose of retracting the legs instantly, so avoiding injury in the event of an emergency ejection and descent by parachute. A blue-grey 'G' suit completes the rig-out. This is an inflating device which restricts circulation around the legs and abdomen, thus delaying a 'blackout' when the pilot executes a manoeuvre at speed which may in effect temporarily increase his weight by six or more times.

Here then was a real twentieth-century monarch, outstanding in his orange flying suit resplendent with heraldic devices and carrying a shiny white jet pilot's 'bone dome,' the modern equivalent of the knight of old, the horse now replaced by a jet fighter. After he had entered the aircraft, there was a final briefing from the Squadron Commander, who explained the multitude of warning lights and the procedure to be adopted should it prove necessary to leave the aircraft in a hurry. The days have gone when an engine's failure meant landing in the largest available field. Now it is a case of 'get out and use your parachute,' because the modern jet fighter will plough its way through field after field before coming to a halt, very likely in many small pieces. Recalling his experience at the controls of an F104, the King confessed his relief that none of the countless red warning lights had illuminated during the flight, but the tremendous surge of power when the Starfighter accelerated down the runway, then climbed steeply to its cruising altitude, made it an exhilarating occasion he will always remember.

The Starfighter has proved something of a 'widowmaker' for some air forces unaccustomed to operating such advanced equipment, and King Baudouin therefore feels justifiably proud of his country's fine safety record with these formidable aircraft. His Air Force is an integral part of N.A.T.O., whose headquarters have for some years been in Belgium.

On 15 December 1960, the King married Doña Fabiola de Mora y Aragon. Queen Fabiola's ancestors were members of the ancient Royal families of Aragon and Navarre. Her Majesty is fluent in Spanish, French, Dutch, English and German. For State visits the royal couple use a DC6 of the Belgian Air Force, but on internal flights King Baudouin pilots himself in his own private light twin-engined aircraft, which he handles with skill. Returning from one such State visit, to Persia, the King and Queen were relaxing in the Royal DC6, late at night over the Mediterranean, when the King's Aide was summoned to the flight deck. The captain told him there was a malfunction of the port outer engine which he had shut down and feathered. Although he would be happy to continue the journey to Brussels on the remaining three engines, he felt it his duty to land at Nice. Hasty arrangements were made with an airline to fly the King and Queen incognito to Paris, where the royal couple would be met by the Air Force and flown to Brussels. On arrival at le Bourget the King spotted a small 'plane and commented with surprise 'There's good taste—

Entering the Starfighter.

someone has painted their aircraft in my colour scheme.' It was in fact his own aeroplane, and it flew him to Brussels!

The demanding nature of his duties as Head of State makes it impossible for the King to keep abreast of all the constant changes and improvements in aviation. Even the practical consideration of keeping up regular flying practice presents difficulties, because there are times when several weeks or even months may elapse between one flight and the next. Even so, his personal pilot never ceases to wonder at the King's ability to go through the various checks and vital actions as though he were flying every day of the week. He flies on the Airways where keeping altitude and position must be of the highest standard of accuracy to avoid any chance of conflict with commercial and other aircraft, and this in turn means that the King must be able to use modern radio aids. These are a study in themselves. Although His Majesty insisted that he should not be portrayed as a very good pilot, enquiries from a variety of sources, military and civil, revealed him to be both able and professional in his approach to flying. This and conversations with him made it clear that he has inherited from his father King Leopold, and perhaps even more from King

Albert his grandfather, a sense of adventure shown by his delight in speed and his love of sport.

King Albert's Europe and present-day Europe represent two different worlds. The tumultuous period between was destined for Leopold III, retired King and father of the reigning Monarch.

King Leopold III lives today in a country residence near Waterloo, a palace of great beauty standing in walled gardens and approached through tree-lined lanes. The palace lodge is manned by uniformed guards. A short drive from the gates leads to a large forecourt, with the palace extending around three of its sides. The entrance hall is dominated by a life-sized painting of King Leopold I. Without ceremony a pair of double doors was opened to reveal the library, a room of grand proportions, perhaps nearly sixty feet in length. King Leopold was dressed casually in a brown sports jacket and slacks. Though born in 1901, he has the look of an athletic man in his late fifties. He now devotes much of his time to his lifelong passion, geography, and in particular the study and conservation of the primitive tribes of the Amazon. His expeditions are far from amateur: full use is made of aircraft, particularly helicopters, and since the King is a talented photographer a very fine pictorial record of his discoveries is kept. In a large basement room at the palace are some 14,000 colour slides arranged according to an elaborate filing system. There is a large screen on one wall and the room may best be described as a workplace, where the King can enjoy the results of fine photography and study in detail the visible aspects of his researches.

On the ground floor immediately above the projection room is the study, its walls covered with photographs taken by the King, the desk deep in maps and reference books. In the adjacent library is an enormous globe which once stood in King Leopold's nursery. As a child he would spend many hours studying its detailed surface, selecting the places he hoped to visit in manhood. Now that most of these ambitions have been fulfilled, it was suggested to His Majesty that he had the best job anyone could wish for—to be retired—for only a professional explorer or a wealthy retired person could follow such an interest. For the first time during the interview King Leopold smiled. 'I am beginning to think that also,' he replied.

Leopold as a Prince was deeply interested in the technological advancements of his day, as his father had been. He went first to Eton, continuing his education at the *Ecole Royale Militaire* (the Belgian officers' Academy). In an age when every youngster expects his own car almost as a birthright, it is worth noting that the youthful Leopold, heir to the throne of Belgium, had to content himself with a motorcycle. It had its advantages—as a young man he visited the United States and was invited to ride in formation with the New York 'speed cops.' They loaned him one

RIGHT Prince Leopold (later King Leopold III) with Lt. Jean Stampe on the occasion of his first flight from the grounds of the King's country residence in August 1919.

BELOW Prince Leopold in the rear cockpit of a Fairey Fox.

of their massive Indian motor-cycles for the occasion. It was seven years before he was allowed his own car and could develop a taste for fast motoring, which found fulfilment in a Bugatti.

Shortly after his solo crossing of the Atlantic in 1928, Charles Lindbergh visited Belgium and was met at the Gare du Midi in Brussels by the Crown Prince, who later presented the lone flyer with a gold medal at a ceremony held at the city hall. Lindbergh's achievement had re-kindled in Leopold an interest in aviation which lay dormant, barely below the surface, but he was never to become a pilot. The idea was unthinkable.

It may seem strange that King Albert, his father, himself such an adventurous man, should have denied the role of pilot to Leopold. He had himself had some experience of parental restraint. Yet, when still Crown Prince, Albert realised his own ambition to fly on a calm day, as early as the year 1907, in a balloon. He stood in a wicker basket, which had been covered in canvas more to give a sense of security than for any other purpose. Ballast was jettisoned and the hydrogen-filled balloon slowly and uncertainly lifted its occupants into the air. Thus concluded many weeks of preparation conducted in great secrecy, because King Leopold II, like so many parents, regarded the aerial exploits of the day with the greatest reserve and would almost certainly have forbidden the flight had he known of his nephew's intentions. However, on that day the young Prince experienced his *baptême de l'air*!

The idea of flying was developing rapidly and he was often to be seen at the 'aerial displays' of the day, in deep discussion with the leading flyers: Blériot, Voisin, Farman and the Wright brothers. Some of the early Belgian aviators had already made a name for themselves as racing drivers or champion motor-cyclists. M. Olieslagers, a motor-cyclist turned aviator, was taken by surprise one day when Prince Albert entered his hangar and asked what was required to become a pilot. 'Plenty of courage, your Majesty, plenty of patience,' he replied. Then, pointing to his badly damaged flying machine, he added 'and plenty of money, too.' This conversation took place at a flying meeting held on 30 October 1909 at the plain of Wilryck. Prince Albert asked the pioneer aviator, the Comte de La Vaulx, if he would take him flying in his small dirigible *Zodiac*. The surrounding officers were horrified at this unexpected request, but no-one would dare contradict the Prince. In any case, he had now made up his mind and was already climbing into the open gondola, a complex network of wire-braced ash beams which hung precariously from a multitude of cables, its only connection with the airship above. The Prince

LEFT H.M. King Leopold, the retired Belgian monarch (*right*) discussing photography with Neville Birch.
Alan Bramson Photo.

watched while La Vaulx cast off. *Zodiac* rose to a height of 100 metres, flew for some 30 minutes, then Prince Albert returned to Brussels, in the certain knowledge that he would face the displeasure of the King, but more than ever air-minded.

In 1909 King Leopold II died, and was succeeded on 17 December by the Prince. The new King, a tall imposing figure with fair hair, the fresh complexion of a Saxe-Coburg and an upright, military bearing, had a talent for bridging the gap between the throne and the people without undermining the dignity of his royal position.

On the occasion of his Coronation with the beautiful Queen Elizabeth, a young Belgian lad and his friends looked down on the scene from a second-floor window. With them they had a large number of paper aeroplanes, and at a given signal, as the royal carriage passed by, they launched them by the dozen into the street below. The boy, Willy Coppens, would in years to come meet his King on the field of battle, and by that time he would be a fighter-pilot of national hero-status. Never again were paper aeroplanes to assume such significance.

But there were to be only five years of peace before the Great War broke out. In the early stages, Belgium was quickly overrun by German troops and the Belgian Army was left with nothing but a small area of land to defend. Only the air pilots were able to see their enemy-occupied country beyond the front line. Once again Belgium had become the 'Cockpit of Europe.'

The King became a regular visitor to his Air Force, flying in French and British aircraft as well as those of his own country, to such an extent that although the Belgian Parliament never allowed him to become a pilot, he was to his subjects their 'Flying Monarch,' a title justly deserved, since King Albert flew against the enemy, sometimes towering behind a machine gun in an open cockpit. At one time there were not many more than a hundred or so Belgian military pilots at front-line readiness and pressure was such that it was often necessary to fly daily on operations without a break. Belgian fighters were based on a series of low-lying fields at Moëres. The elite of their fighter squadrons, equipped with Nieuport biplanes, was commanded by Colonel Jacquet. On 18 March 1917 he received orders to prepare their only two-seater, a Farman F 40 with a 130 h.p. Renault engine and so much wire bracing that it was irreverently known by the pilots as the 'hen coop.' The squadron's personnel waited in anticipation while Jacquet sent for the largest fur-lined suit that could be found. Then the King arrived and it all became clear—he intended to fly with his leading fighter squadron. He put on the fur-lined suit, then Jacquet loaned him his newest flying helmet, as yet only faintly smelling of the castor oil lubricant flung into the slipstream by the aero engines of the time.

The lumbering Farman took off, staggered into the climb, then made for the front line, surrounded by the best pilots of the squadron in their Nieuport fighters. They flew in formation over the German trenches, attracting salvo after salvo of anti-aircraft fire which burst around them like little black clouds. Throughout this pandemonium King Albert stood in the open gun turret, peering through his goggles at his battered country some 10,000 ft. below. It was a grey, hazy and depressing sort of day but the experience deepened the King's interest in his Air Force, won for him great admiration and stirred the Belgian pilots to still greater efforts. They had defied the enemy in the presence of their King.

On 7 April 1917, King Albert again flew with Jacquet, this time penetrating an enemy sector patrolled by the feared and respected Von Richthofen 'circus.' Although the escorting Belgian fighter pilots were later reported to have been somewhat nervous (not without good reason) one of them performed a series of loops at

King Albert of the Belgians in the front cockpit of a Farman F40. The picture was probably taken early in the first World War.

low level over the infantry-filled German trenches 'just to show the King.' A third flight was made on 5 June, this time in a Handley-Page 0/200 bomber of the British Royal Naval Air Service. King Albert was so impressed by these massive twin-engined biplanes, spanning more than 100 ft., that within a few days another flight was arranged so that he could be accompanied by the Queen.

The King would arrive unexpectedly at his front line squadrons, mixing informally with the mechanics and air crews. He would listen to their exploits, his enormous frame brimming with scarcely-contained enthusiasm, eyes twinkling behind his pince-nez. Jacquet, who was commanding his elite squadron at Moëres airfield, lived with his wife at a rented farmhouse nearby. Service regulations strictly forbade pilots being accompanied by their wives while on duty and it was therefore with some embarrassment that Jacquet looked up from his garden one day to find the tall figure of his King beaming down at him over the hedge. 'Your Majesty has caught me out, I have my wife here' admitted Jacquet. With great understanding and a knowing smile, the King replied 'I'm here with mine, too.' Before the Belgian fighter ace had collected his wits the King was bidding him farewell and striding away towards the hangars.

Willy Coppens, who on that Coronation day had showered the King and Queen with paper aeroplanes, had by now fulfilled his ambition and become a fighter pilot in the Belgian Air Force. On 6 July 1917 (which incidentally was his birthday) Coppens, having a few hours off duty, went into the local town to buy chocolate. Back at the squadron they searched for him in vain—King Albert had arrived and asked for a flight in a Sopwith. Another pilot, Lieutenant Jacques de Meeus, took his place and Willy Coppens later wrote, 'All my life I shall regret my greed—I missed the only occasion offered me to pilot my sovereign.'

The Sopwith, surrounded by a formation of other aircraft, flew over Nieuport, Dixmude and Ypres, but King Albert wanted to fly deep into German-held territory. Apparently the squadron had been warned of His Majesty's zeal on these occasions and instructed to take every precaution. De Meeus pretended not to hear. Back on the ground the monarch told his pilots that the flight had been a successful reconnaisance but for his taste, rather tame, whereupon one of the pilots begged the King not to risk his luck any further in future. 'So you think it would be nice to die in one's bed?' replied the King. Nine days later, Jacques de Meeus was shot down and killed behind the enemy lines.

King Albert had on several occasions ascended in the basket of an observation

RIGHT The Air Gunner King. Seated behind a machine gun, King Albert prepares to fly over enemy lines in a Spad of the Belgian Air Force.

balloon. This was generally regarded as a hazardous occupation and once nearly proved fatal for the King, who narrowly escaped being shot down by a German fighter aircraft. But his main interest was the aircraft of his Air Force and those of the Allies. The King and Queen Elizabeth of the Belgians flew with leading pilots of the French *Cigognes* group and later accepted the squadron emblem, a stork, but his exploits with the British were to bring him greater honours.

No. 48 Squadron of the Royal Flying Corps (later to become the Royal Air Force) was commanded by Major Shield, then only 22 years old. The Squadron was based on Leffrinckoucke and equipped with the Bristol Fighter, an outstanding biplane and without doubt the best two-seater fighter on either side during the Great War. It could dive vertically at a speed of over 230 m.p.h., when the noise was 'like a million sabres cleaving the air' (thus wrote Major Vere Bettington from France on 13 May 1917). Nearly 5,000 were built in Britain alone. Of the two examples still in existence, one is on display at the Imperial War Museum, London, and the other, immaculate example (service number D8096) is maintained in flying condition by the Shuttleworth Trust, a source of great pleasure to the air-minded public whenever it performs at air displays.

His Majesty King Albert visited 48 Squadron early in 1918 and in great secrecy occupied the gunner's cockpit of a Bristol Fighter with Major Shield as pilot, flying over Ostend, twelve miles into enemy-occupied territory. This, and a subsequent flight, were after the war to inspire a unique occasion; but more of this later.

On 5 July 1918, a car flying the pennant of the Commander-in-Chief of the Belgian Army drove up to a seaplane squadron at Calais. The fighter dock, known at the time as 'The Gull Puddle,' was the home of two squadrons, one French and the other Belgian. Their tasks were hunting U-Boats, protecting convoys and searching for mines. King Albert and Queen Elizabeth had tea in the officers' mess and then boarded two seaplanes. Lieut.-Pilot Tony Orta was detailed to fly the King, and the Queen's pilot was Adjutant-Pilot Victor Boin.

They took off at 18.25, their destination unknown to all but the pilots and a handful of senior officers. After 50 minutes the 'planes landed together at a point between Dover and Folkestone, where an Admiralty launch awaited their arrival. A French seaplane, sent ahead for the purpose, radioed the message to Calais: 'Mission Accomplished.' The Belgian sovereigns were welcomed aboard the launch by Admiral Sir Roger Keyes (of the legendary Zeebrugge raid) with the words, 'Here are the first royalty to have arrived on an English coast from the skies.' The Queen took photographs of the occasion, unique because, war or no war, the Belgian King and Queen had arrived to attend the Silver Wedding celebrations of King George V and Queen Mary. When he later introduced the royal couple to the cheering crowds of London,

Queen Elizabeth about to join King Albert, seen here in the cockpit of a Caproni C.A.42, a massive Italian Triplane bomber built in 1917. Wing span nearly 100 feet, more than 20 feet high and with its three 400 h.p. engines (one behind the cockpits) capable of only 88 m.p.h. The bomb racks are visible below the cockpits.

Lord Curzon commented, 'The exploit of the Belgian sovereigns at the height of war will remain an historic one.'

Queen Elizabeth certainly endeared herself to the British public. She was regarded as one of the great beauties of her time and a contemporary writer described her as 'frail and delicate, with the sweet unselfconsciously attractive eyes of a young girl, and a fine sensitive mouth.' That she had flown across the Channel, defying war conditions in a seaplane so noisy that her only communication with the pilot was by means of a slate and chalk, earned her the admiration of the British, French and Belgian peoples.

During the closing stages of the Great War, when Belgium saw the liberation of her despoiled country, the King and Queen were to travel a great deal by air. By now the King's personal pilot was Lieut.-Aviator Henri Crombez and it was more or less daily routine for a Spad biplane to land on the beach opposite the royal villa at La Panne. The tall figure of the King would stride across the sands, fastening his fur-lined flying suit. He would climb aboard the aircraft, pull down goggles over his pince-nez and take off for the Front. On Armistice Day, 11 November 1918, Crombez piloted the Queen over the battlefields, while King Albert flew alongside as a passenger in another Spad. By now Queen Elizabeth was very much at ease in an aeroplane and before landing, Her Majesty asked Crombez to do a spin. Those

King Albert (in Army cap) looks on while Queen Elizabeth (facing camera in flying helmet) talks to Belgian pilots after flying over the front during the 1914-1918 war.

LEFT King Albert with his personal pilot, Lt. Crombez.

BELOW Queen Elizabeth about to fly over the Western Front.

watching from the ground were horrified to see the Spad with its royal passenger flick into a nose-down attitude, spiralling through a number of turns before recovering. Queen Elizabeth was the first royal person to experience the manoeuvre which only a few years previously had been regarded as highly dangerous and possibly fatal. To commemorate the incident, the Queen presented Crombez with a cigarette-case depicting the outline of a spinning aircraft, and bearing her initials and the date.

After the Armistice the King was committed to spending a lot of his time in Brussels. The palace still bore evidence of its wartime use as a hospital and in consequence Queen Elizabeth lived most of the time at La Panne. Twice a week, King Albert would fly to the royal villa in a Spad piloted by Lieut. Jean Stampe, who by then had taken over from Crombez as his personal pilot. As they approached La Panne, the lone figure of the Queen would be seen waiting on the sands and Stampe would arrange his landing so that the Spad came to rest opposite Her Majesty. As the propeller jerked to a halt King Albert would jump from the gunner's cockpit to embrace his wife. It was, of course, necessary to ensure that a landing would coincide with low tide, but on one occasion Stampe arrived a few moments too early. He flew over the beach at low level, looking for the shallowest water, chose his landing area, then touched down, the big wheels of the Spad sending up cascades of spray. Leaning forward from the rear cockpit the King slapped his pilot vigorously on the shoulder, pointing in alarm to the spray. Being rather short-sighted, he was convinced Stampe had landed by mistake in the sea, where they would presumably sink at any moment.

The friendships of war are often enduring, particularly those resulting from a life-and-death incident. In November 1917, for example, Willy Coppens had come to the assistance of a lone British aircraft engaged in a running battle with seven German fighters. It later transpired that the British pilot was the same Major Shield who several months after flew King Albert over the enemy lines in a Bristol Fighter. Shortly after the Armistice, Willy Coppens visited London and met Major Shield, who told him of the King's secret flights with 48 Squadron. The discussion ranged over his other sorties in aircraft of the Belgian, French and British Air Forces, then someone suggested that King Albert should be awarded a decoration in recognition of his bravery. Air Marshal Sir Hugh (later Lord) Trenchard readily approved of the idea, which was soon put into effect.

On 24 February 1921 H.R.H. The Duke of York (later King George VI) sailed into Ostend in the destroyer *Walker*. He boarded King Albert's personal railway carriage that afternoon and was later met by the King of the Belgians at a private railway station within the estate of the Royal Chateau of Laeken, where he was to stay. On the following afternoon an informal ceremony took place at the British Embassy in Brussels, when the Duke of York presented to King Albert the Distinguished Flying Cross in recognition of 'His Majesty's personal gallantry in flying over the enemy lines in 1918.' To this day he remains the only monarch of any nationality to have been awarded the decoration.

There is no doubt that, from its inception, King Albert readily accepted the aeroplane as a practical means of transport. In the years of peace following the Great War he used it increasingly for what must then have been regarded as long-distance flights to various parts of the world. He flew from Casablanca to Toulouse, for example, then boarded a night train to Paris where Lieutenant Stampe piloted him to Brussels, the entire journey being completed in a day and a half; perhaps not very fast by modern standards, but this was more than forty years ago. He flew across the Syrian desert to Mesopotamia, along the Nile to the Belgian Congo and across great areas of South America, all before the advent of modern radio aids and reliable engines. He was the first monarch to fly in an autogyro and by his example the King encouraged civil aviation in his country, making possible the formation of Belgium's renowned national airline, Sabena.

King Albert in the Bristol Fighter presented to him by the British Government at the end of the war. The Queen was given a similar aircraft.

Jean Stampe was to found the aircraft manufacturing company Stampe et Renard, whose most famous design, the SV4 Stampe biplane, was used in considerable numbers as an elementary trainer for the Belgian and French Air Forces. After World War II, it won conspicuous success in international aerobatic competitions and to this day is considered by the knowledgeable sporting pilot to handle superbly. Now over eighty years of age and retired, Stampe lives in a house of his own design situated in a fashionable part of Brussels. It is a home which reflects the eventful years when he was a pioneer pilot to an outstanding monarch. There are awards, mementos and numerous signed photographs of the Belgian royal family. Among them is a picture taken in August 1919 of King Albert's son, Leopold, standing in front of a DH4 light bomber of the type used during the Great War. M. Stampe has some delightful stories of his days as King Albert's personal pilot.

One morning, for example, he was flying the King to the fashionable resort of Deauville. In those days there was no airfield at Deauville, although the beach was sometimes used by visiting aircraft. For once he had failed to check his tide tables, with the result that on arrival he was acutely embarrassed to find the beach covered by the sea. He turned inland and very soon flew over a small airfield, with a solitary hangar, called Tancarville. They landed to find the place deserted, so Stampe requested his King to remain with the aircraft while he went to find transport into Deauville. He came across an angler, fishing beside his little 5 h.p. open car, and asked if he would be kind enough to drive him and his passenger to Le Havre. Fishermen dislike having their sport interrupted and this one was no exception. He refused—that is, until Stampe told him the name of his passenger. Then he hastily packed up his fishing tackle, jumped into his car and drove to the airfield to find King Albert waiting patiently by the aeroplane. During the drive to Le Havre, the angler kept apologising for his fishing clothes. Despite the King's repeated assurances that he quite understood, and was in any case grateful for the lift, the car stopped at his cottage where they all got out. There were three downstairs rooms but no hall. With much ceremony the King and Stampe were invited to sit in the middle room. Then panic seemed to reign around them. Bells rang and people scurried from room to room, carrying various pieces of clothing. Finally the angler presented himself in triumph, this time clad in a frock coat and white tie and announcing himself at last properly dressed to drive His Majesty to Le Havre.

King Albert of the Belgians, loved and admired by so many besides his own countrymen, died tragically on 17 February 1934 while climbing a rock-face at Marche-les-Dames. He had inspired his nation in time of war, and when peace returned had laid the foundations for civil aviation in Belgium. He was Europe's loss.

The Shahs of Persia

Iran, the modern name for ancient Persia, is a country considerably greater in area than Britain, France and both East and West Germany combined. Its recorded history goes back some six thousand years and the Persian Monarchy, the oldest in the world, has existed over two and a half millenia. Here is a civilisation that makes Magna Carta, the Roman Empire, the Ancient Britons and even the Bible seem recent by comparison; the great book contains many references to the Medes and the Persians.

Persia was blessed with some outstanding Kings: Cyrus, Cambyses, Xerxes and Darius who ruled an empire which, at its height, stretched from Afghanistan to the Aegean. Alexander the Great, who later conquered Persia, modelled himself on Cyrus. In the sixteenth century, Shah Abbas the Great was to develop friendly relations with the Christian West.

After the seventeenth century Persia declined and for several hundred years floundered under the doubtful leadership of succeeding Shahs of the Quajar dynasty.

Early in the 1920s Colonel Reza Khan of the Iranian Cossack Brigade summarily dismissed the Czarist officers then dominating the Persian Army, sending them back to Russia before a weak, ineffectual Teheran government could react to his boldness. He rose quickly to the rank of General, then, gathering around him a contingent of like-minded officers, early in 1921 Reza Khan marched on Teheran at the head of a relatively small army. Ahmad Shah Quajar, the reigning monarch, offered little resistance and soon agreed to radical changes of government and the appointment of Reza Khan as Minister of War and Supreme Commander of the Persian Armed Forces. Within two years he became Prime Minister and it was during this time that Ahmad Shah went on an 'indefinite' visit to Europe, never to return.

The stage was set for extraordinary events. Would Persia follow the example of neighbouring Turkey and become a republic or could another King be found? Popular opinion called for the end of the Quajar dynasty and by special act of parliament Reza Khan was proclaimed Reza Shah Pahlavi, an elected King who was to lead Persia back on the road to its former splendour. He was tough. He was ruthless and he cut like a scythe through deep-seated prejudice and corruption.

During World War II Iran was invaded by Britain and Russia and the proud Reza Shah rejected the role of 'puppet monarch,' handing the throne to his older son Crown Prince Mohammad, the present Shah of Iran.

RIGHT His Imperial Majesty the Shahanshah of Iran on the flight deck.

CHAPTER 4

IRAN

Absolute Monarch and Jet Pilot

Night over the desert in a modern jet is something to remember, for there is no scene like the barren wastes of Africa or the Middle East, viewed from 30,000 to 40,000 ft., when no moon shines. The velvet carpet of darkness below may be broken by the flaring burn-off from an oil rig, or the twinkling lights of a tiny settlement—lights unreal and without human association to passengers in the jet above: home to the Bedouins on the ground.

Less than two hours after departure from Beirut your jet is on finals, at Teheran, whistling in towards the runway with flaps fully extended. The engines subside, revealing the true silence of flight while the monster skims along with its great wheels a few inches from the runway. A protesting squeal, as motionless rubber makes contact with fast moving tarmac, and you are on the ground. Most of the procedure—immigration, customs—follows the usual pattern of airports. Only outside does the babble of many languages arise, including the traditional cry of the taxi-driver, jockeying for position and imploring you to give preference to his cab to take you to your hotel. Pandemonium, yes, but everywhere smiles, smiles right from immigration to the greetings of the hotel staff, because the Iranian is a friendly and hospitable soul.

Long before other peoples had began to form into nations Persia was a homeland of scholars, scientists and poets like Omar Khayyam. It is bordered to the north by the Caspian Sea: along its southern shores lie the Persian Gulf and the Gulf of Oman. To the west are the arid deserts of Turkey and Iraq and in the east are the highlands and mountainous regions of Afghanistan and Pakistan.

It is a land of many climates, from desert heat to mountain snow, with all manner of temperate and tropical crops. Economically the country may be regarded as the bridge between East and West, crossed as it was by the ancient silk caravans as they made their way to and from China. Certainly this early link between the ancient worlds of Asia and a semi-barbaric Europe placed Persia in the role of defender: defender of the ancient oriental civilisation and of the trade route between East and West—the very route later used by Marco Polo in the thirteenth century. Because of their unique position the ancient Persians developed two outstanding talents, an ability to organise themselves into a highly developed civilisation and a military genius which for centuries withstood the might of the Roman Empire.

By the sixth century B.C., the Persians had won for themselves an Empire stretching from Afghanistan in the east to the Aegean Sea in the west. They freed the Jews from Babylonian oppression and were renowned for their mercy and generosity. Today, Iran is one of the few Muslim countries to tolerate the Jew.

Alexander the Great, by defeating Darius III, brought the first Persian Empire to an end. Conquests by other invaders followed, but not only did the Persian people somehow survive: the disasters were regarded as opportunities to learn new trades and talents, especially in architecture. When Islam came to Persia and attempted to influence its famous style, the Persians replied by exerting their own talents, particularly on places of worship. There is no more beautiful mosque, many say, than a Persian mosque. 'A Sovereign without religion is a tyrant' was a quotation of one of Persia's early rulers. Another saying, of Abalshea the Sassarian, runs: 'There can be no power without an army: no army without wealth: no wealth without agriculture, and no agriculture without justice.'

Other Kings had other interests and one of them, strangely enough, is said to have been concerned with flight. According to the 'King-Book,' or 'Shah-Nameh,' written in the tenth century, King Kai Kaoos became obsessed with the problem of achieving human flight without attaching wings to the body.

He consulted his personal astrologer, who advised him thus: 'Four young eagles must be stolen from the nest, reared with care and fed upon invigorating food.' This was the first requirement. While the birds were under training, as it were, an 'aircraft' was to be constructed from 'Alose-Wood' and designed in the form of a single seat within four uprights, supporting a curved roof.

When the time came for the first test flight, the King sat in the pilot's seat with a goblet of wine before him. The four Eagles were then tethered with leads to the corners of the 'aircraft.' Meanwhile, four large pieces of goat's meat had been fixed in its roof above their heads. On becoming hungry, the eagles flew up to the extent of their leads which then prevented them reaching the food. They continued flapping and raised the frame with its royal pilot until, the chronicler continues:

'After a long and fruitless exertion their strength failed them and the whole fabric came tumbling down from the sky, and fell upon a dreary solitude in the Kingdom of Chin, where Kai Kaoos was left a prey to hunger, alone and in utter despair.'

In inventions, Persia was a land of many 'firsts'; the first observatory, the first sundials, the first calibration of a clock face and the first rose trees. In medieval times the Persian Avicenna founded the science of antibiotics. Persia reached the zenith of her power and achievements in the seventeenth century. Then followed a decline, in part self-inflicted, which was to reduce this wealthy and talented people to a nation of paupers and beggars. The once-great Persia remained a country of apathy and corruption for several hundred years.

But enough of ancient history. The object of this modern journey from London was to meet the present Shah, and to learn of his beliefs, his hopes for the future of his land, and his personal love of it. As he has expressed himself in his autobiography *Mission for My Country*:

> 'We cherish the gardens and the poetry and the family life and hospitality of Persia. We acclaim this land of deserts and snow-capped mountains, of cedars and plane trees and rivers and fountains and tiled water-courses, and roses and orange blossoms and nightingales, and we are proud of our political and social institutions.'

This was the opportunity to talk with the Shah about something close to his heart, a subject on which he can speak with equal authority—flying. It is amusing to contrast King Kai Kaoos and his four unfortunate eagles with a King who has nearly 7,000 hours' flying in his log-book, and as much pilot experience as many an airline pilot. There are two royal palaces in Iran. In Teheran is the Golestan palace, the official residence. The summer residence, the Palace of Saheb Gharaniyeh, is situated a little way outside Teheran, where the countryside rises towards the mountains. As can be imagined, the gardens are the first sight to impress any visitor. Wide, perfectly-kept lawns are flanked by tropical flowers and trees. There is a scent of jasmine and roses in the air, and all is peace and quiet. A red-carpeted marble staircase leads to this palace, where officials wait to conduct the visitor to the apartment of the Marshal of the Court, a most imposing room with priceless carpets. There is a large rosewood desk, adorned with a huge vase of perfect roses, and an enormous gilt chandelier. It has over a hundred lights, but today, of course, they are electric. The grey carpet is Wilton. The walls, of pale blue, have a satin finish to them, and the scarlet chairs have gold tassels.

In these beautiful surroundings the visitor enjoys a traditional Persian welcome, lemon tea, while simple rules of protocol are explained.

Double doors of enormous proportions are opened, a quiet introduction is spoken by one of the officials, then the visitor is ushered into a magnificent room of gilt and glass to find the Shahanshah (King of Kings) of Iran coming towards him. He is of medium height, slim waisted and broad shouldered with a shock of grey hair which he later explains was acquired prematurely in the course of his demanding royal duties.

There is no need for an interpreter. At times the Shah pauses for a while before replying, but when the answer or the explanation comes, it is in perfect English, and flows on as if almost an extension of his thoughts. Here and there a little humour breaks through the conversation—especially when he is talking of his early flying predicaments. At times, however, his expression will change dramatically while he describes some incident out of one of the more difficult times in his life and it is not hard to imagine him controlling, with a word here and glance there, a meeting of quarrelsome ministers.

True, his mode of living now has a majestic splendour about it, and the power he wields in his country is supreme; but these cannot hide a past that has often been uphill, and a life which has at times been not without personal danger.

Under the guidance of strict but nevertheless kindly parents, and a devoted French governess, Madame Arfa, the Shah enjoyed a happy childhood at home, where his favourite game was 'cops and robbers.' His love of flying and deep interest in aviation probably started not long after he became Crown Prince, when he was taken to see a Junkers passenger aircraft then operating between Teheran and the Soviet border. His father, the formidable Reza Shah, believed in what he called a 'manly' education for his son. He founded an elementary military school especially for him, at which the boys wore uniforms, and were subject to military discipline. His leisure hours, according to his own book, were largely occupied in building models with his Meccano set. Later he continued his education at Lausanne, in Switzerland. Here a talent for sport, particularly tennis, soon became evident. He became fluent in French and English and made a general success of his studies. Throughout his schooling, despite the change to a European background, he maintained a deep interest in the history of his country and this knowledge was to prove invaluable to him in the task ahead. He gained his diploma, and returned to Teheran in 1936. Although Reza Shah had founded the Persian Air Force in 1928 and clearly recognised the importance of the aeroplane as an instrument of defence he resolutely forbade flying by the Crown Prince. The Army was another matter and he was encouraged to join the Military Academy in Teheran where he later took a commission.

Meanwhile Reza Shah was rapidly changing the old order. Persia had fallen behind the advancing peoples of the world by the equivalent of several hundred years. There were no real communications and most of the population was illiterate. In 1927, Reza Shah undertook what has sometimes been described as the most remarkable feat of railway engineering ever to be completed, the Trans-Iranian Railway—900 miles through some of the most impassable country in the world. It involved the construction of 4,100 bridges and the cutting of 224 tunnels, yet the railway was in use within eight years and completed by 1939. The entire project was financed without foreign aid. So Persia began to move into the twentieth century, led by a King of her own choosing.

Ironically it was the Trans-Iranian Railway which was partly to cause the downfall of Reza Shah. By 1941 the conflict between Germany and the Allies had embraced Russia and Iran, still a poor country, found herself an innocent bystander in the line of fire.

The bystander was soon to be involved. Soviet Union forces advanced from the north, since their Arctic supply route had been severely cut by bad weather and Nazi attacks. The British and Persian Governments exchanged notes, in which Reza Shah asked Britain to explain herself. The explanation, never given by Churchill or Wavell, was that the Allies were determined to make use of the railway to supply the hard-pressed Red Army. But words were useless: force followed, despite the Shah's protests, and the British moved in from the south. The Crown Prince, according to his biographer, Ramesh Sanghvi, was prepared to mediate, but his father was a proud man. On 16 September 1941, he sent for his son, to meet him for the last time, and to abdicate in his favour, saying 'I cannot be the nominal head of an occupied land, to be dictated to by a minor English or Russian officer.'

It is against this tragic, war-torn background that His Imperial Majesty Mohammad Reza Shah Pahlavi became Shahanshah of Iran. It was a daunting prospect

The Shah of Iran receiving his pilot's wings from General Ahmud Nakhjevan, Iran's first pilot.

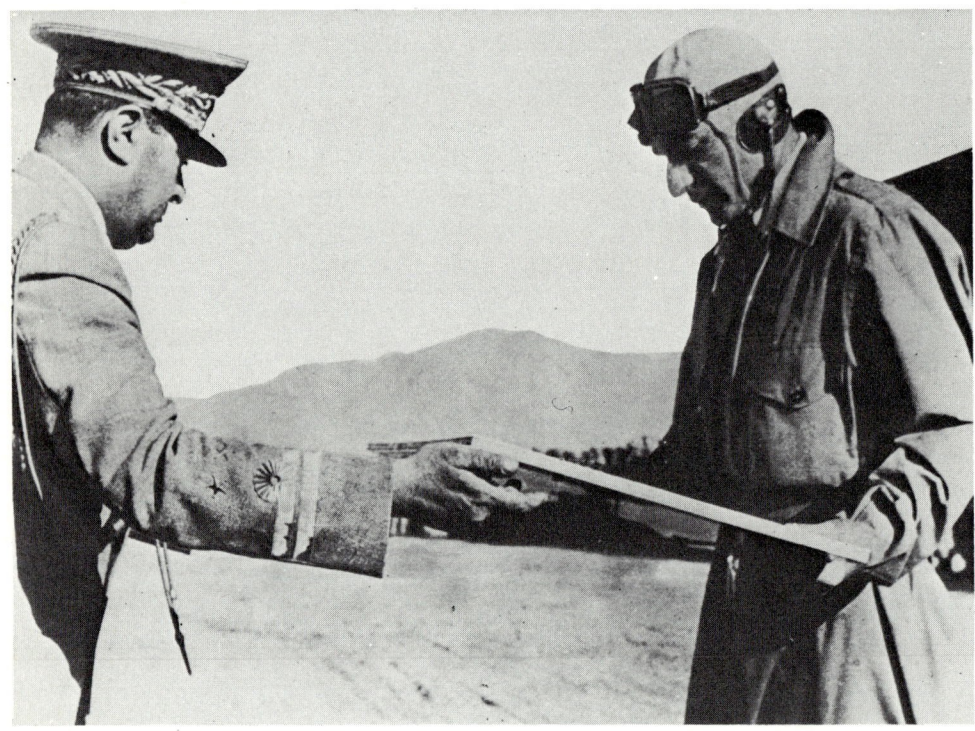

for a young man in his twenty-first year. For several days the succession was not even recognised by the Allies.

He was the inheritor of a poor backward country under the heel of two powers who, however friendly and whatever the circumstances, were nevertheless occupying his Kingdom by force of arms. His was a country of more than twenty million subjects, of many religions and several tongues. Because the work of his father was incomplete, the majority were poor and illiterate. Corruption among the rich and intrigue among religious and political institutions were rife. Such was the economic position that it is doubtful whether at the time Persia could have afforded a coronation but in any case the thought was far from the mind of the young Shah, who refused to be crowned 'ruler of a nation of beggars.' The coronation could wait; he was committed to the rebuilding of a nation.

It was on 18 September 1942 that Wendell Wilkie, President Roosevelt's envoy to Persia, gave the Shah his first flight in an aeroplane. The occasion was particularly memorable because it coincided with the first anniversary of his accession to the throne. Whether or not he was impressed by the experience, it was not until 1945 that the Shah could find the time to start learning to fly. His first lessons were in that universal workhorse, the Tiger Moth, a masterpiece of rule-of-thumb engineering which had emerged without proper drawings from the parts of other de Havilland aircraft. The little biplane found a home in nearly every corner of the world and trained more pilots than anyone would dare to compute.

Some nine thousand examples were produced and the law of averages demands that when large numbers of aeroplanes are flown by even greater numbers of pilots, many of them under training, sooner or later an accident is bound to occur. While accidents in modern jet aircraft can on occasions prove serious, incidents of this kind in Tiger Moths are sometimes funny.

The Tiger is no respecter of persons, royal or otherwise, and such was the case when in 1948 the Shah flew to Kuhrang near Isfahan, where a dam was under construction. The nearby airstrip was small—so what better choice of aircraft than the royal Tiger Moth? It was decided that on the return journey His Imperial Majesty would give a lift to the local military commander, a General of the Iranian Army. It seems almost blasphemous to say this of a Tiger Moth, but within ten minutes of take-off, the engine stopped! It was a mountainous region, and the ravine below looked unhealthy by aeroplane standards: but there was no alternative. With little height remaining, the royal pilot found himself hard pressed to clear a barrier of rather solid-looking rock before landing in an area of relative flatness. It was unfortunate that a large boulder should have been in the way, for this tore off the undercarriage, leaving the Tiger to continue the landing run on its belly. Before the dust could settle another boulder executed the *coup de grace*. The aeroplane stood on its nose, then slowly and deliberately settled on to its back. The Shah's own description of the scene ends:

'There we were, hanging by our seat belts in the open cockpits, but neither of us had suffered so much as a scratch. I remember the scene amused me so much I burst out laughing but my upside-down companion did not think it was so funny!'

Meanwhile, an accompanying Tiger had landed at a nearby village, and the Shah was anxiously looking at his watch, protesting that he must have the other aeroplane, to keep a tennis appointment in Isfahan. By now a crowd had gathered. It is not every day that the good country folk of the mountainous regions have an opportunity of seeing their Shah, and rare indeed that he should emerge from an inverted Tiger Moth expressing concern about missing a tennis match. A group of officers and senior citizens from the village were doing their utmost to persuade His Imperial Majesty not to attempt a departure from the unprepared ground, and when the Shah climbed aboard the other Tiger and started the engine they all lay down in front of the aircraft to prevent him taking off. This dramatic gesture, intended to safeguard their King, was successful as far as flying was concerned, but the Shah then drove to his tennis in a borrowed car, at times flat out on an unmade road—and, incidentally, won his match!

On another occasion, this time while flying a twin-engined Beechcraft, the Shah found himself surrounded by mountains, as the weather began to deteriorate. The situation was the more unnerving because he was in a ravine with little room to manoeuvre. Every instinct told him to hold up the nose of his aircraft in a frantic effort to outclimb the fast-rising ground below and so clear the mountains at the end of the ravine. By now the airspeed was low—too near stalling for comfort. The point of no return had arrived, bringing with it a choice of evils: the chance of hitting the mountain ridge ahead or the risk of making a steep turn away at low airspeed, the classic ingredients for a spin, which in a twin-engined aircraft would prove difficult or even impossible to stop. The Shah made a quick choice, threw the wheel over into a steep turn and as the Beechcraft shuddered around on the verge of aerodynamic collapse a wing tip narrowly missed one side of the ravine—but he was through.

The margin between a frightening experience and total disaster is sometimes very small. It is quite impartial, knowing no social distinctions, recognising only human

RIGHT Visiting the McDonnell factory in the U.S.A.

error, or a combination of factors so often called luck. As a boy the Shah had contracted typhoid, diphtheria and malaria. The illnesses made him face the possibilities of death, and this seems to have had a profound effect on his character. It strengthened a religious belief which has continued through his life. Perhaps his faith was reinforced by deliverance in those two flying incidents. Certainly he is firmly convinced that the famous attempt on his life failed by the will of God.

The attempted assassination occurred on the anniversary of the foundation, by his late father, of Teheran University. A ceremony had been arranged during February 1949 and the Shah was to address the students. He arrived dressed for the occasion in his military uniform and was about to enter the Faculty of Law building when a gunman, masquerading as a press photographer, drew a revolver, took aim and fired at short range. The first three bullets went through the Shah's army cap, miraculously without touching him. A fourth shot then entered his right cheekbone and departed from under his nose. The next few seconds are described by the Shah in his book *Mission for My Country*:

'What should I do? Shall I jump on him? But if I approach him, I shall become a better target. Shall I run away? Then I shall become a perfect target to be shot in the back.'

By now the man was but two paces away, aiming at the heart. Although grievously wounded the Shah, maintaining both courage and presence of mind, began weaving about like a shadow-boxer. Another shot, this time wounding him in the shoulder—then the gun jammed. The would-be assassin tried to escape but by now the crowd had gathered its wits and closed in. Within seconds, he was killed by some infuriated Army officers, which meant that the identity of his organisation was never discovered. He may have been a member of the Tudeh party, a Communist guerrilla movement active in Persia at that time, or one of the Fadyan, a fanatical religious community. To this day the Shah's bloodstained uniform may be seen on display at the Iranian Officers' Club in Teheran.

It would be very easy to build up a picture of the Shah as a rather serious person, courageous, deeply religious and perhaps so involved in the urgencies of state affairs that he had neither time nor inclination to let off steam and enjoy himself. In fact the Persian King has in his character a good measure of what the British Royal Air Force call 'the press-on spirit'. He is always ready to try his hand at a new type of plane, however large or complex. At one time he flew a private Hawker Hurricane,

RIGHT The Shah of Iran at the controls of a Phantom jet.

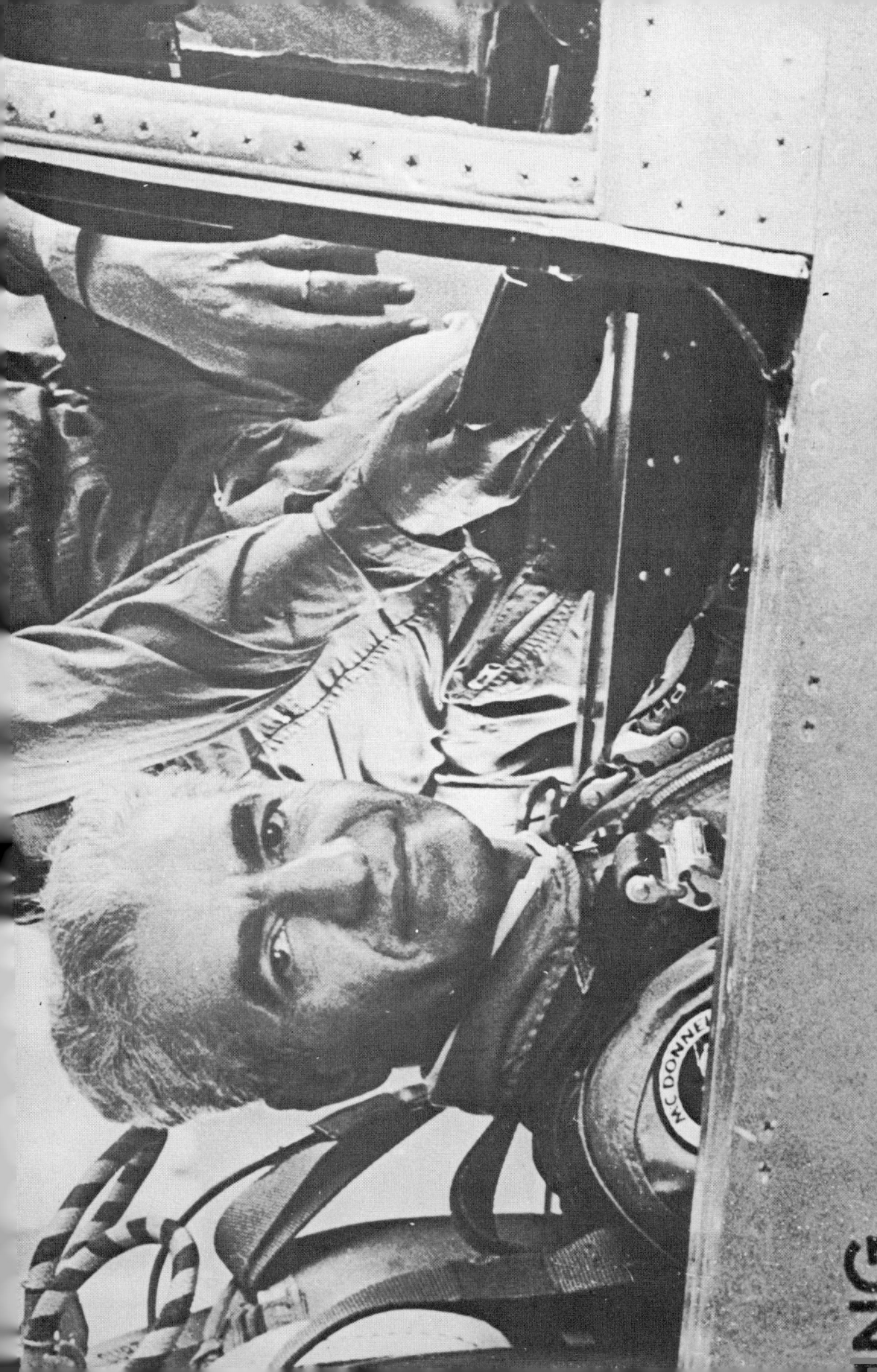

Preparing to fly an F5 jet at the Northrop factory in California.

the immortal Battle of Britain fighter. In August 1948 he accompanied Bill Waterton, chief test pilot of the Gloster Aircraft Company, in a Meteor Mk. VII twin-jet fighter. This was the company demonstration model, painted carmine and cream and carrying civil registration letters G–AKPK. The Shah, dressed in a tan-coloured flying suit, flew the aircraft and kept repeating 'wonderful—wonderful' as they 'beat up' the airfield at Filton, near Bristol.

Some years later he bought a Morane-Saulnier Paris, an exciting little four-seat aircraft powered by two small jet engines. It was many years ahead of its time, capable of speeds well in excess of 400 m.p.h. The Shah would delight in flying his little jet at high speed near the ground, causing anxiety among his friends and consternation at the palace. His friend and fellow-flyer Prince Bernhard of the Netherlands begged him to give up this practice, reminding him that a split-second error while flying low in a fast aircraft can prove 'incredibly final.'

During his Tiger Moth days the Shah took up aerobatics and gliding, but these sporting aspects of flying have of necessity given way to the more serious business of

RIGHT His Imperial Majesty with Queen Farah in one of the Royal helicopters.

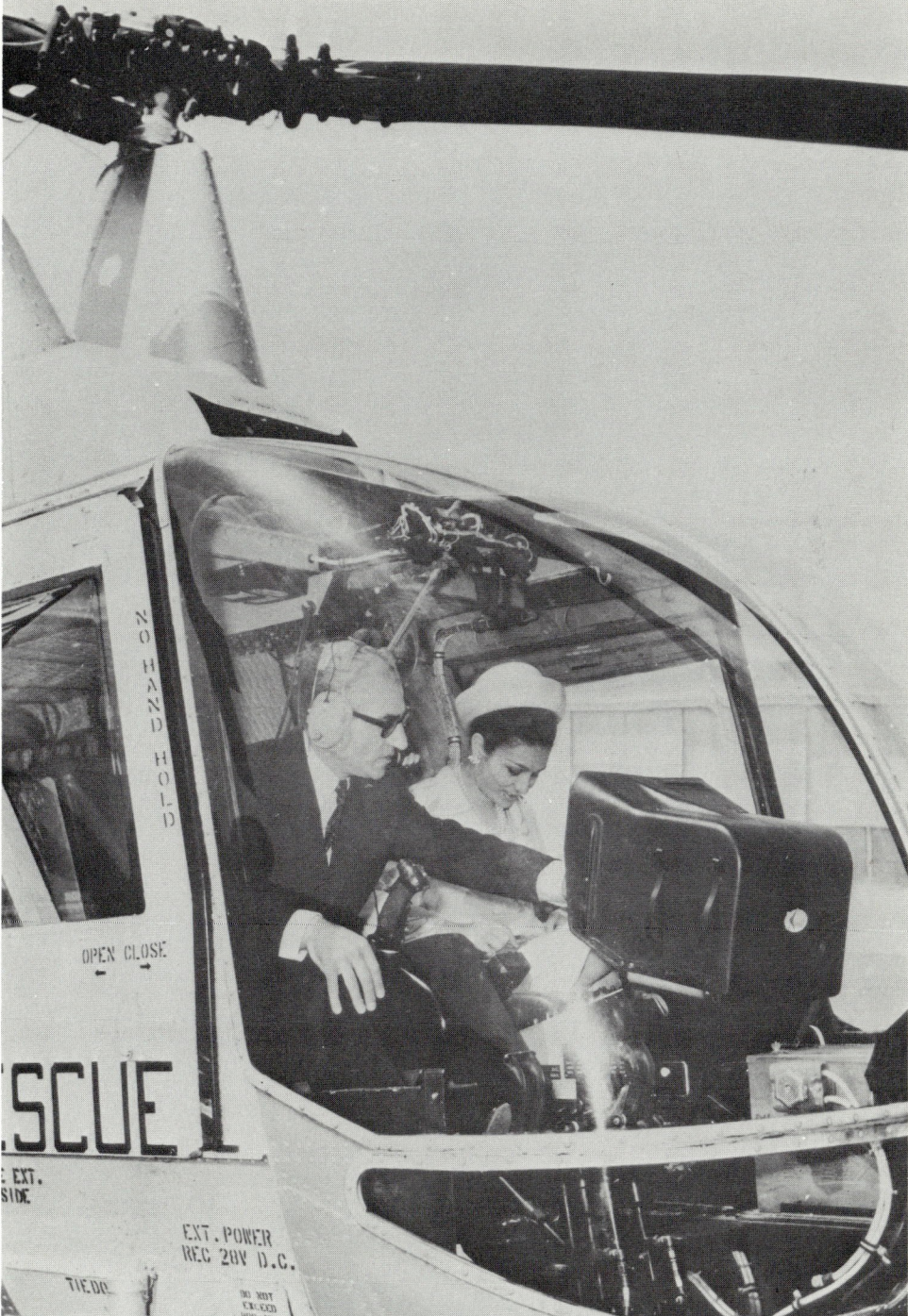

The Shahanshah and Queen Farah with the Crown Prince, watching an air display.

piloting his various transport aircraft. He also flies a helicopter, as naturally as others would drive a car. The helicopter is of course a remarkably convenient, time-saving vehicle, but its mastery demands special tuition, even when the pupil is a very experienced 'fixed-wing' pilot. The Shah is often to be seen flying his Queen, Farah Diba, in his helicopter, but its single engine has been a cause of some misgivings in court circles and perhaps he has by now fulfilled his intention to replace it with a twin-engined machine '—to ease the anguish of my entourage,' as he put it.

When longer distances have to be covered the helicopter is no substitute for a fast aeroplane and in 1957 the Shah took delivery of a Vickers Viscount. This four-engined turbo-propeller airliner is well known to the travelling public the world over, but the royal aircraft was no ordinary Viscount. In place of the usual rows of seats there was a bedroom and accommodation limited to twelve people. The interior was beautifully appointed with, among other luxuries, a 200-piece Crown Derby dinner service incorporating the Shah's coat of arms, crystal glass, silver cutlery and best Irish linen.

Over the years aeroplanes have become jet-propelled and faster, and the spaciousness of the Viscount was sacrified for the speed, quietness and all-weather comfort of the Lockheed Jetstar, with its four rear-mounted engines, looking for all the world like a scaled-down VC 10. The superb Jetstar will cruise over long distances at speeds in excess of 500 m.p.h. It has very comprehensive radio, air conditioning, pressurisation and in fact practically all that an airline pilot would expect to find in his modern long-distance passenger jet. As with any other complex aircraft of modern design, the flight deck of a Jetstar is no place for the amateur pilot. It carries a flight engineer and handling it is decidedly a two-pilot operation. Furthermore, these pilots must be up to the highest standards of technical knowledge and skill, so that bearing in mind his many other commitments, it comes as something of a surprise to learn that the Shah flies the Jetstar himself. The transition from the usual run of light aircraft to this type of equipment can involve an experienced pilot in several weeks of ground study and examinations before even setting foot in the plane, when he must learn how to control it under emergency conditions with perhaps only two out of four engines functioning. In flying there are no short cuts. Either you can do it or you are not up to the task.

It must be remembered that the Shah has so transformed Persia that his personal standing among his people is perhaps without comparison in other countries. In attaining these spectacular advancements he has at times been accused by his enemies of being an aloof, disinterested King albeit a liberal one. Many would of course emphatically disagree with this assessment but contrary to the more general trend among world royalty, his personal power has grown over the years. One might wonder, therefore, if, while his all-powerful and revered monarch was learning about a new type of aircraft, the check-pilot would feel able to make any criticisms. The possibility that awe may overcome frankness on these occasions is one which has not escaped the Shah and in answer to the question he will admit: 'So far everything has gone well, but I don't know, I can't say.'

The guest list of V.I.P.s who have flown with the Shah in his Jetstar is impressive. His passengers have included not only the Presidents of neighbouring countries, but people like the King and Queen of the Belgians, who accompanied him through snow and ice from Shiraz to Teheran. On this trip the compass became suspect, and they had to call up Teheran for radar assistance. On another occasion, the experienced Prince Bernhard flew the aircraft with the Shah while Queen Juliana of the Netherlands enjoyed the quiet comfort of the cabin.

Visits to foreign countries have in the past enabled the Shah to fly a number of supersonic fighters. In the U.S.A. he tried a McDonnell Phantom and early in 1965 a visit to Britain gave him the chance of a thirty-minute flight at the controls of an R.A.F. Lightning at over 1,200 m.p.h. On landing there was the usual 'ten ton'

The Royal Jetstar.

ceremony when he received a scroll and a tie admitting him to the 'Thousand Miles an Hour Club.'

To Persia, with its vast mountain regions and great distances between cities, air transport has become vital, and the Shah has encouraged the expansion of the national airline network just as his late father saw a need for the Trans-Iranian Railway. Thus has history repeated itself. However, there is perhaps almost as large a gap in technology between jet travel and space travel as there is between the railway and the jet. Moreover, the space-travel achievement is enhanced by the miracle of modern communications. Millions throughout the world watch and listen to the astronauts on colour television. It should be remembered that for several hundred years the clock had stood still in Persia. Then the nation awoke in a modern world and there must in consequence be many people in Iran who have experienced within living memory the transition from a seventeenth century way of life to a world of electricity, motor cars, aeroplanes, radio, television and all manner of things so often taken for granted by citizens of other countries. Because the Shah has been and still is the prime mover behind his people's spectacular advancement his views on the subject of space travel take on a special interest:

> 'Since the time that Daedalus and his son Icarus took off our soil to go into the air, this—the conquest of space—has obviously been the greatest achievement in man's imagination. It is a fantastic achievement to be able to land on the moon, such a distance, within such a small radius. It's incredible. And to come back again at a pre-determined point, again within that range,—that really is fantastic. It couldn't have been done without the computer, obviously, but after all, man created the computer as well as the machine to take up the module. As a scientific achievement it is almost beyond belief—but where do we go from there? I don't know—is it worth spending all this money when there is still in our world disease, poverty, hunger? This is a debatable question. If we want to be very practical, even narrow-minded, we should say "Well, let's do these things after we have already put our own world right." On the other hand, if we don't engage ourselves in adventures like this, science would never develop as it has. And finally, if we believe in the intelligence of man (and we should, otherwise it's hopeless, for when there's no hope there can be no life) we must believe that science would be of service to humanity and help it to solve more easily the problems that we are actually facing.'

Although the Shah is clearly impressed by the great achievements of the astronauts, his prime concern has to be the improvement of life on earth, particularly as it affects his subjects. More schools, universities and hospitals must be built, educational standards improved and social reforms initiated. And this may often be in the face of opposition from vested interests.

The Shah derives great pleasure from meeting his subjects. At any time the Prime Minister, Foreign Minister or other key officials may have access to the King. As Commander-in-Chief of the armed forces, too, the Shah devotes two mornings a week to meeting his senior officers. He is anxious that they should feel free to express frankly their views on all military subjects, and a suitable atmosphere for these discussions is ensured by interviewing the officers one at a time. Once a month there is a press conference, after which journalists are given an opportunity of meeting the King. The palace routine is broken by outside journeys of every kind—visits to new factories, hospitals and orphanages and inspections of military units. Invariably the Shah pilots himself in his helicopter.

An entrance to the Golestan Palace, Teheran. *London Express Photo.*

In effect the Shah may be described as a 'super-manager' controlling the affairs of his nation. Unlike his late father, when confronted by a problem he prefers first to obtain the views of many people from all walks of life before deciding on a course of action, rather than rely upon expert advisers, whose opinions may on occasions be tainted by self-interest. Part of his management technique is based upon what he calls 'plurality of administrative channels.' In other words, he is never dependent upon one official only, because if that official fails to carry out an instruction there is always another ready to act for the Shah.

Had he been a lesser man the growth of the Shah's personal power could well have proved disastrous for Persia, but he is sensitive to the dangers inherent in an authoritative form of government and he is on record as saying, 'Discipline without democracy is authoritarianism, and democracy without discipline is anarchy.'

The Throne Room at the Golestan Palace. *London Express Photo.*

In contrast, the Shah's earlier days on the throne were by no means secure. For example, there was the Azerbaijan disturbance of 1946 when he flew himself over the rebel positions, assessed their strength, then sent in his loyal troops who quickly restored order. Some years later there occurred under the nationalist leadership of Mossadegh a more serious threat to the throne and the very life of the royal family. To those living outside Persia, Mossadegh was hardly to be taken seriously. He was rarely seen by the press other than lying in bed wearing striped pyjamas, and his passionately anti-Western outbursts were accompanied by floods of tears. His association with the Tudeh party was later proved, as was their intention to murder him when the party came into power. On 22 August 1953, Mossadegh was forcibly removed from office by General Zahedi. The Shah's reaction was characteristic. In order that the Persian people could decide freely on the future of the Monarchy, the Shah flew himself and the Queen to neighbouring Baghdad. His voluntary absence helped to result in an overwhelming display of loyalty which has enabled him to lead his country from success to greater success.

The growth of Iranian prosperity has been accompanied by a remarkable absence of inflation. The spread in literacy has been equally remarkable. There are new schools, new hospitals, new industries to supplement the wealth derived from oil, modern airports and roads, but alongside these new developments traditional crafts have been encouraged to continue as before, including magnificent silverware and incomparable carpets.

The Shah realises too the important role of women in the new life of Iran and it is his ambition one day to provide a State dowry for every girl marrying at the legal age.

Teheran, the capital, is today a city of over one and a half million people. It is set against the Elburz mountains which in Spring and early Summer lie snowcapped to the north, providing a 13,000 ft. backcloth of great beauty and a potential hazard commanding the respect of all airline pilots. The splendour of this fine city, an intriguing mixture of old and new, is enhanced by the womenfolk who must be among the most beautiful in the world.

His Imperial Majesty Mohammad Reza Shah Pahlavi, Aryamehr, Shahanshah of Iran, is an impressive title for an impressive monarch but the name most coveted by the Persian King is that given him by his people—Aryamehr. The story behind the name is of interest, because it confounds a misconception held by many who believe that the Aryan race emanated from Germany. In fact it originated in Central Asia, at a time generally accepted to be 2,000 B.C. It was during their wanderings that the Aryans settled in the great plateau to the south of the Caspian Sea, and this they named Iran. Although they are now of the Moslem faith, the Iranians have never

Climax to a glittering coronation. His Imperial Majesty the Shahanshah of Iran placing the crown on the head of his Queen while Crown Prince Reza looks on. *London Express Photo.*

forgotten their Aryan background and because the Shah had led them from decline to prosperity the people proclaimed him Aryamehr, 'Light of the Aryans.'

By 1966 Iran had become an economic pace-setter among the developing nations and the time had clearly arrived for the Shah to accept his crown. The coronation was held on 26 October 1967, in the Hall of Mirrors at the Golestan Palace. An Indian journalist later described the scene as 'like walking into the heart of some enormous diamond.' In an atmosphere of intense emotion the Shah put on his crown. Then followed an important break with tradition, when the young Empress Farah, (who though Persian by birth, was educated at the Sorbonne in Paris, and like her husband is thoroughly modern-minded) became the first woman in 25 centuries of Persian history to be crowned alongside the reigning King and the young heir to the throne, Crown Prince Reza Cyrus.

Emperor, soldier, social reformer, sportsman and pilot of the highest calibre, the Shahanshah rose to speak to his people. He could look back with pride on great achievements and there was no need to make promises for the future. But on that day he made this vow to the nation:

'My only goal in life is the ever-increasing ascendance of the land and people of Iran, and I cherish no other wish than to safeguard the independence and sovereignty of this country, helping the Iranian nation to catch up with the most progressive communities of the world, and reviving its ancient grandeur and historical glories. Towards this end I will not spare anything, not even my life, just as I have not spared it in the past.'

The House of Orange-Nassau

Before the establishment of a monarchy in Holland the country was ruled by Stadthoulders or Princes, the most famous being William the Silent. He is generally regarded by Dutchmen as their greatest patriot. Holland's history has followed the pattern of many other European countries in the shift of power and conflict over religious and other issues. These conflicts have not always been to her advantage. For example the Netherlands have been annexed by the Romans, plundered by marauding Vikings and embroiled in the quarrels of their neighbours. While other countries may have suffered all this and more, the Dutch have at the same time been fighting a constant battle with the sea. A modern reminder of this battle is the notice at Schiphol, Amsterdam's fine airport, which says 'Ten feet below sea level.' But the Dutch are a solid, resilient race and Holland today has become one of the most stable and developed countries in the world.

It has been ruled in turn by the Burgundian and Habsburg dynasties, then became a republic in 1684. There was a period of hated rule by Spain and the Duke of Alba, then in 1814 the monarchy was restored with William I of the Franco-German House of Orange-Nassau. He abdicated in 1840 and was succeeded by William II and then William III. The Dutch were not altogether happy with their three Kings but when William III died in 1890 he was survived by a ten-year-old daughter, Wilhelmina, who acceded to the throne on her eighteenth birthday. The new Queen's inauguration (there is no coronation ceremony in Holland) marked the beginning of a fifty-year reign which reconciled the throne and the people, and endeared her to the nation.

During World War I Holland was a neutral country. Twenty-one years later, German troops with massive air support invaded Holland and Queen Wilhelmina and members of the Dutch Royal Family were evacuated to England by the British Royal Navy. Looking after the Royal Party was a young German Prince who on 7 January 1937 had married the Queen's daughter Princess Juliana. He then assumed Netherlands nationality. His unsparing efforts for the good of his adopted country form the subject of the next chapter.

In 1948 Queen Wilhelmina insisted on abdicating in favour of her daughter, the present Queen Juliana, when her husband Bernhard took the title Prince of the Netherlands.

RIGHT The Prince of The Netherlands.

CHAPTER 5

HOLLAND

Fighter Pilot to Inspector-General

The royal palace at Soestdijk, which is in the country east of Amsterdam, near the village of Baarn, is a beautiful building, just off the main road, and has always been the favourite residence of the Royal Family. It is surrounded by trees and lawns, and compared with the original palaces in the Hague and in Amsterdam, which are now used only for certain public functions, it is a real home, where the four daughters of Queen Juliana and Prince Bernhard grew up, and were educated at the local village school.

Royal guards—from the famous Koninklijke Mare-Chaussee regiment—stand guard at the entrances, but there is little formality once your credentials are known. The left wing of Soestdijk Palace is the more formal one, for state occasions, and glitters with chandeliers and mirrors and statues, but the right wing is the real residence, with everything up-to-date, including a private cinema and kitchens which would be the envy of every housewife.

Many of the palace walls are adorned with hunting trophies. There are also signed photographs from the famous—Queen Elizabeth, Churchill, Eisenhower and many others, all personal friends.

The Prince had changed his beribboned tunic of Inspector-General for the comfort of a brown sports jacket and spotted handkerchief, but he was still wearing his uniform trousers. A friendly greeting preceded an invitation to take tea on the verandah which overlooked the beautiful grounds. A lake provides sanctuary for wild life nesting in its reeds, while swallows make long swooping flights, the tips of their crescent wings almost touching the water. From time to time a palace clock chimes, an elusive, pleasant sound peculiar to great homes in park-like surroundings; in all a delightful setting for an interview. The Prince's friendly, enthusiastic manner and keen sense of humour immediately puts one at ease. He talks freely about his flying experiences, never hesitating to tell a story at his own expense, and it is soon evident that the few wrinkles on his suntanned face are more from laughter than the years. For nearly two hours he reminisced, turning the pages of four massive photograph albums devoted entirely to his aviation activities since 1940.

He expresses himself rapidly, in perfect English, with the suggestion of a transatlantic accent, the fruit of some years of wartime in Canada. Prince Bernhard celebrated his 60th birthday in 1971 but has the look, manner and energy of a man fifteen years his junior.

As consort to the Queen, Prince Bernhard takes precedence over all members of the Royal Family in Holland, and his official title is H.R.H. The Prince of the Netherlands. Born at Jena, Germany, on 29 June 1911, he was christened Bernhard Leopold Frederik Everhard Julius Coert Karel Godfried Pieter. His late father, Prince Bernhard of Lippe-Biesterfeld, was a great believer in public education, at a time when other princes were cosseted at home and handed over to the sometimes valueless instruction of a private tutor. Higher education at the Universities of Lausanne, Munich and Berlin culminated in his gaining a law degree, enabling him to take up an executive appointment with I. G. Farben in Paris.

Soestdijk Palace, residence of H.M. Queen Juliana and H R.H. Prince Bernhard.
Doeser·Photos.

After his marriage, Prince Bernhard assumed Dutch nationality and became a Captain in the Netherlands Army. Today he is Inspector-General of the Netherlands Armed Forces and holds directorships on the boards of such leading Dutch companies as Royal Netherlands Aircraft Factories, Fokker and is an adviser for K.L.M., Royal Dutch Airlines. He is Patron or President of so many institutions and societies that the complete list runs to some fourteen typed pages. He is also the most experienced royal pilot, with over 8,000 hours in his log book.

The Prince's first interest in flying was awakened in, of all unlikely places, the kitchen. A new cook engaged for the Royal household used to go about his task wearing a uniform of the German Air Force, the first ever seen by the six-year-old prince, and it created such a lasting impression that he determined to fly as soon as he was big enough to reach the controls. That was 1917. The war was all but lost for Germany and many years were to pass—but let the Prince tell the story:

It is 1934, and the countryside is blooming under a warm sun and a blue sky. The scene is one of peace and tranquillity. A tiny speck appears just above the distant horizon, followed by the gentle splutter of a low-powered aero engine. The speck, growing larger quite rapidly, is soon recognisable as a Klemm monoplane trainer. It weaves and turns aimlessly while the two occupants enjoy freedom of a kind only known to those fortunate enough to fly for fun, with nowhere in particular to go. They pass over a lake, its undisturbed waters like a sheet of glass reflecting the blue sky above. Simultaneously the pilots catch a glimpse of a duck flapping its way on its own final approach to land. It is almost as though someone has sounded the 'Tally Ho,' for in an instant the little 'plane is in a dive, the airspeed rapidly increasing, the altimeter winding down until the wheels speed only a few inches above the surface of the lake. In comparison with other birds, the duck is generally considered to be a reluctant flier, but this one quickly proves that he knows more of the art than the two pilots because he is now aware of the aircraft and turns almost within his own length, to disappear in another direction. At that moment there follows a loud splash and a rending, tearing, disintegrating noise of the most expensive variety as machine and pilots spread fan-like over the surface of the lake. The pilots are in no mood to dwell on their sudden and undignified change of element from air to water! The lake is not only deep but very cold and they are a long way from land. The two wheels float by, convenient lifebelts grabbed by the dazed airmen, as they swim out for the side of the lake. They were to suffer no more than a mild attack of 'flu but retribution followed, both from the flying school and the anxious parents of the junior partner in this escapade—Prince Bernhard!

The accident occurred while the young Prince was learning to fly, at a time when

The Prince in an open cockpit, without a helmet, flying a Tiger Moth during his early training. *Prince Bernhard's personal album.*

he had completed no more than a few hours of instruction. As a result he was forbidden by his parents to continue flying, and it might all have ended there but for his marriage into the Netherlands Royal Family and Holland's involvement in the war.

As the Storm Troopers overran the flat plains of Holland in 1940, the Prince took Queen Wilhelmina and the Royal Family on a British warship to the relative safety of England, then rejoined the Army, fighting on the Continent until the fall of France.

Back in England, there arose an opportunity to renew his latent interest in flying. He was posted to No. 1 Elementary Flying Training School at Hatfield, where along with other pupils, most of them R.A.F. cadets some years his junior, he flew Tiger Moths. Flying training in Britain and throughout the Commonwealth was based upon a brilliantly conceived syllabus, the work of the Empire Central Flying School. The course provided foundations for the more complex instruction to come, when the cadet progressed on to advanced trainers and, eventually, aeroplanes of the type he would fly on operations. In common with the young cadets, Prince Bernhard was introduced to the world of 'circuits and bumps' (a take-off followed by a circuit of the airfield and a landing, sometimes not without intense moments), cross-country flying, night-flying and aerobatics. It was low flying that really stirred the imagination of those young men under training. In no other mode of flight was the thrill of speed so vivid, even in a Tiger Moth and although pupils were forbidden to practise the exercise without a flying instructor, the sight of an express train streaming its wake of smoke and steam was to Prince Bernhard quite irresistible. No longer was he in a Tiger at 90 m.p.h.; he saw himself in a Spitfire with cannon roaring. Down he would go, the wind buffeting around the open cockpits of the little biplane as speed wound up in a dive, flashing past the engine to the consternation of the 'enemy,' an astonished driver and his fireman crouched within their cab and armed with nothing more deadly than lumps of coal. There are early pictures in the Prince's photograph albums, obviously taken over a train while flying below embankment level, and others showing a Tiger Moth emerging from between trees. Clearly he was no stranger to the joys of illicit low flying.

At the end of the course, pupils were graded 'below average,' 'average,' 'above average' or on rare occasions 'exceptional.' The Chief Flying Instructor at Hatfield was Wing Commander 'Clem' Pike A.F.C., and although he gave the Prince an 'exceptional,' it was qualified with the words: 'This pupil is so overconfident that in my opinion he will not live to see 1,000 hours.' Prince Bernhard felt he had earned his 'exceptional' and although he considered the additional remarks unfair at the time, he is inclined to agree with them now.

There was a sequel to the Wing Commander's comments. Shortly after the war the Prince borrowed a Vampire jet fighter and made a low pass over Hatfield, narrowly missing a chimney on the roof of his former Chief Flying Instructor's house. He landed at Hatfield then telephoned 'Clem' Pike and said 'This is Prince Bernhard speaking. I've got 1,800 hours now and I'm still alive.' He received the reply, 'After what you did this morning, you won't live to see 2,000!'

Prince Bernhard went solo in Tiger Moth N-6919, completed the remainder of his training, and was awarded R.A.F. wings on 24 April 1941. On the instruction of the late King George VI he was promoted to the rank of Air Commodore and subsequently appointed Chief Netherlands Liaison Officer with the British Forces. It was a task that suited him admirably, involving as it did a lot of flying within Britain and to most theatres of war. His personality and temperament made him acceptable to everyone from the most senior officer to cadets under training.

On one occasion he acted as co-pilot in a Liberator being ferried from the U.S.A. to Prestwick in Scotland. Several hours out over the bitterly cold Atlantic the oil pressure on number one engine dropped to zero and the Prince, who was then flying, tried to feather it but it would not stop turning. Shortly after that they became aware of a slight vibration which could be felt through the control columns. The crew checked the instruments, load, trim, in fact anything that could be examined in flight yet nothing irregular could be found. Soon after that, the automatic pilot ceased to function. Hour after hour they sat on the flight deck, while the controls continued to shake with increasing intensity. As time passed they began to wonder just how long the aircraft could withstand the vibration before breaking up. Despite the cold they perspired fiercely as their clammy hands gripped the shuddering control wheels while hardly a word was exchanged to relieve the tension. Then out of a grey dawn the Scottish coast appeared and they made a normal landing at Prestwick. 'Two crew members kissed the tarmac,' recalls the Prince.

On examination it was found that a pipe had fractured, spewing hydraulic fluid out into the intense cold of a winter's night over the Atlantic. It had carried back in the slipstream to freeze on to the elevators, causing an out-of-balance condition. Flying controls on an aircraft are very sensitive to changes of balance and the build-up of ice had radically altered the distribution of weight on the elevators, causing them to 'flutter,' a condition that might well have resulted in the disintegration of the entire airframe.

Prince Bernhard's liaison duties continued into 1943. Some idea of the extent of his work can be seen from one trip which began with a visit to the Ascension Isles

At General Montgomery's desert caravan.
Prince Bernhard's personal album.

on 2 March. Two days later he was in Nigeria, then on the 5th he flew to Egypt. He made a tour of the desert airfields and had a meeting with General Montgomery in his famous caravan on 10 March. Within forty-eight hours he was with General Eisenhower in Algiers. On 14 March he flew back to England, breaking his journey at Gibraltar in order to meet King George of Greece. Within a few weeks he was off to Canada again and so it went on, exacting, tiring but interesting work, at times not without hazard.

Shortly after he was appointed Senior Liaison Officer the Prince paid another visit to his old flying school at Hatfield, where his ex-flying instructor casually mentioned a field he had noticed in the area. It was a very small field and he was willing to bet that the Prince would be unable to do a practice forced landing into it without hitting something on the way in or running into the trees at the end. Prince Bernhard was hardly likely to ignore a challenge of this kind and without hesitation replied, 'I'll take you on, for a fiver.' They took off in Tiger Moth T-7414 and flew towards the field. It was certainly small. Three quarters of the perimeter were surrounded by woods and the other quarter was lined by a fairly tall hedge.

In a practice forced landing the throttle is closed to simulate engine failure. The pilot must then glide into the field and land into wind. It is an exercise calling for accurate judgement of height, distance and wind strength. The smaller the field, the greater the degree of skill required. In Prince Bernhard's own words:

'I said to myself, "If he [the instructor] can get in, I can get in," so at 2,000 feet we cut the engine.'

Every yard of the field would be needed if he was to avoid running into the trees at the far side, so the Prince came in low, his wheels brushing through the hedge.

'I heard him say "Damn it, you've made it!" but unfortunately there was a hidden tree stump which caught the wheels and flung us over on our back. I let myself out carefully but he was so scared when the petrol started dripping that he opened his straps and fell on his head. The Tiger Moth was a complete write-off but I claimed I had won my five pounds, because I had got into the field.'

Needless to say the bet was never paid.

One day a Spitfire landed at Biggin Hill, the famous Battle of Britain fighter station. It taxied to the area set aside for visiting aircraft, the engine stopped and the

RIGHT The bet he almost won.
Prince Bernhard's personal album.

Hatfield. Sept. 12th, 1941
One complete write-off.

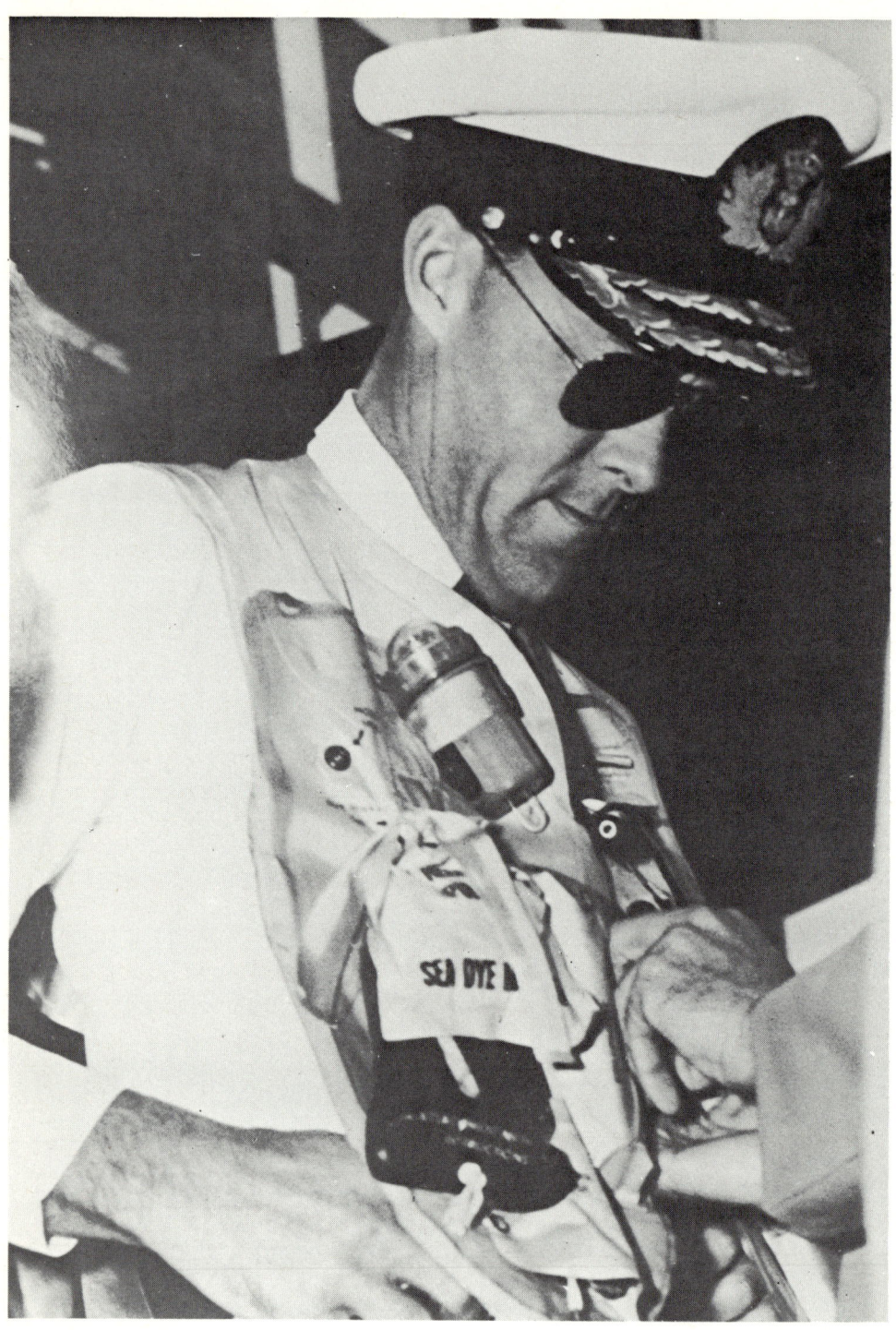

canopy slid back to reveal a figure in a bowler hat. A crowd of airmen gathered, disbelief written on their faces as the bowler-hatted pilot climbed out of the heavily-armed fighter standing there. He was dressed like a stockbroker, complete with umbrella, briefcase and spotted tie. Possibly it was the white carnation in his buttonhole that did it, because they sent for the R.A.F. police who promptly arrested the intruder and took him before the station commander, Group Captain (later Air Marshal) Atcherley. He and his twin brother were themselves merciless practical jokers and a legend within the R.A.F., but Atcherley had to admit to the station police that, for once, he was on the receiving end. The 'city gent' in the Spitfire was his old friend Prince Bernhard—who nearly always wore a white carnation.

On one of his liaison tours the Prince flew with his staff to the Caribbean in a

LEFT Preparation for flight.
Prince Bernhard's personal album.
BELOW With his dog 'Pilot Officer Martin.'
Prince Bernhard's personal album.

Lockheed 12, a small, twin-engined transport aircraft. For some reason they arrived two hours earlier than expected and the entire island defence system let fly. Fortunately the gunners' enthusiasm exceeded their marksmanship, most of the shells bursting some distance behind the landing aircraft. Far from being angry about his unfriendly reception Prince Bernhard indulged in some good-natured leg-pulling when later he met those concerned.

His next call was Puerto Rico. As they flew towards the airfield ominous flashes could be seen coming from some warships moored in the harbour. Following his experiences in the Caribbean the Prince had become rather sensitive about being shot at by those who, according to the rules, were supposed to be on his side and on landing he complained to the resident Senior Naval Officer that he had been fired upon while approaching to land. The Navy reported that no shot had been fired and that, according to the Army, the Prince must have seen sparks from an electric welding plant. The Prince, who knows a tracer bullet when he sees it, remained sceptical of this explanation.

In one way or another this was an eventful trip for Prince Bernhard. Soon after, while flying in clear air, he noticed some isolated cumulus clouds and it occurred to him that it might be fun to fly through the top of one that was floating dead on track. His co-pilot was quietly reading a book as the Lockheed brushed through the top of the cloud. Instantly, it dropped several hundred feet. The Prince had some time previously unfastened his safety belt and was lifted out of his seat with such force that he cut his head on the cabin roof and was unconscious for several minutes.

Between visits to Dutch and British squadrons Prince Bernhard got himself checked out on a Miles Master advanced trainer in preparation for conversion to Spitfire and Hurricane fighters. These superb thoroughbreds were a never-ending source of enjoyment to him and any excuse to fly them was good enough. For example, he wanted to view Scapa Flow from the air so, in formation with another Spitfire, he headed north. After a while, cloud obscured the ground below, making them uncertain of their exact position. They elected to let down through a gap in the cloud which had conveniently presented itself. It so happened that under that very gap was a convoy steaming at ten knots or so, its gunners alert and trigger-happy. The sudden appearance of two Spitfires from out of cloud was too much for them. It was no time to indulge in the finer points of aircraft recognition and they

TOP RIGHT King Peter of Yugoslavia (*centre*) preparing for his first solo flight. Smiths Lawn, 19 July 1944. *Prince Bernhard's personal album.*

RIGHT King Peter of Yugoslavia (*2nd left*) with Prince Bernhard and the Payne brothers who taught them to fly. *Prince Bernhard's personal album.*

opened fire with alarming accuracy while the Spitfires hastily regained the safety of cloud cover and returned home bearing marks of the encounter!

During 1943 Prince Bernhard attended the Royal Air Force Central Flying School and qualified as an instructor on Mosquito aircraft. He had become friendly with King Peter of Yugoslavia who was learning to fly at No. 18 Elementary Flying Training School, based at Fairoaks aerodrome in Surrey. Wing Commander Cyril Arthur A.F.C., for many years commanding officer at Fairoaks, remembers the Queen of Yugoslavia as a most beautiful young woman sitting in a car parked at the edge of the airfield while her husband, the exiled King, became acquainted with the idiosyncrasies of Tiger Moth flying. The Queen would wait for hours, politely declining all offers of tea. When King Peter did his first solo flight it was from Smith's Lawn, a satellite airfield near Windsor. Prince Bernhard was there to lend moral support. On gaining his R.A.F. brevet the King returned the compliment by presenting his flying instructor and Wing Commander Arthur with pilot's wings of the Royal Yugoslavian Air Force. Later the British Air Ministry provided him with a Harvard aircraft for his personal use.

Prince Bernhard contrived to fly on a number of operational sorties before the Air Ministry became alarmed.

> 'I was told, "If we ever catch you doing any illegal operational flying, we'll ground you, because we don't want to have any responsibility with your people." I knew they meant it too! So I got my operational flying from the Americans, with the help of a bottle of Bourbon and a note from Jimmie Doolittle [war-time commander of the American Air Force in Britain] whom I knew very well.'

As a guest of the U.S. Army Air Corps he accompanied Liberator and Flying Fortress crews on bombing raids, such as that on 21 June 1944, when he flew in a Liberator which bombed some German rocket sites. Occasionally, he would borrow a massive P47 single-seat fighter, fly across to enemy-occupied Europe and go 'train busting.' By this time the Germans had captured a few British and American aircraft and they were not beyond using them in their original squadron markings for the purpose of 'hit-and-run' raids. Soon it became necessary to treat as hostile all solitary aircraft approaching the coast, whether or not they were of British or American origin flying in their national markings. They were to be shot at without hesitation—questions could be asked later. No longer could Prince Bernhard embark on his lone 'beat-up' of the enemy-held railway across the Channel. It was the end of his kind of private war.

The invasion of Western Europe by the Allies on D Day, 6 June 1944, encouraged

Undercarriage failure can happen, even to a Royal Prince. *Prince Bernhard's personal album.*

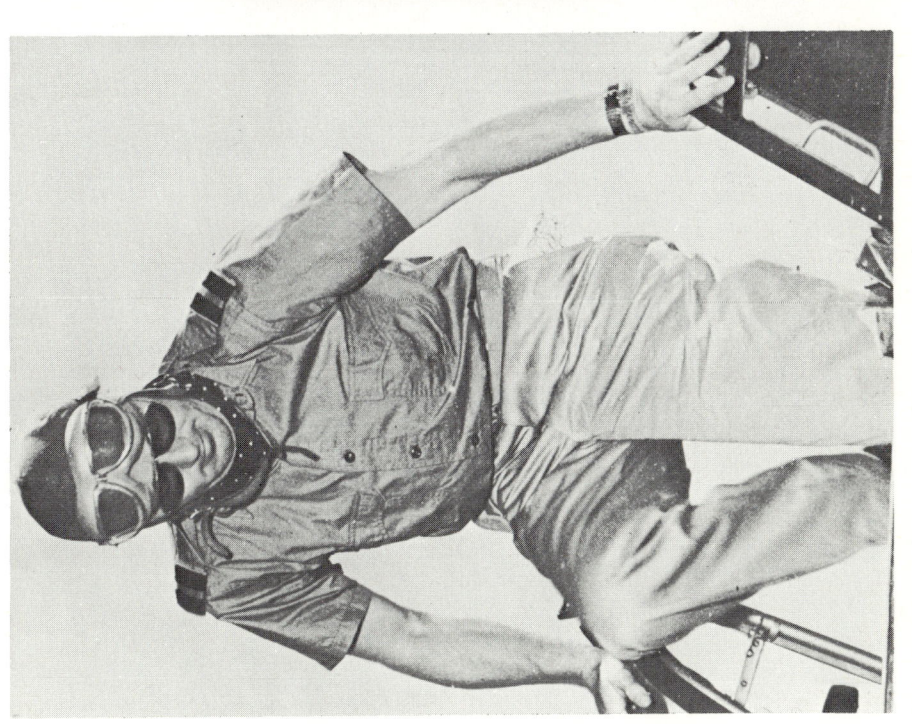

Leaving the cockpit of a Canadian Hawker Hurricane Mk XII (6 July 1943). *Prince Bernhard's personal album.*

resistance movements to still greater activities against the occupying German forces. Throughout the war Prince Bernhard had maintained close contact with the Netherlands underground organisation—one of his proudest moments was when he was officially appointed as Chief of the Dutch Resistance. After the invasion he became increasingly involved with their activities and in recognition of the important part he had played in the liberation of Holland he was invested with the G.B.E. by King George VI.

During the war, squadrons of the Royal Netherlands Air Force flew alongside British pilots and they have always valued their association with the R.A.F.

A particularly interesting example of this association is 322 Squadron. It was formed at R.A.F. Station Woodvale, near Liverpool, on 12 June 1943. The Squadron Crest incorporates a parrot named Polly Grey who has been the squadron mascot since 31 July 1943. At first there were only 8 Dutch pilots among the total strength of 31 but eventually all except the Squadron Commander and one Flight Commander were from the Netherlands. They flew Spitfires on various operational missions and on 12 June 1944 Queen Wilhelmina visited the squadron, just before it flew across the Channel in support of the allied forces invading Normandy. Later they shot down

LEFT With Air Chief Marshal Sir Sholto Douglas.
Prince Bernhard's personal album.

RIGHT 322 Squadron badge showing mascot 'Flight Sergeant Polly Grey.' Motto: 'Deeds not words'

110 V1 flying bombs directed against London by the Germans in their final desperate attempt to terrorise the civilian population. In 1945 the squadron was the first to return to Holland since the German invasion. After a varied post-war career it is now flying F-104 Lockheed Starfighters.

In the closing stages of the war Prince Bernhard was never far from the fighting and during September 1944 he flew over the front in a light aircraft of the type used for artillery spotting. On 7 May 1945, the very day that hostilities in Europe came to an abrupt end, he flew to Amsterdam, landing his Vigilant aircraft near the city on one of the main roads. He had returned to his adopted country burning with a desire to help in the rebuilding of Holland and the lives of the Dutch people. With his confident manner, enthusiasm and ready wit the Prince was a natural leader, re-

Prince Bernhard with Polly Grey. The Squadron mascot has just bitten the Prince's first finger. *Prince Bernhard's personal album.*

establishing civil institutions and taking a leading role in the re-organisation of the Netherlands Armed Forces.

At a time when aircraft without propellers were as yet something of a novelty, in 1954, the Prince became a jet pilot. He visited Edwards Air Force Base in California to be checked out on the F86 Sabre fighter. After the Americans had given him a thorough dual check and pronounced him qualified to fly the aircraft, he was sent off on his own to enjoy himself without the searching eye of a check pilot. He climbed to 40,000 ft., dived through the sound barrier and generally let his hair down before descending to 2,000 ft. in preparation for the landing. At this moment the F86 commenced a violent porpoising motion. It was quite unexpected and the more alarming because, try as he might, the Prince was unable to stabilise the bucking aircraft. Conveniently positioned on the control column is a 'transmit' button for the radio and this he inadvertently pressed while struggling to bring some order to the F86. In consequence, the air traffic control staff at Edwards base could hear a by now somewhat bewildered Prince Bernhard breathing heavily and exclaiming 'Jesus, Jesus' through clenched teeth. Fortunately one of the local test pilots was in the control tower at the time. Picking up the microphone he advised the Prince, 'Let the stick go.' The Prince lifted his hand off the stick and the F86 resumed level flight as though nothing had happened. After landing Prince Bernhard was met by the commanding officer at Edwards Base. 'I see you have had the J.C. effect' said the Brigadier. Apparently the characteristic was well known to F86 pilots: 'They usually shout "Jesus!" when it happens the first time.' Experience had devised the simple remedy of letting the aircraft fly itself 'stick-free' in the event of porpoising which, if mishandled, could result in disaster.

From Tiger Moth to Lockheed Starfighter represents a speed range of 90 to 1,400 m.p.h. To fly such a variety of aircraft requires a degree of pilot skill and technical knowledge not usually associated with the splendid surroundings of a royal palace. The Prince has gained his competence like any other pilot, by constant practice, followed by periodic checks of every kind. Asked if his instructors or examiners were ever less than frank with him because of his royal rank, His Royal Highness was most emphatic:

'Never, never, never, otherwise they would be no good as instructors. This is the reason I advised Prince Philip to get his wings in the normal way. The [British] Air Ministry and a lot of people were very upset about it and said "You shouldn't have done this" and talked about a lot of responsibility. My answer was, "Have you got good instructors, yes or no? If he makes the grade normally with a good instructor, that's fine, and if they say 'No, he's no good,' they will say he won't make the grade. So what have you to worry about? Either your whole system is no good or it will apply to him just as it would apply to me, or anyone else, and I have never had any trouble about that."'

A similar question had been put to His Imperial Majesty The Shah of Persia, who could not be so sure about his check pilot's frankness. 'I know that it did not apply to the Shah when he learned to fly the Jetstar,' said the Prince:

'When he had had his for about a year we came to Teheran and he flew me and my wife and his own wife and my daughter. He said, "You come and sit up front, you've flown it before." Funny thing is, he called his co-pilot forward to start it. Then the co-pilot was put right in the end of the fuselage, last seat but one, and we flew it for two days. He flew it brilliantly—he's really a first class pilot—but I wasn't happy that, had a red light flashed, he would have known exactly what to do. I wrote him a letter saying, "Your flying is OK but if you want your own life to be reasonably insured by your own actions, it would be a good idea to take a few hours to be completely checked out"—and he did this. There it did not apply, because nobody had said to His Imperial Majesty, or perhaps dared to say to him, that he needed a full check-out on the aircraft.'

In the course of flying the royal aircraft, first a Dakota and then its replacement, a twin turbo-propeller Fokker Friendship, Prince Bernhard is required to conform to airways procedures and air traffic instructions just like any other pilot. He must therefore hold an instrument rating. Much of the practice flying inseparable from maintaining this very exacting qualification may be effected without leaving the ground and various simulators have been devised for the purpose of enabling pilots to practise radio navigational and landing procedures at a fraction of the cost involved in flying a real aeroplane.

The Link trainer was among the first of the simulators to find widespread use and its acceptance as a training aid saw the emergence of a specialised breed of teacher known as the 'Link instructor.' They sit behind a large, glass-topped desk, watching the trace left by a moving pen which obeys the speed and direction flown by the pilot under practice, sitting in his little imitation aeroplane with its complete instrument panel and working controls. Pilot and Link instructor are in contact with one another through microphones and headsets, so that the illusion of radio is created and the most complex procedures may be flown while the flight path is traced on the glass desk.

Prince Bernhard did much of his instrument training with K.L.M. Royal Dutch Airlines, where his particular Link instructor was Edward Walton, an ex-R.A.F.

Final briefing in an F104 Starfighter.
Prince Bernhard's personal album.

officer settled in Holland after the war who later returned to England and entered the church. The Reverend Walton has, among other accomplishments, some skill as a linguist and it was his practice to pass air traffic instructions to the Prince in a variety of accents intended to create realism and accustom him to the radio jargon likely to be encountered when flying in various parts of the world. Prince Bernhard is a natural mimic and he would acknowledge his instructions in a perfect French, American or German accent, or whatever his instructor was using at the time. He is an exceptionally good instrument pilot, better in fact than many an airline pilot known to Walton, who says:

> 'He wouldn't accept second best—ever. He has always been determined to get things right and he welcomes criticism. I must have given him 80 hours instruction, and I have never come across anyone who was so devoted to flying and who was absolutely set on getting things one hundred per cent; 99 per cent wasn't good enough.'

At home on the flight deck—the most experienced Royal pilot.
Prince Bernhard's personal album.

As a family man, too, he expects perfection. Some years ago the royal children were walking back to the palace. One of the Princesses went into an orchard and helped herself to some apples. Back at the Palace, Queen Juliana and Prince Bernhard wanted to know how the children had got the fruit and with utter frankness they confessed. The Queen and her Consort took them to the local police station. 'What do you normally do with children who steal apples?' they asked the officer in charge. 'Oh— we sort of lock them up for a bit to make them feel frightened,' the man replied. To his astonishment he was requested to put the Princesses behind bars for a period which was short, but nevertheless long enough to teach them a lesson.

To some it is inconceivable that a royal pilot should under any circumstances be frightened by the weather. Could it be that aviation for the royal pilot is perhaps smoother than it is for other pilots, that fog is less dense for a Prince and cumulo-nimbus cloud more hospitable? Is the risk of airframe and engine icing any less

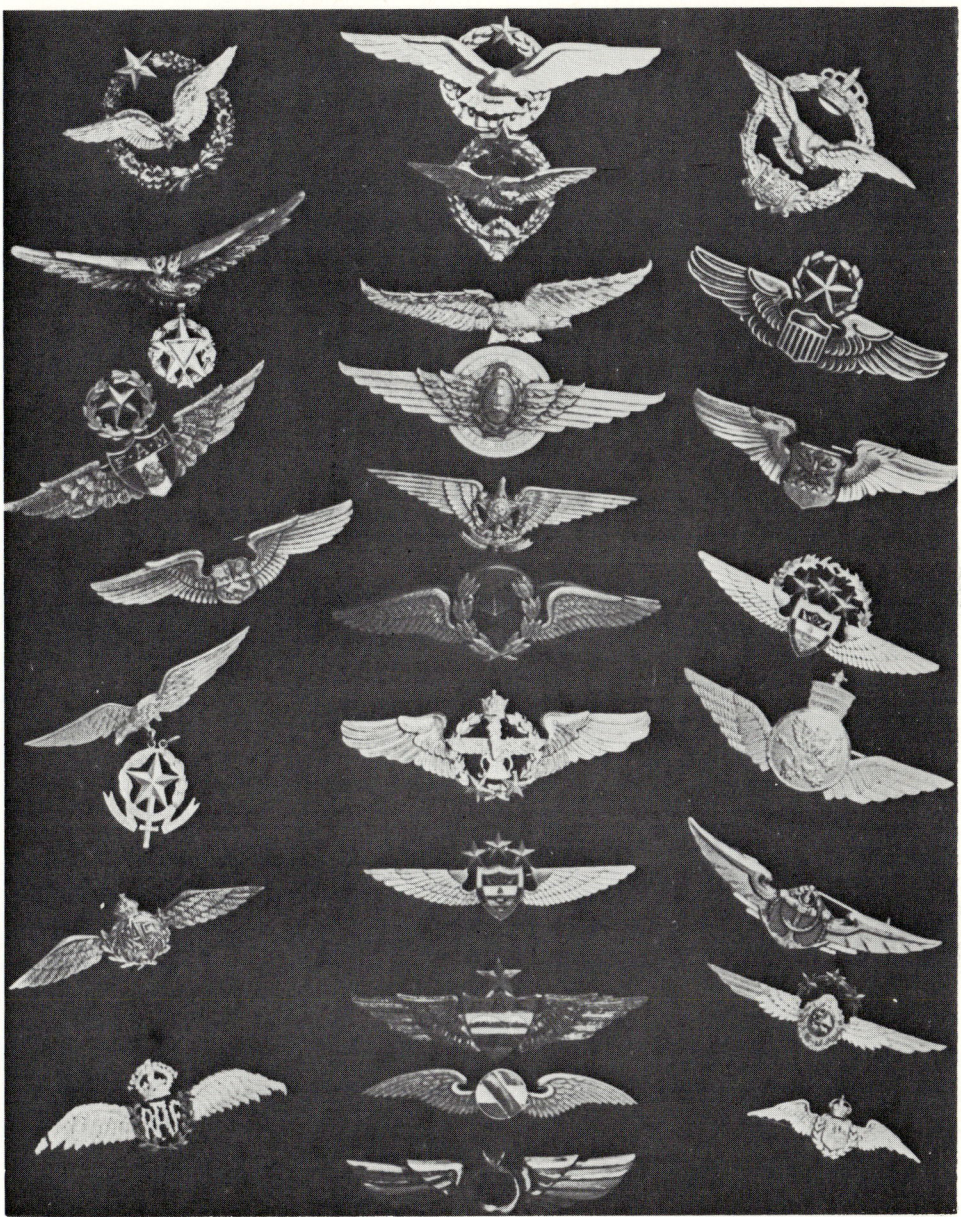
Twenty-six different pilot's wings awarded to the Prince of the Netherlands.

severe for the royal pilot than it is for an airline captain? It is, of course, an irrational line of thought and Prince Bernhard rapidly dispelled all such illusions when he was asked if he had experienced any anxious moments. 'Never mind anxious moments,' he replied, 'I can tell you when I was good and bloody scared.' The capacity to be good and bloody scared is an essential quality in all competent pilots. To be scared breeds discretion and without discretion any pilot, whatever his breadth of experience, is a menace. The Prince considers that one becomes scared in a car on many more occasions than while flying and he has done more than enough piloting to back up such an opinion. Nevertheless he has had his emergencies both as a military pilot and while flying in a civil capacity. It is the way these incidents have been handled that identifies him as a pilot of exceptional ability, because by adopting the correct procedure he can turn a potentially dangerous situation into an unpleasant few moments, no more, no less.

There was the day he was flying the Fokker Friendship over Belgium. Ice began to form on the aircraft with such rapidity that it became necessary to call up control, advising them of the situation, and requesting an immediate let-down into warmer air. Both airspeed indicators had stopped working and the aircraft was being flown by reference to the attitude instruments. When eventually they landed at Schiphol the best part of a ton of ice fell off the aircraft and those present found it unbelievable that the aircraft could have flown in such a condition.

On another occasion, this time not long after leaving Bangkok, the Prince's 'plane entered the monsoon and flew into some thunder clouds buried in the murk. Air Traffic Control had been unable to re-route the royal aircraft around these violent clouds and His Royal Highness had to press on while his alarmed passengers tightened their seat belts.

During a tour of the Far East, while flying close to the Himalayas at 19,000 ft., one of the two engines failed in a rather audible manner. Without delay it was shut down and its propeller feathered to prevent windmilling and the possibility of causing further damage. The Chief Pilot of Pakistan Airways was flying with the Prince as crew member and when they landed at Rawalpindi he felt moved to compliment his royal captain on a fine performance in the air, culminating in a perfect landing on one engine. Prince Bernhard replied that he had welcomed the incident as an opportunity to practise his emergency drills. As for the landing, he jokingly added, they were always perfect as a matter of form. Several days later, after the engine had been changed, he flew into Manila and dropped the 'plane on the runway so hard that he was grateful no one but his usual crew had witnessed the landing.

Prince Bernhard is currently flying some 250 hours a year, mainly in the royal

Fokker Friendship. The only restrictions on his flying are self-imposed. He will no longer fly a modern jet fighter, for example, unless he is accompanied by another crew member—a realistic limitation for a man in his sixtieth year who has had little involvement in this type of flying.

He does the same instrument-rating renewal and competency checks as any professional pilot and deliberately engages in training practice during fading light or indifferent weather, when conditions are most testing. When his many other commitments permit, he devotes time to practising advanced exercises in one of the modern jet simulators at Schiphol airport, which accurately reproduces the flight deck and handling characteristics of a DC 9 transport aircraft. He seeks no special royal privilege and complies with all licensing and flying regulations, civil and military. He is a member of the Airline Pilots' Association.

Some time ago on American television, the Duke of Edinburgh took part in a discussion on the future and problems of unions. He remarked that he was a member of the smallest union in the world, in fact there was only one other member besides himself, Prince Bernhard. Asked for the name of the shop steward, Prince Bernhard replied that as he could not remember whose turn it was, perhaps the question should be put to the other member!

A stranger meeting Prince Bernhard without knowing his identity could very easily mistake him for an international businessman or perhaps an eminent surgeon. His accomplishments include the holding of so many important business and public appointments that it is impossible to list them here. Not only has he achieved the highest professional standards as a civil pilot, but he is so well regarded by military authorities throughout the world that twenty-six foreign air forces have presented him with the badge worn by their own pilots, the coveted wings that are the pride of every service pilot, whatever his nationality.

One leaves Soestdijk Palace with a very clear impression of the Prince, a man whose interests range from Inspector-General of the Armed Forces of his country to the Presidency of the Wild Life Association. His confidence, his enthusiasm and spontaneous wit are vital qualities which he brings to his job. He has never sought the privileges his royal position can secure and this is evidenced in his flying. Never, for example, does he use Purple Airways, those special aerial highways which royal rank can command.

Above all there is his personal courage; Prince Bernhard had no need to fly on operations during World War II. One cannot but admire this man whose example and way of life have endeared him to the Dutch people and marked him as an outstanding man of his time.

The Chakri Dynasty

The Thais originated some six thousand years ago in a narrow belt of land between the Yellow and Yangtse rivers. They remained under the rule of minor princes while the Chinese became warriors and developed a great empire. To avoid domination the Thais migrated through Indo-China and built their first city, Sukhot'ai (Happy Thai) in the centre of Thailand.

The first monarchy was founded in A.D. 1238 under King Sri Int'ratit. In 1350 a rival prince built the city of Ayutthaya, proclaimed himself King Rama Tibodi and later conquered Sukhot'ai. There followed a line of wise Kings who managed to avoid foreign domination while neighbouring countries became European colonies.

In 1518 the Portuguese were the first Europeans to visit Thailand, followed in 1608 by the Dutch and by the British in 1612. On 25 January 1593 the Crown Prince of Burma was killed by Prince Naresuan of Thailand in a duel fought on elephants, bringing to a temporary close the constant state of war that had for centuries existed between the two countries.

In April 1767 the Burmese destroyed Ayutthaya, at the time a city of over one million inhabitants. It had been the Thai capital for 417 years under 33 Monarchs.

Chinese attacks against the Burmese soon forced their withdrawal from Thailand. But the Thai Monarch, King Taskin, was becoming insane, praying constantly that he might fly like a bird. In 1782 there was a revolt and Chao P'raya Chakri, a highly-regarded General, was elected King Rama I. It was the beginning of the present Chakri dynasty.

The small fishing village of Bangkok was rebuilt as a replica of the old capital and Thailand began to flourish again. King Mongkut, the fourth of the Chakri monarchs (who was depicted in the popular musical 'The King and I') in 1868 led an expedition to Southern Thailand for the purpose of observing the total eclipse. He contracted fever and died within a few days. His son Chulalongkorn became Thailand's greatest reformer, abolishing slavery and establishing a postal service. He built a railway, introduced currency and re-organised the Army. He commissioned the first Thai police force, built the first hospitals—the list is endless.

In 1910 he was succeeded by King Vajiravudh who was educated at Oxford, founded the Thai Boy Scouts and translated Shakespeare's plays into Thai. He died childless in 1925 and was succeeded by his brother King Rama VI, uncle of Prince Varanand, one of the subjects of the next chapter. In 1935 King Rama VI abdicated. His nephew Ananda succeeded and reigned under Japanese occupation during World War II but in 1946 he was found shot under mysterious circumstances. His brother is the present King Bhumibol.

Prince Birabongse, an early postwar photograph. *The Autocar.*

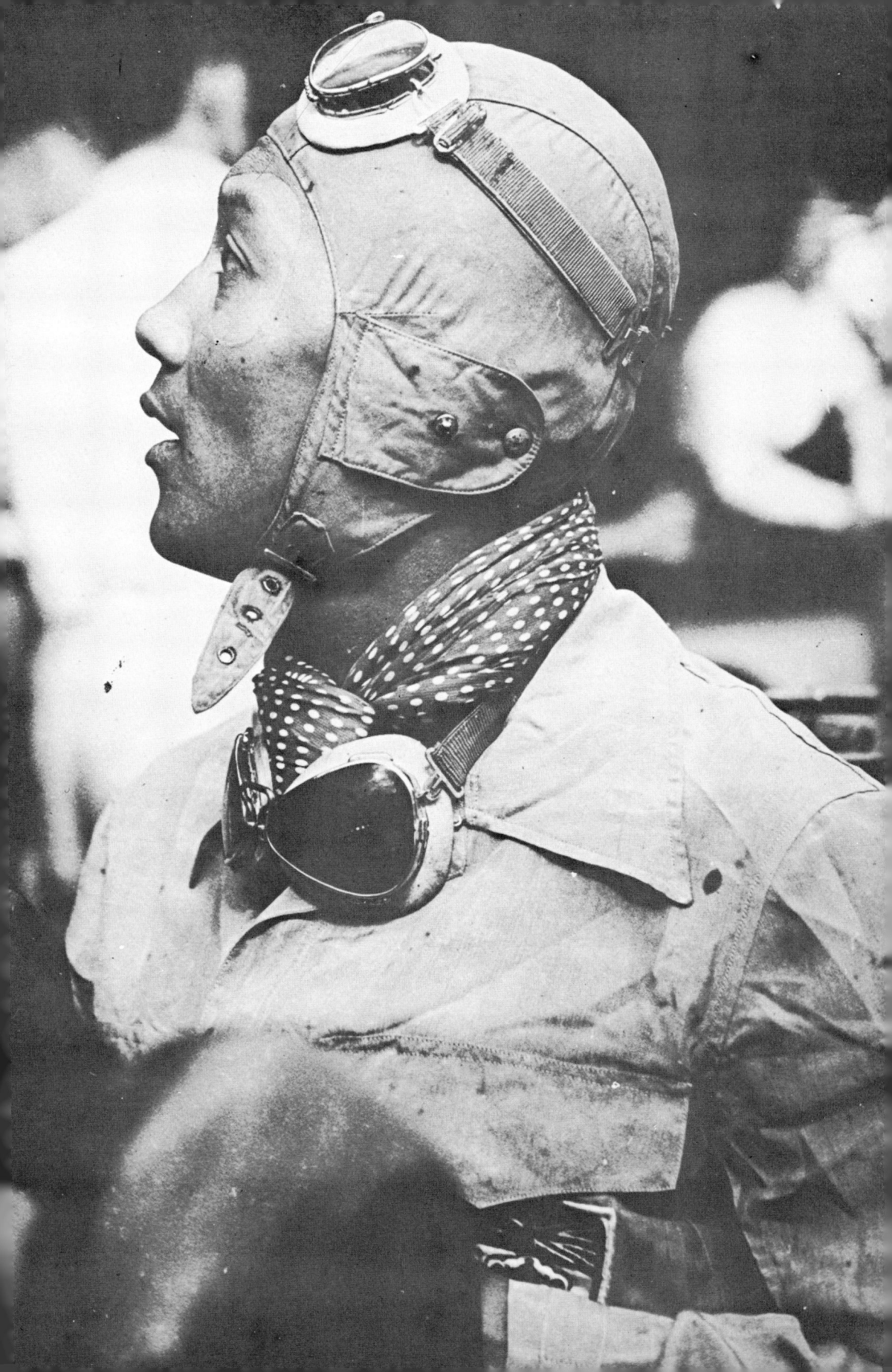

CHAPTER 6

THAILAND

Pilot Princes and the Flying Princess

The scene could be any of the famous motor racing circuits of Europe in the mid-nineteen-thirties. By modern standards the cars hurtling around the track are tall, conveying an impression of top-heaviness. At intervals a car pulls into the pits to be descended upon by an army of mechanics. Within seconds the wheels are off and others, shod with new tyres, are being tightened on their hubs. Fuel is poured in, the driver swallows a quick lemonade, then eager hands push the monster into life and it roars off around the track once more, while an anxious team manager surveys his stop watch.

At this very moment a hyacinth-blue ERA is about to commence the ritual. It has the name Romulus and a white mouse painted on its sides and the driver is wearing a matching blue overall. Helping in the pit is an attractive blonde, typically English and contrasting rather strikingly with the driver, who has pushed up his goggles to reveal a round, boyish face of Eastern origin. It is the famous face of a famous racing driver, B. Bira or more correctly His Highness Prince Birabongse, Bhanudeg Bhanubandh, royal prince of Thailand. Under the management of his older cousin and guardian, Prince Chula Chakrabongse, he carried away a roomful of trophies from the racetracks of Britain and Europe and established himself as a legend among spectators and participants alike. The organising genius of Chula and the driving skill of Bira made a formidable combination and to this day there are many associated with the track who credit the two princes with the introduction of new standards to motor racing. The team was very much a family enterprise, with Bira as driver and Chula's wife Elizabeth (H.H. Princess Chula Chakrabongse) the English girl helping with the split-second organisation at the pits.

In boyhood Prince Birabongse had served in the royal palace as a page to King Rama VI. Following an elementary schooling in Bangkok, the Prince was sent to Eton, the King's *alma mater*. On the death of his father in 1928 he came under the guardianship of Chula, another, older great-grandson of King Mongkut and grandson of Chulalongkorn. Chula was a generous guardian, and it was his gift to Bira of a potent Riley Imp sports car at the age of eighteen that provided the inspiration

The first aeroplane to fly in Thailand, a Farman biplane. Crown Prince Chakrabongse accompanying a French pilot about to take-off from what is now Don Muang International Airport (1911). *By permission of Princess Chula Chakrabongse.*

Prince Birabongse in the famous E.R.A. 'Romulus,' with his cousin and racing manager Prince Chula Chakrabongse.

for Bira's racing career. Not long after he had started with the Imp, Bira took an eminent motoring journalist for a breathtaking ride around London which ended in a 180-degree skid—rather appropriately outside St. George's Hospital. By the time he was 21, Bira had progressed from the little Riley to 'Romulus,' the ERA racing car which made his reputation, and in which he won his first European race at Dieppe in 1935. Bira's skill with his hands was not confined to driving. In the same year, 1935, he studied sculpture under Sir Charles Wheeler and his work was exhibited at the Royal Academy.

The Bira-Chula partnership succeeded without the advantages of a motoring tradition, for none existed in Thailand, although King Chulalongkorn introduced the motor car to his fellow-countrymen as early as 1902. Apparently this affinity for the mechanical was shared by his senior wife, Queen Saowabha (polygamy was practised until 1932). Her Majesty would buy, from various countries, perhaps twenty or so cars at a time. They would be driven slowly around the palace gardens

RIGHT The winner! A jubilant Prince Birabongse at the end of the 1936 International Trophy Race. The Autocar.

while the Queen reviewed her private motor show, deciding on merit which car should be presented to those fortunate enough to be on her list.

At the beginning of World War II there were several Thai princes in Britain and they were forbidden by their King to become involved in the conflict, whatever their sympathies, because initially Thailand was a neutral state. She remained so until the Japanese invasion of December 1941. Then the situation changed and B. Bira, racing motorist, sculptor and royal prince, tried to join the British Royal Air Force so that he might become a pilot.

At the time there were few Siamese pilots, although Thailand had been one of the first royal houses to show interest in aviation when, in 1911, Crown Prince Chakrabongse, father of Prince Chula, flew with a Frenchman who brought the first aeroplane to Siam. There being as yet no established flying kit, the Crown Prince decided that cavalry uniform and spurs would be most appropriate for the occasion! His half brother Prince Purachatra flew later that day and the site chosen by the Crown Prince for the demonstration later developed into Bangkok International Airport (Don Muang). It was a wise choice because, in a country noted for its rainfall, Don Muang is never flooded.

Bira, however, was denied the opportunity of becoming a pilot in the R.A.F. because of defective vision. It is perhaps not generally known that he wore corrective lenses in his goggles while motor racing and, although this was an eminently practical solution to the problem, there were circumstances, such as possible emergencies, which made corrected goggles for pilots unacceptable to the R.A.F. This was a bitter disappointment, particularly since his younger brother, Prince Chirasakti, was by now flying with the Air Transport Auxiliary, ferrying aircraft from the factories to the squadrons. He was later killed while engaged in this important work.

Following his rejection Prince Birabongse joined the Home Guard; he took up gliding and very soon began teaching the art to A.T.C. cadets, schoolboys waiting to join the R.A.F. It paved the way to other things and sharpened his interest in aviation to the extent that, on the resumption of private flying after the war, he went to Marshalls, the famous school of flying at Cambridge, going solo after only 3 hours and 35 minutes dual instruction (the minimum is usually seven hours). On 7 January 1946 he became the first pupil pilot in Britain to gain a post-war 'A' Licence, the equivalent of a present day Private Pilot's Licence. He had caught the flying 'bug' and was beyond all cure.

His first aeroplane was an Auster bought for him by the ever-generous Chula who, despite his willingness to encourage light aviation, steadfastly refused to fly in the machine. This was not motivated by mistrust of the Auster so much as a general aversion to flying as a means of transport. However, the light aeroplane had become

Bira's prime means of getting to racetracks in rapid succession. He had been quick to realise that even a relatively slow private aircraft can provide the nearest answer to the problem of being in two places at once. Today, many of the leading racing drivers use an aeroplane in this way. An acute shortage of labour and materials in the immediate post-war years was more a challenge than a frustration to the prince, who set about preparing a small private airfield near Tredethy, the Cornish estate of his cousin Chula. A little hangar was built for the Auster, which was soon replaced by the larger and more comfortable Miles Messenger. The Messenger could lift four adults and their luggage out of small fields that were inaccessible to most other aircraft. Essential flying between motor races was supplemented by a continued interest in gliding, and to this he applied his usual professionalism. In 1946 he achieved a flight of 187 miles (at the time just 22 miles short of the world record). Three years later he won the South American Gliding Championship, held at Buenos Aires. He developed an expert eye for the weather and, although some regarded his flying in marginal conditions as foolhardy, his flights were always carefully planned and decided upon only after lengthy discussion with the 'met' man.

When finally Prince Chula could be persuaded to fly with his younger cousin, there must have been times when he regretted ever changing his mind. It should be remembered that until more recent years light aircraft radio has been limited in scope and reliability, so that bad weather flying in the fifties was often a case of 'press on, use your watch, compass and altimeter, and hope for a hole in the cloud at the other end.' There was the day Prince Bira set off for a race meeting in Monte Carlo accompanied by Princess Chula Chakrabongse, who enjoyed flying, and her husband Prince Chula who, it will be remembered, did not. They took off in a haze that got steadily worse until nothing could be seen except the water immediately below. They flew on and on while a nervous Prince Chula studiously read a book until finally he could stand it no longer. Turning to Bira he said 'Shouldn't we have crossed the Channel by now?' Bira then admitted that the weather was unfit, adding 'I have turned back and we shall be landing at Lympne in a few moments, when we can wait for the weather to improve and have another try for Monte Carlo.' Prince Chula insisted on taking his wife by public transport but Bira took off again and his was the only light aircraft to land at Nice that day.

On another occasion they flew to Southampton. Queen Rambai was returning to Thailand in the liner *Willem Ruys* and they were there to see Her Majesty safely and comfortably on board. As the ship pulled away from its berth the two princes quickly found a taxi and made for the airport. Within minutes they were airborne and heading out after the *Willem Ruys*, now leaving Southampton Water. The Queen stood on deck acknowledging the frantic waves of farewell so clearly visible through the windows of the low-flying aircraft, which circled the liner several times at porthole level before turning for land. Waving from the bridge, but in a rather different manner, was the Captain. He had taken exception to the little fly buzzing around his great ship and an unfriendly radio message was sent to Southampton Airport forthwith. It was never received by the two princes because after leaving the ship they flew to their private airfield in Cornwall.

Among royalty living in Britain, Prince Birabongse may be regarded as a pioneer on the post-war flying scene. Even by 1948 there were only two other members of royal families with Private Pilot's Licences, neither of them British. One of these was Prince Alexander, brother of the late King Peter of Yugoslavia, and the other was Princess Windisch-Graetz of Austria.

On 3 August 1949 Prince Birabongse was in his glider, being towed by an aircraft of the Plymouth and District Aero Club, flown by Wing Commander R. J. B. Pierce, O.B.E. It was just after midday when the prince cast off at a point near the Cornish town of Launceston. Almost immediately he experienced freak conditions of extreme turbulence, so bad in fact that he decided to land as quickly as possible. He found a suitable field and came in low, barely missing some power cables, but just as he seemed to be making a perfect landing, strong gusts of wind caught the sailplane which crashed and was wrecked. Bira crawled out from the pile of splintered plywood, having suffered no more than the temporary loss of his gold watch, which was later found for him by the local police.

By now Bira had replaced his single-engined Messenger with a Miles Gemini, the first light twin-engined aircraft of post-war design to be produced in any country, and in many ways an ingenious little aeroplane, incorporating the wings and many other components of its single-engined cousin, the Messenger. It was powered by a pair of Cirrus Minor engines of only 100 h.p. each and it had an electrically-operated retractable undercarriage. Even by modern standards the cabin was large, offering saloon-car comfort for four adults. Luggage went in a nose compartment and under the seats. It could carry 66 Imperial gallons of fuel, enough for some 950 miles range, but with that amount of petrol, only three passengers could be accommodated. Otherwise the take-off and subsequent climb-out was an experience few pilots would want to repeat. As a convenient base for the European racetracks, the prince had a villa near the airport at Cannes, and it was his delight to 'beat up' the beaches at full throttle in the Gemini until an embarrassed airport manager issued a tactful word of discouragement.

It was while Prince Birabongse was staying with his cousin at Tredethy that an ambitious scheme filled his imagination to the point where sleep or indeed normal conversation became impossible. After many years away from his country, he would fly his Gemini right from London to Bangkok. He would take his Argentine-born wife, Chelita, and their West Highland Terrier, Tich. They would visit so many wonderful places on the way that it would be a trip never to be forgotten.

Prince Chula was horrified at the idea. Even the air-minded Princess Chula did her best to dissuade Bira, drawing to his attention the vast areas of water to be covered. True, the Gemini had two engines but, unless it was lightly loaded, height could not be maintained in the event of an engine failure and in the hot climates likely to be experienced this already marginal single-engine performance would become still worse. But Prince Bira is a determined character, and soon the floor of the large study at Tredethy was covered in maps. At least one-third of the journey would be over water, and for the first time he began to realise that, although our world may be one tiny planet in a vast universe, to a light aeroplane it is a very large place indeed.

The Gemini was painted in his racing livery of hyacinth blue, with the famous white mice on either side of the nose and yellow registration letters G–AJWH. He took with him a spare propeller, extra tyres and a replacement magneto. Spread across the two rear seats was a small mountain of luggage topped by an inflatable dinghy, which made a comfortable bed for Tich.

The Gemini at Beirut. 4 a.m. departure for Baghdad en route for Bangkok.

At 16.39 on 15 October 1952, the little blue Gemini accelerated down the runway at London's Gatwick Airport before heading for Paris, the first stop. In his book *Blue Wings to Bangkok* the prince describes the flight in some detail.

Certainly there were moments to remember, the uneventful contrasting with the dramatic. During the leg to Athens, the Gemini was thrown about rather badly over Corfu, and Tich jumped down from his perch on top of the dinghy, taking refuge on his mistress's lap with an expression of disenchantment on his shaggy white face which was more eloquent than any words. At Athens Airport they met two young Englishmen who were flying a rather tired-looking Auster with the words 'Kuala Lumpur or Bust' painted on its sides. After a pleasant flight to Rhodes there were some terrifying moments in a thundercloud before landing at Cyprus.

A night landing at Beirut was followed by a take-off in the early hours of the morning, intended to avoid the mid-day build-up of violent thunderclouds on the way to Baghdad. The utter darkness of an Arabian night made way for the sun, climbing over scattered clouds and sending down fingers of light which brushed the featureless sand below. It stretched in all directions to the limit of vision. There had as yet been no map-reading and no radio aids, just a watch and the compass for navigation. Yet, dead on time a pipeline appeared below, guiding them to their destination, as the Gemini flew on and Bira fought to stay awake in the hot atmosphere. Sandstorms rose to a height of 5,000 ft., and these had to be avoided because petrol engines are allergic to sand even when it is mixed with copious quantities of air.

The flight from Baghdad to Basra revealed some views of true magnificence. To the left were the mountains of Iran while on the right was the Iraqi desert. The river Tigris was directly below, snaking its way through a narrow strip of fertile land. King Feisal had sent telegrams from Baghdad to his various royal friends on the route to Bangkok warning them to expect a flying Siamese Prince and his Argentine wife. As a result the Sheikh of Kuwait made elaborate preparations for their arrival. They climbed out of the aircraft to be received by two Sheikhs and an Arab guard of honour, standing to attention around a magnificent Persian carpet spread out over the sand of the desert aerodrome. At Sharja, the next stop, the British Major in command of the Arab Guard insisted that Bira, dressed as he was in sports shirt and bright red shorts, should inspect his men. It was here that Sheikh Saga gave Princess Chelita a priceless gold necklace studded in colourful gems.

And so the flight continued with stops at Jiwani, where they had to put motor fuel in the Gemini, followed by a lifeless, depressing leg to Karachi and on to Indore, where they stayed with the Maharaja of Holkar.

From Indore they flew on to Allahabad with its tree-lined approaches, then to a

Calcutta so overpopulated that it was difficult to walk at night for people and cattle lying asleep on the pavements.

The flight from Calcutta to Akyab involved a 130-mile crossing over isolated marshland, the breeding ground of crocodiles and in the opinion of Prince Bira this part of the earth could only be described as 'the sore on the earth's skin.' The beauty of Akyab's white beaches gave way to the rugged coast of Burma, its endless scatter of little islands and fishing boats with sails of various colours. They landed at Rangoon where the Burmese looked so like his fellow-countrymen to Prince Bira that instinctively he tried without success to converse in Thai. Rangoon, the capital of Burma, Thailand's ancient enemy of countless wars! It is perhaps symbolic of this turbulent history that over the very route used by the invading Burmese the Gemini gave cause for concern for the first time since leaving London. With so much of the journey behind him, it was to Bira more infuriating than alarming when the starboard engine began to shake and misfire. The temperature was high, thinning the air and causing the little aeroplane to lose height on the remaining power of the live engine, which under the strain soon began to overheat. After fifty minutes they had descended to 1,500 ft. over the jungle—then the engine cleared itself. They landed at Bangkok to a tumultuous welcome. It had been a fine achievement; 7,319 miles involving more than fifty-nine hours of flying at an average speed of 121 m.p.h. He had used 718 gallons of petrol.

Prince Birabongse later received an invitation to drive for Maserati. It was a difficult choice between remaining among his people and returning to the freedom of motor racing and the South of France. He flew back to Europe in his Gemini.

The Chula-Bira partnership was, alas, finally broken by the death of Prince Chula Chakrabongse towards the end of 1963. Prince Birabongse is now once again in Bangkok, operating Bira Air Transport, an air charter company which made the headlines when one of its Cessna light aircraft was hijacked by an American who forced the pilot to fly him to Vietnam.

* * * * * *

Among other Thai princes living in England at the outbreak of World War II was His Highness Prince Varanand, another grandson of King Chulalongkorn and a cousin of Bhumibol, the present King of Thailand. He is at first meeting a perplexing man because, although unmistakably Siamese in appearance, in his accent he is typically British and readily recognised as a product of the R.A.F. He was born in Bangkok on 19 August 1922 (corresponding to the Buddhist year 2465). Early schooling at the Chitrladda Palace was followed by a year in Washington, U.S.A., where he attended Sidwell's Friends' School. In 1935 he came to England, went to preparatory school for one year, then became a pupil at Marlborough College.

By now thoroughly Anglicized, he entered into life at Magdalene College, Cambridge, with some relish, trying his hand at most of the non-academic activities available to undergraduates. This enthusiasm for the Cambridge way of life rather conflicted with his studies for the science tripos. Later he turned to medicine but by now World War II had started. Thailand had been drawn into the turmoil under the heel of Japan, and Prince Varanand therefore felt himself free to take sides. It was the beginning of 1942 and many of his friends were leaving university to join up. The Prince had no need to join a British fighting service but would often remember the good times he had enjoyed with his school and university friends. Now that circumstances were less happy, he wanted to join them in uniform—and at the same time escape the embarrassment of learning about 'interesting' examination results. It was a lighthearted enough conversation which made him decide to go to war in a foreign uniform:

'A particularly close friend said to me, quite jokingly, "How about you, you old villain, are you still just enjoying life? You're a lucky devil aren't you, not having to join up!" Well [Prince Varanand continued] boats make me seasick, so the Navy was out. I didn't like walking so the Army was out. What else was there left?—the Air Force.'

In case the Royal House in Bangkok withheld consent to join the R.A.F., Varanand conveniently 'forgot' to ask permission. Instead he went through the machine like any other cadet.

He got his R.A.F. wings and was commissioned as a Pilot Officer on 24 June 1943. Soon he was flying Spitfires on shipping patrol. The serious business of enjoying himself really started again when he joined 132 Squadron and went with it to France on 25 June 1944. They were a wild bunch of fighter boys in 132, determined to make a great nuisance of themselves, dive-bombing V1 flying bomb sites, shooting

RIGHT Prince Varanand of Thailand.   *Alan Bramson Photo.*

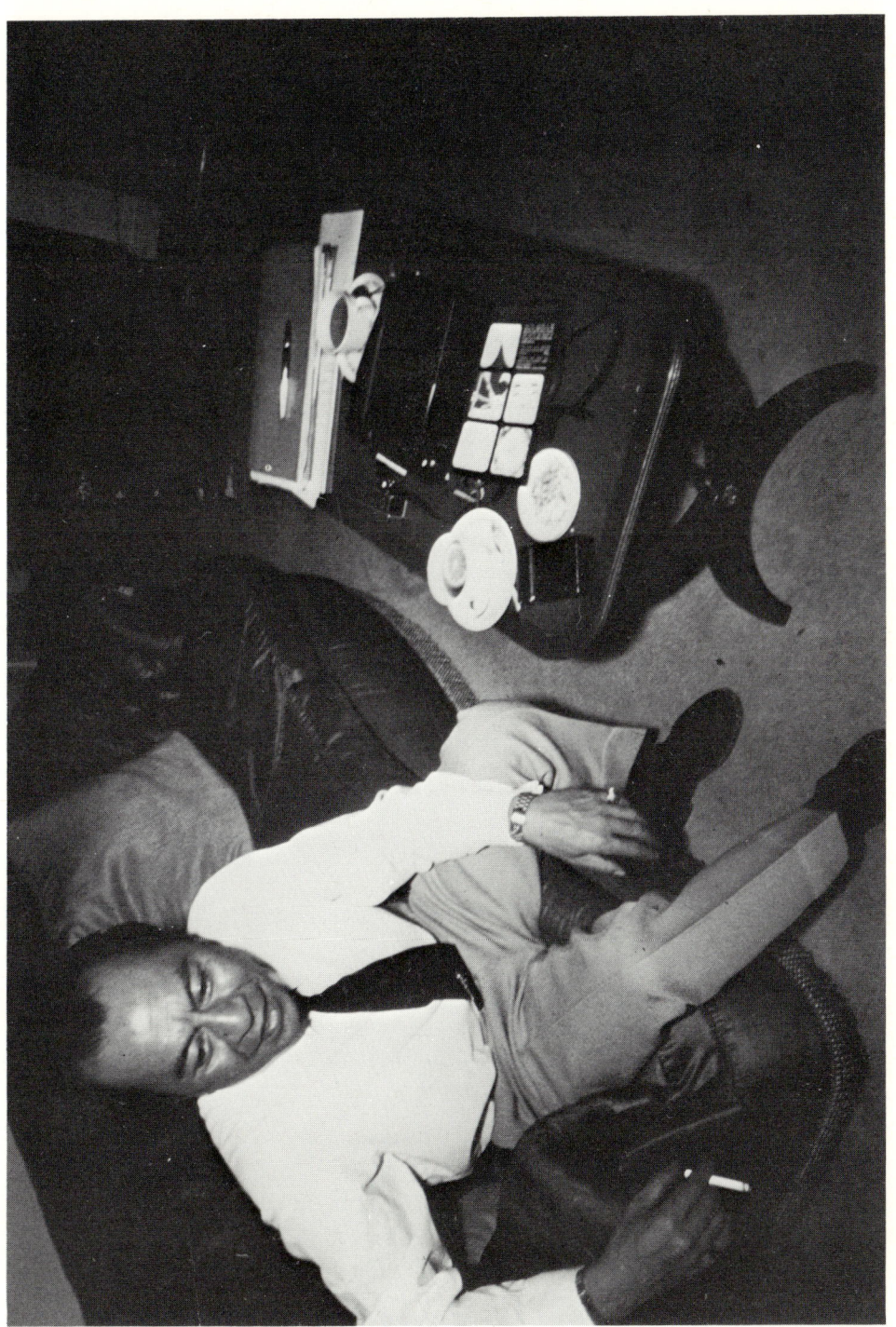

up trains and generally mixing it with the now-defensive Luftwaffe. 7 July was a particularly fruitful day for the pilots of 132 Squadron. They scored 6 aircraft destroyed, 2 'probable' and 4 damaged. Prince Varanand was flying in 'Blue' section which shot down 2 enemy aircraft, claimed 2 'probables' and damaged 3 others, although he is quick to say, 'Personally, I did not even get a near miss.' He did, however, put himself at the wrong end of a Messerschmitt 109 with its cannon blazing and he was lucky to return with the remainder of the Squadron. Clearly 132 had cause to celebrate and very soon the town of Bayeux resounded to the strident singing of unprintable R.A.F. songs from the celebrating fighter pilots.

Prince Varanand, known by now to his fellow-pilots as 'Nicky,' had formed the habit of flying with his battledress worn over pyjamas—'It was less itchy that way.' In his anxiety to enter the town in triumph with his colleagues, he forgot to change into a shirt and tie. As the evening progressed, a rather drunken officer wearing R.A.F. battledress, pyjamas, flying scarf and flying boots, yet for all that looking decidedly un-British, suddenly came face to face with an officer of the military police. This worthy had never seen anything like it before. The gently swaying figure confronting him was unable to produce his identity card or discs and that was enough; Prince Varanand was arrested. After two hours behind bars some pilots from 132 Squadron were ushered into the gaol and asked if they could identify the oriental gentleman claiming to be a real R.A.F. fighter pilot. They even brought in the leader of 'Blue' section, who had been in the dog-fight with Prince Varanand that very afternoon. Of course they all disowned him, at first with perfectly straight faces, until a burst of hilarious laughter spoiled the deception. 'No, we don't know old Nicky,' they protested. Then, turning to him, they added 'Don't be late for readiness to-morrow.' On the strength of this the Prince was released.

Fighter sweeps continued during the Allied advance but apart from a rudder damaged by enemy fire Varanand was very lucky: 'I went through the war without even a nosebleed.'

With the war in Europe drawing to a close, Prince Varanand was posted to the Far East on 'cloak and dagger' operations, ferrying agents behind the enemy lines. Before the work could become interesting it was decided that, in the light of Japanese withdrawal from many fronts, Thailand should receive Allied assistance. Someone who spoke Thai should be parachuted into the country to find suitable airfields for the Free Thai Forces and at the same time determine the strength of the Japanese. Who better qualified for the task than Flight-Lieutenant 'Nicky' Varanand? They sent him to Jessore for his parachute course. At 7 a.m. he was shown how to land without breaking his neck and by 5 p.m. they had pushed him out of a Dakota. It was his first real jump.

Shortly afterwards he met the Commanding Officer over a cup of tea. 'When do I get my next six jumps?' he asked. 'As far as I am concerned,' was the C.O.'s reply, 'you have done the course. You didn't break a leg here and I couldn't care less what happens now. You are not going to break anything at my school. If you are going to break a leg you may do it in the field!' Thus ended, in one day, a course that should have lasted three weeks, yet without further preparation His Highness Prince Varanand, Flight Lieutenant pilot in the Royal Air Force, was given the code name 'Nid' and dropped out of an aeroplane into north-east Thailand. The local peasants had no idea who he was or why he was there but he lived in a field for seven days, collected information about the Japanese, located suitable airfields for the Free Thai Forces, then departed in a Dakota of 257 Squadron which had obligingly flown in to pick him up.

Prince Varanand ended the war on staff duties in Kandy, Ceylon. He had served in one of the most dangerous branches of the fighting services and after three years in what to him was a foreign air force it would have been reasonable to expect him to accept his demobilisation gladly and return to his country. There were many princes and princesses in Thailand, often with very tenuous connections with the monarchy owing to the practice of polygamy, but Prince Varanand could, at one time, have acceded to the throne.* He was no junior prince and many of his friends would therefore have expected him to involve himself in the activities of the royal house of Thailand, but he was now used to squadron life and proud of his association with the R.A.F. He elected to remain in the service as a peace-time officer. Until March 1946 His Highness was a liaison officer with the British Military Mission stationed in Thailand. He spent an enjoyable six months flying Spitfires around Bangkok before returning to England for a staff course at R.A.F. Digby. When later he was posted to 54 Fighter Squadron, he helped to organise the first crossing of the Atlantic by jet aircraft, Vampires of 54 Squadron.

The de Havilland Mosquito was in 1949 still performing a useful role within the R.A.F., primarily on photographic survey and map-making, and by May of that year Prince Varanand had completed his conversion training on these fine war-time aircraft. His association with the Mosquito continued until 15 January 1951, when he took off from Benson in Oxfordshire with instructions to photograph Munich. While crossing the Channel he carried out a routine check of the engine instruments and immediately realised that his starboard motor was about to fail, possibly in a rather spectacular manner. It was promptly shut down, the propeller feathered to prevent further damage and since this was the engine driving the generator he

* Prince Chula Chakrabongse, *Lords of Life*, pp. 300, 302.

The end of a Mosquito. An unsuccessful single-engined landing at R.A.F. Benson. The runway is still wet with the remains of 500 gallons of petrol. Flight Lieutenant Prince Varanand's torn parachute is in front of the wreckage.

requested the Navigator to obtain a position before switching off the radio, it being vital to conserve the battery. By now he had already turned for home.

They flew on until Benson was only 15 minutes away, then switched on the radio and requested clearance for an emergency landing on one engine. At this point the battery died and they never received the reply, warning Prince Varanand that a forty-knot wind was blowing across the runway and advising a diversion to nearby Abingdon, which had a more suitable runway available. No other aircraft were flying around Benson and they naturally thought that control had cleared the circuit for their benefit. Indeed, this would be the usual procedure when an emergency landing was imminent.

Prince Varanand brought his crippled Mosquito round the turn on to final approach. He came in on one engine—the other lifeless, with its propeller immobile. The wind was strong, drifting him to one side of the runway ahead. As he struggled to line up with the approach they struck a tree. He continues the story:

'I consider myself very lucky to be alive because there were so many things we did that we should not have done. Firstly in the pilots notes they recommended that in a Mosquito if you have to do an emergency landing be sure to feather the port engine even if it means doing a "dead stick" [no power] landing, otherwise you have the danger of the propeller breaking off, coming in and cutting off your legs. And with a Mk 34, what we called the "pregnant belly" [a reference to the long-range fuel tank under the floor] even if the tank is empty you must never do a belly landing. Bale out because sparks could make it explode if the undercarriage collapsed.

Instead of the port propeller coming in and cutting off my legs the entire engine broke away from the wing and went on for another two hundred yards. I still had 500 gallons of fuel left on board and the thing just burst open without catching fire.'

The navigator was killed and Prince Varanand suffered a broken back and a crushed ankle, yet by August of that year he was flying again.

In the nine years following his near-fatal accident the prince managed to fly most of the 'first generation' jet aircraft entering R.A.F. service; Meteors, Vampires, Venoms and the massive Javelin all-weather fighter that weighed more than a pre-war air liner.

Flight Lieutenant Prince 'Nicky' Varanand in 1955.

Central Fighter Establishment

Fighter Combat School

FLIGHT LIEUTENANT N. VARANAND

successfully completed No. 1 Course at the Fighter Combat School and is awarded the category Fighter Combat Leader.

Date of Course
12th MAY, 1958
to
18th JULY, 1958

Wing Commander
Commanding
Fighter Combat School
Central Fighter Establishment

Fighter Combat Leader certificate gained after completing No. 1 Course at the Fighter Combat School.

When the cold war in Europe between East and West was at its height, he took one-hour turns sitting in the cockpit of a Javelin while it stood near the end of the runway at two minutes 'readiness.' Within those 120 seconds, he and his squadron colleagues would have had to start the engines, take off, climb away and be ready for immediate action against enemy raiders.

On 29 February 1960 a somewhat disappointed Prince Varanand retired, at his own request, from the air force he loved. He had served as a pilot in war and peace for eighteen years. Realising that he was an officer in a foreign air force, he never aspired to greater ambitions than to be a squadron commander but even this was not to be. In retrospect, the Prince will say he was something of a 'Walter Mitty' and very much 'one of the boys' so that he never rose beyond the rank of Flight-Lieutenant. But there are many in the British Air Force today who still talk of Nicky Varanand with great affection. He left behind many friends, when the time came for his return to Thailand, and 54 Squadron are still wearing the tie he presented to them.

Prince Varanand is now married to Her Celestial Highness Princess Galyani, sister to the reigning monarch, His Majesty King Bhumibol. A Celestial Highness is in Thailand the most senior rank among Princes or Princesses, followed by Royal Highness, Highness and Serene Highness, in descending order of precedence.

Princess Galyani was born in London. As a girl, she was educated in Switzerland where her brother Prince Ananda Mahidol, a boy in poor health, was under treatment. At the age of ten he was acclaimed the eighth King of the Chakri dynasty, but on 9 June 1946, while still a young man, he was found shot, apparently with his own pistol. After a trial lasting several years two of the royal pages were executed for their connection with the assassination. King Ananda Mahidol was succeeded by his younger brother, the present King Bhumibol. His only sister, Princess Galyani, a tall attractive woman of great charm, is inclined to be rather shy at first meeting. The Princess speaks French as well as her own language and her English has a slight French accent, but equal fluency. As sister to the reigning monarch she has official functions to attend, but like all Thai royalty Her Celestial Highness has an occupation, teaching French at a Bangkok university.

There were only two women pilots in Thailand in 1957, when in August of that year the Princess began flying instruction on a Tiger Moth belonging to the flying club run by the Thai Air Force, based on Don Muang Airport. She qualified for her civil pilot's 'wings' the following December. When a King's sister learns to fly it would be reasonable to expect every precaution to be taken, even to the point of over-caution, but there was little interference other than a request by the authorities that 'first solo' should be postponed until the Princess had completed eighteen hours of instruction, whereas her flying instructor would have let her fly alone some six hours earlier. Since gaining her pilot's licence Princess Galyani has flown a number of British and American light aircraft, including the Chipmunk and the Piper Cub. She has also made a flight as second pilot in a T-33 jet aircraft of the Thai Air Force. Her ambition to land on glaciers—thus combining her old love, skiing, with her new-found interest—has yet to be fulfilled.

As a member of any royal house other than his own, Flight-Lieutenant Prince Varanand, R.A.F. retired, would have returned home to a life of official functions, but, as already mentioned, in Thailand even those close to the King are working Princes and Princesses in the true sense. Princes are to be found holding important positions in every walk of life and it was therefore considered quite natural for Prince Varanand to become a professional airline pilot with Thai Airways International, a subsidiary company of Scandinavian Airlines System. He joined the airline at the beginning of June 1962 and a year later went on a course in Stockholm for his Airline Transport Pilot's Licence, the highest category of professional pilot's licence.

It says a lot for Prince Varanand's skill and concentration that, despite the reduction of his course from thirteen to only seven weeks, he passed the final examinations and gained his A.L.T.P. Within a few years he had become a Captain on Caravelle jet aircraft and, although there have been other royal airline pilots, few have gained a captaincy.

To Captain Varanand, flying scheduled routes with Thai Airways International was rather like serving in a foreign air force, in that most of the key personnel were not his fellow-countrymen. He desperately wanted to see a truly Siamese airline, run, maintained and flown by Thai personnel, even if in the short term foreign help would be needed to establish the enterprise. Thailand is imagined by many people living in the western world to be a little country; it is actually rather larger in area than Spain. Its only rail link is with Malaysia and, although the roads are improving, long-distance motoring is still something of an adventure. The aeroplane provides an immediate answer to the problem of internal and external communications and these days 90 per cent of all visitors to Bangkok arrive by air. Against this background, and spurred on by his desire to see the development of Thai aviation, Prince Varanand resigned from Thai Airways International on 31 August 1965 and founded his own air transport company, Varan Air-Siam, which is now called Air-Siam. It was the first private-enterprise airline to be established in Thailand.

The formation of a new airline is a major task, since its life-blood, the route structure, usually involves agreements with other countries at government level. Then there is the vital matter of purchasing the correct type of aircraft. After visits to Canada and the U.S.A., Prince Varanand came to Britain and chose the Super VC10

ABOVE Princess Galyani after gaining her pilot's wings.

ABOVE, LEFT AND MIDDLE LEFT Her Celestial Highness Princess Galyani learning to fly in a Tiger Moth.

BELOW, LEFT Flying a Chipmunk.

BELOW Jet pilot Princess.

Prince Varanand and Princess Galyani arriving at Don Muang Airport, Bangkok.

as being the long range civil transport most suited to his operation. Negotiations were started with the manufacturers, the British Aircraft Corporation, a preliminary contract being signed on 21 April 1966. At a fully-equipped price in excess of £3 million per aircraft the purchase of three VC10's was in itself a mammoth commitment for an airline that had not even started to fly.

There were many things to be done before a final contract could be signed. Thai government support had to be obtained so that negotiations could be commenced with other countries, otherwise Varan Air-Siam would have no routes to fly. Then there was the problem of staff; there were few skilled maintenance engineers of Thai nationality and still fewer licensed aircrew. Furthermore, there were no Thais with the commercial experience applicable to a modern airline. To meet these difficulties Prince Varanand adopted the enlightened procedure of inviting foreign experts between the ages of 55 to 60 to join him in Bangkok. They would be paid attractive salaries in return for training bright young Thais in their respective jobs, with a view to handing over in about five years' time when, in any case, retirement on pension would be due. He was, of course, buying experience and passing on the learning of a lifetime to his fellow-countrymen. One of the old hands chosen for his expertise and specialist knowledge was Ivor Gregory, for many years Chief Maintenance Engineer with British European Airways. During the short time he was in Bangkok, Gregory formed a very high regard for his boss. He reports:

> 'The thing that impressed me most about Nicky was that he is an enthusiast and, you know, enthusiasm does generate a splendid bunch of people. He had around him a number of Thais who were really keen, and what they didn't know they would learn quickly because of the enthusiasm he had inspired in them. I felt he had unique characteristics. He was very sincere. He communicated well, and when he approached you on a subject to get your advice he went to extreme measures to ensure that you knew the whole of the problem.'

With his background of wild days at Cambridge and still wilder ones in the Royal Air Force, the sceptic could be forgiven for questioning Prince Varanand's ability to run an airline and, even more unlikely, to start one from scratch. But he seems to have inherited considerable clarity of thought and shrewdness of judgement, often tinged with the idealistic. For example, in a letter to the Minister of Communications in Bangkok the Prince said:

> 'Your Excellency can rest assured that Varan Air-Siam will, in every respect, keep alive and maintain the Thai national characteristics of gentleness and amicability towards all countries and peoples who extend to us these reciprocal traits of friendliness.'

In an imperfect world the success of a commercial enterprise is contingent upon more than just enlightened sentiments. Unfortunately Varan Air-Siam encountered difficulties with its route network, the VC10's were never delivered (they went instead to Ghana Airways Corporation) and the airline made a more modest start with smaller aircraft and an all-cargo service. Nevertheless, Prince Varanand has achieved one of his prime aims, the establishment of a Thai airline. Once again the initiative has been taken by a member of the royal family, maintaining the innovative tradition of the Chakri dynasty.

The Hohenzollerns

For many hundreds of years a substantial part of Central Europe consisted of provinces, states and small kingdoms individually governed by ruling families who devoted much of their time to quarrelling among themselves. Many of these states and kingdoms formed part of the Holy Roman Empire. Among the more powerful of these ruling families were the Hohenzollerns who originated from Swabia. The dynasty was founded by Buchardus in 1061 and continued by a long line of Brandenburg Princes. By the beginning of the seventeenth century they had gained possession of the lower Rhine in the west and the Dukedom of Prussia in the east. For some time attempts had been made to form a united Germany and it became the practice for an elite of princes, three Spiritual and four Temporal, to elect an Emperor or Kaiser. The Hohenzollerns were among these 'Electors of State.' However, with land and power concentrated in the hands of the Church and the nobility trouble fermented over the centuries which came to a head with the emergence of Protestant teachings and the possibility of a Protestant Kaiser. Against this background, in 1618, commenced the Thirty Years War. As a result the provincial princes became independent of the Emperors who were now regularly elected from the House of Habsburg. While the Habsburg Emperors extended Austria, their homeland, further to the south and south-east, Prussia was, in the north, growing at an even faster rate. Under Frederick the Great it became an important European power. Napoleon destroyed the old realm and in consequence the Habsburgs were confined to Austria.

The German princes, always inclined to be disorderly and quarrelsome, became even more so when Napoleon fell. With the Habsburgs no longer able to assume leadership the princes accepted the Hohenzollern Kings of Prussia and towards the end of the nineteenth century Germany achieved the unity it had long sought. In 1871 Wilhelm I became the first Kaiser of the new Germany and his rule, coupled with the superlative statesmanship of Bismarck, saw the country enter a period of remarkable growth in power and prosperity. Another branch of the House of Hohenzollern provided Rumania with its first Kings.

Wilhelm I was succeeded by his son Friedrich III, father of Kaiser Wilhelm II whose aspirations were to culminate in World War I.

RIGHT H.R.H. Prince Louis Ferdinand of Prussia, head of the house of Hohenzollern, seen here wearing his badge of the 'International Order of Characters.'
Georg Schmidt Photo.

CHAPTER 7

GERMANY

The Kaiser's Flying Family

The Armistice in 1918, confirming the defeat of Germany's armed forces, brought with it revolution. Such was the mood of the people that Kaiser Wilhelm II abdicated and watched from exile in Holland while the country became a republic. So the monarchy in Germany ended, but one influence remained: the Kaiser's traditional dominance over the Hohenzollern family. For example his son, the Crown Prince, had four sons, Wilhelm the eldest being born in 1906. When the second boy arrived on 9 November 1907, the parents wanted him christened Michael after his grandfather, the Archduke Michael, arguing, too, that the Archangel Michael was the Patron Saint of the German people. This was of little consequence to the Kaiser, who overruled the parents on the grounds that the name sounded Russian. Instead, insisted the Kaiser, the infant Prince should be named Louis Ferdinand, after the highly talented nephew of Frederick the Great.

Even in exile the Kaiser continued to exercise iron control over his family and when his oldest grandson Wilhelm became engaged to a commoner, it was made clear that he could no longer be regarded as a future head of the House of Hohenzollern, though by now German royalty existed in title only, with no legal standing. The Kaiser, of course, regarded the revolution as lacking legal standing and upheld the claim of his House to the Imperial crown. Naturally any marriage of his successors would have to be in accordance with the principles of princedom—a predictable enough reaction for the Kaiser, who was once alleged to have said that marriage between a prince and a commoner 'is as biologically impossible as a union between a swan and a goose.'

Extreme views perhaps, but in the Kaiser's days of power such a marriage would have been unthinkable, and exile in Holland was to him no reason for changing his beliefs. He proclaimed that Prince Louis Ferdinand would be the future head of the family, and no one dared disagree. In World War II fate seemed to endorse his decision, since Prince Wilhelm was killed in action in 1940 while fighting in France.

Today, Prince Louis Ferdinand, head of the House of Hohenzollern, lives in a quiet residential district of Bremen. His home, while modest in size, is nevertheless most elegantly furnished and the sounds of farm and domestic animals in neighbouring fields convey a rural atmosphere, though the centre of Bremen is only a short drive away. The Prince is a tall, kindly man, with a friendly approach and a sense of humour which is entirely different from the popular concept of a Prussian prince. He speaks perfect English in a slow, deliberate manner, pronouncing his words with the slightest of accents.

In conversation it soon becomes apparent that outside influences have had a profound effect on the Prince's character. His childhood days were spent in a palace near Danzig, situated on the shores of a great lake, with gardens in the English tradition. All over the world these were formal times and Prussian ruling circles were probably the most formal of all, so that it is surprising to learn that Prince Louis Ferdinand's favourite childhood game was tobogganing. There was nothing particularly undignified about this, except that it was performed not on ice, but down the grand staircases of the Palace on a tea-tray! He was often joined by his brothers and various members of the family—they even persuaded visiting generals and high dignitaries to take part in the sport. At least it relieved the tension of maintaining a dignified façade over long periods.

The young Louis Ferdinand had an English governess, Miss Grimble, and it is to her that he owes his excellent English. An otherwise happy childhood was marred by a somewhat strained relationship with his older brother Wilhelm. Their temperaments were so different. The older boy had the traditional Prussian fondness for military discipline while Louis Ferdinand was more retiring. Moreover Wilhelm gave the impression of being continuously aware of his position as future heir to the throne. To Prince Louis Ferdinand he seemed at the time to be taking advantage of his seniority and this developed in him a rebel attitude and a strong individualistic character. World War I, which started when he was six, meant little to him, but a few years later, at the age of ten, he was commissioned as a Lieutenant in the Prussian Imperial Army. He was of course the youngest officer in the whole Army, although it was considered quite normal at the time for a royal child to start his military training within a few years of leaving the nursery. It ensured that by the time he was eighteen a prince would be ready to command a company. But the war ended and so did the charade, leaving the boy Prince to continue his education in peace.

He went up to Berlin University and a full life of study, drinking and duelling. One incident was brought to the notice of the exiled Kaiser and as a result duelling for Prince Louis Ferdinand was forbidden, although one last meeting was allowed, on a point of honour, because the duel had been accepted before the Kaiser had said 'verboten.'

By now Prince Louis Ferdinand had developed an interest in political and social science and in furtherance of his studies a visit to the Americas was arranged. He met Henry Ford and later worked at the Ford plant in Buenos Aires. His background conferred no advantages and he worked on the production line like any other semi-skilled employee, assembling cars and experiencing the particular brand of monotony that only a repetitive task can inflict. The unbelievable had occurred—a Hohenzollern Prince becoming a worker, rubbing shoulders with the masses and, even more extraordinary, the Kaiser, autocrat supreme, actually admiring him for it. The experience enabled Prince Louis Ferdinand to learn at first hand what went on in the minds and hearts of the workers and it provided him with valuable material when he returned to Berlin University and wrote his Ph.D. thesis.

To the smart set of Buenos Aires, flying was 'out.' It was unfashionable, not to be compared with horseriding and the racetrack and despite its costliness fit only for the working classes. Even Henry Ford did not like his managers flying but since Prince Louis Ferdinand was an ordinary worker on the production line he decided he would learn to be a pilot. He joined the local flying club at Flo Field where the other student pilots were waiters, taxi drivers and all manner of tradesmen with money to spend on the 'unfashionable' sport. The club operated an elderly Curtiss Jenny biplane with speaking tubes which worked only from the flying instructor to his pupil, who was therefore unable to defend himself against verbal abuse by answering back! There was no family opposition to his learning to fly: on the contrary the Kaiser was proud of his favourite grandson's flying. This cut no ice with his flying instructor, a fiery Spaniard who had once earned his living as a taxi-driver. When the Prince was asked if his royal background had protected him from criticism during training, he replied emphatically:

> 'No, no—by no means. Especially this Spanish instructor of mine—he was extremely rude. Nevertheless, I think I owe him my life, because for all his rudeness he pounded into me the safe way of flying. He was an awfully nice man on the ground but up in the air—!!'

Could he remember clearly his first solo flight?

> 'Yes—very much. I was very happy to be rid of this man—he couldn't shout at me any more.'

Nevertheless, Prince Louis Ferdinand planned a return visit to South America, so that he might celebrate his forty years as a pilot with his old instructor.

The ground subjects, limited as they were in 1930, did not come naturally to the

Prince but he gained his pilot's licence in August of that year. On his return to Germany, the authorities required him to convert his Argentinian qualification to a German pilot's licence. This involved very little; in fact, all he had to do was to make three spot landings (a glide from some specified height followed by a touchdown within a prescribed area of the airfield). For the test he borrowed a Klemm monoplane from Seible, the aircraft manufacturer, then he completed the landings in the presence of an official observer at Tempelhof, Berlin's international airport. As he taxied back to the terminal buildings and got out of the aircraft he was astonished to hear the old Imperial Anthem blaring out over the airport's loudspeaker system. It was the same tune as the British 'God Save the King' and this rather embarrassed the Prince, because after World War I it had been laid down in the German constitution that royal titles and prerogatives should be abolished. He decided to have a word with the Airport Manager about this politically doubtful gesture—besides, he wanted to know if the playing of 'God Save etc.' was an implied criticism of his landings! The airport manager, however, assured him that he intended nothing more than to mark the occasion of Prince Louis Ferdinand's qualification as a German pilot by playing the British National Anthem, as there had been many British aircraft visiting Tempelhof of late . . .

This was 1931 and a busy year for the Prince. He had gained his Ph.D. at Berlin University, obtained his pilot's licence and started taking violin lessons from some of the most distinguished musicians of the day. He continues to find great relaxation both as a musician and as a composer. Many of his works have been performed in the concert hall.

In the course of a number of visits to the U.S.A. he became firm friends with Franklin D. Roosevelt, both before and during his Presidency. Aviation in the vastness of Northern America had of necessity developed more rapidly than in Europe, with its frequent train services and relatively short distances between important centres. The Prince was impressed by what he saw and made up his mind to devote himself to flying as a career. In 1935 he joined Lufthansa, the German commercial airline. By that time he had a professional pilot's licence and a multi-engine rating and, although employed in an executive capacity on air route developments, he managed on occasions to fly as first officer on internal and some international routes. The great Rickenbacker invited him to do a survey of civil aviation in the U.S.A. It was a fascinating project, involving a considerable amount of passenger flying over the extensive route network of America. As a result he gained a clear insight into the remarkable progress in airline operation achieved by his American hosts during the 1930's.

Naturally his report to Lufthansa reflected great admiration for civil aviation in

Prince Louis Ferdinand and Princess Kira at their wedding reception on 4 May 1938 held at Doorn, Holland. Standing behind them is the ageing Kaiser Wilhelm. *Prince Louis Ferdinand's personal album.*

the U.S.A. but by now the political mood had changed in Germany. Hitler was at the helm and his 70 million people embarked on a collision course which was to shake the world. The civil airliner had little to offer the Nazis.

On 2 May 1938 Prince Louis Ferdinand married the Grand Duchess Kira of Russia. The original ceremony was conducted at Cecilienhof, but later the Prince and his bride travelled to Doorn in Holland for another marriage at which the exiled Kaiser and other members of the family were present. It was a glittering occasion, reminiscent of the old Imperial days. As if two marriages were not enough, the royal couple went through yet another ceremony in Potsdam, where the Mayor presented them with a copy of *Mein Kampf!* In later years Princess Kira never ceased to enjoy relating the story of her three marriages to one husband.

During 1939 the Führer led his people into ever more lunatic adventures and in September war was declared on Germany, following her invasion of Poland. Some four years before war broke out, Prince Louis Ferdinand had begun his training as a reserve pilot at Neurappin in Brandenburg. Later he qualified as an instrument flying instructor. His own instructor at Neurappin, Otto Kurnika, the only N.C.O. to be awarded Germany's highest honour, the *Pour le Mérite*, was so short-sighted he could barely see the instruments. Now the Prince was called up as a Lieutenant in the Luftwaffe and stationed at Tempelhof. At first he served with a transport squadron, flying Junkers JU52s, the German equivalent to the ubiquitous Dakota. To achieve rigidity, the entire metal outer surface of the JU52 was corrugated and in Britain it was often referred to as 'the flying Nissen Hut,' yet despite its somewhat grotesque appearance it was nevertheless a splendid aeroplane with an excellent safety record. It could fly well on any two of its three engines and the only mechanical failure remembered by Prince Louis Ferdinand was when one undercarriage leg refused to lock down; the aircraft finished the landing chasing its tail in an uncontrollable ground loop. No one was hurt and there was little further damage to the machine, but on another occasion a complete radio failure in bad weather could very well have produced a different outcome.

The Prince was flying from Elbing to Stuttgart, returning from weekend leave, when it happened. The visibility was almost nil, snow was falling and they were picking up a good deal of ice. With no means of communication, desperate attempts were made to maintain visual contact with the ground. By now uncertain of his exact position, the Prince began to descend into the murk—it was a classic flying hazard, possessing all the possibilities of a fatal accident.

During the war, air forces on both sides still used medium-frequency radio and this required a long aerial. To overcome the problem, they used to winch out a length of aerial wire which terminated in a small lead weight. Suddenly this trailing aerial was torn away from the winch. It had caught in a tree! Then, miraculously, a familiar if indistinct sight appeared, almost obliterated by snow and fog. Seconds later they could breathe again, as the wheels of the Junkers rumbled over the frozen surface of their home airfield.

The Hohenzollern family commanded respect to such an extent that even at the height of his power Hitler was known to stand somewhat in awe of the ex-Crown Prince. On the occasions when they met he always addressed Prince Louis Ferdinand as 'Your Royal Highness.' The death in action of Prince Louis Ferdinand's elder brother Wilhelm attracted attention and sympathy to the deposed Royal House, in conflict with the Nazi Party, which regarded the Hohenzollerns as a possible challenge to its supreme control and leadership of the German people. Their anxiety reached a higher pitch on the death of the old Kaiser, early in 1941. Such fear of public sympathy for the Royal Family may well have appeared, to more balanced minds, as symptomatic of the neurosis of Nazi fanatics, but there was some basis for their anxiety, as events were later to confirm.

All this reflected on Prince Louis Ferdinand. The true depth of Nazi feelings was revealed when he was summoned before his Commanding Officer to hear his confidential report for the preceding twelve months, a procedure similar to that practised by the British Royal Air Force. 'It would appear,' said the C.O., 'that you do not seem to be a very enthusiastic supporter of the Third Reich,' adding, in confidence, that he could hardly blame him for that. The Prince asked what his future with the Luftwaffe was to be, and his C.O. replied, 'You are particularly fortunate to have been flying but this will soon have to end. Under the circumstances, would it not be a good idea for Your Highness to transfer from active service to the reserve of officers?' It was not just a hint; he was being advised to resign before he became an embarrassment to the Nazis.

So in December 1941, with the war still in Germany's favour but by no means ended, the Prince discarded his uniform and moved with his family to their estate at Cadinen in East Prussia. By now he had become head of the House of Hohenzollern, and he took up residence in a castle which he regarded as no more than a large farmhouse, a place where he and his family could live in peace. Certainly life was relatively quiet in East Prussia and at times it was hard to remember that Germany was still at war. Once again the Prince could pursue some of his interests: a little hunting, some music, but no flying, because civil aviation for private pilots had been curtailed as an essential war measure. Prince Louis Ferdinand was conscious of the fact that he and his family were under constant observation by members of the Nazi Party. They had some reason to fear him, for a growing body of opinion regarded the later adventures of Adolf Hitler as nothing short of disastrous to Germany and he was a natural target for overtures emanating from certain quarters. As a possible leader of any attempt to overthrow the regime, the Prince could hardly have been a more ideal choice. His pre-war experience in the Ford factory and his known sympathy for the working man assured him acceptance by the progressive element of the German people and, of course, the labour movement as a whole; his royal background made him equally acceptable to the armed forces, and the fact that he had remained aloof from the Nazis as soon as he recognised their gross inhumanity still further strengthened his position in the eyes of his many close friends, some of whom were extremely

RIGHT Father and son admiring 'Preussenadler' (Prussian Eagle) the new aircraft decked in flowers after the naming ceremony.
Georg Schmidt Photo.

influential.

It took a major incident to provoke the Nazis into direct action against him. By the summer of 1944 the Allies had re-entered Europe and the outcome of the war was becoming painfully obvious to the realists in the German High Command. On 20 July a group of officers made an audacious attempt on Hitler's life. A bomb was secreted into a top-level meeting and left in a briefcase near the Führer. It killed several of those present and although the heavy table diverted much of the blast and saved Hitler from death, he was never the same man again.

Prince Louis Ferdinand was not involved in the plot, but he was immediately contacted by the Gestapo. They wanted to see him at his home and there could be no mistaking the reason for their request. In the circumstances, the prospect of a visit from the Gestapo was a particularly alarming one and the Prince had to search his mind as well as his personal belongings, to ensure that he could explain his movements at the time of the attempt. There were certain documents to be put away, of a kind that could be deliberately misinterpreted by the Gestapo. It was no secret that he had been a close friend of President Roosevelt, for example, and the signed photograph so prominently on display was hardly likely to set the tone for a friendly meeting with the secret police. They arrived at the castle, familiar, sinister figures in their long black leather coats, bearing themselves with an arrogance encouraged by the knowledge that the regime gave them its complete support. The Prince received his unwelcome visitors, seating them in a part of the room where a large painting of the late Kaiser seemed to be looking down in disapproval, and he admits this gave him moral support during what started as a difficult interview. The men from the Gestapo questioned and cross-questioned, insinuating in coldly polite tones. Much would depend on the Prince's answers. He offered them wine and this they accepted, again and again. It was a particularly good wine and it soon began to have a devastating effect. The atmosphere began to change; hostility gave way to back-slapping cordiality and in time the Gestapo men were so incapable that Prince Louis Ferdinand had to type his own report on the forms they had brought for the purpose—he even signed them himself! Seven hours after their arrival the Gestapo staggered into the night, shouting farewells and good wishes to their royal suspect. It was a case of self-recommendation being a good thing. The report he had written must have satisfied the authorities, because the Prince was not bothered again.

Before long the final German resistance faded before the advancing armies of the Allies. In the parcelling out of areas of responsibility, Prussia in its entirety fell to the Russians, becoming part of East Germany. Prince Louis Ferdinand had of necessity

RIGHT Prince Louis Ferdinand Jnr. at the controls of 'Preussenadler.'
Georg Schmidt Photo.

Ex-King Michael of Rumania, a picture taken when he was European sales manager of an aircraft firm.

to leave the family estate and it remains to this day behind the 'Iron Curtain.'

Another member of the Hohenzollern family remained behind that 'Curtain' at the war's end. He was King Michael of Rumania, who had come to his throne at 19 years of age, on the abdication of his father, King Carol, in 1940. Rumania was allied to Germany through the influence of her all-powerful Prime Minister, General Antonescu, at whose hands the young King suffered constant humiliation.

In 1943, King Michael had taken a course of flying lessons, probably with the thought of escaping this intolerable situation. He was a keen pupil and an apt one, going solo after only twenty days' instruction. Such precautions proved unnecessary as the German forces in Rumania cracked under the Russian advance. In a remarkable *coup d'état*, the King ordered the arrest of Antonescu and his supporters. With them out of the way, he quickly made peace with the Allies.

The Russian 'liberators' were not inclined to leave Rumania, and their presence soon became as intolerable to the King as his previous constraint. This time, there was no answer to their superiority and in December 1947 King Michael was forced to abdicate. Only a month before, he had stolen the headlines in British newspapers when he flew his twin-engined Beechcraft to London for the wedding of Princess Elizabeth.

The ex-King lives in Geneva now, a businessman with a continuing interest in the air. He has over 1,000 hours of flying time in single and multi-engined aircraft.

For Louis Ferdinand, too, life immediately after the war was far from easy. During the first years of peace he moved from place to place with his wife and seven children. At one time they were living in an attic, often with insufficient food to eat and without enough fuel to keep the family warm. These were years of real hardship, contrasting markedly with the conventional picture of royal comfort. Later, rapid improvements in Germany's economy and her recovery from the chaos of war enabled him to repossess those parts of the family estate which remained outside East Germany. In addition to his house in Bremen, there is a fine castle built on a mountain-top not far from Stuttgart.

In 1955 Prince Louis Ferdinand was among the first to obtain a pilot's licence, when private flying was permitted again in Germany. He bought a Cessna 172 which he called 'Zollernadler' (Zollern eagle) and had the name painted on the aircraft along with the family crest, which incidentally incorporates an eagle. He said of his flying, 'It gives me great satisfaction. You feel so extremely independent and close to the Creator.'

As a method of transport he finds the light aeroplane far more relaxing than driving on the Autobahn, which he regards as a form of suicide. Not all of his family share this view—the late Princess Kira disliked flying, although she always encouraged the Prince in it and often flew with him. Some of Prince Louis Ferdinand's children are likewise not at all impressed by light aircraft although his third son (also named Louis Ferdinand) qualified for a private pilot's licence in 1970.

The Prince has recently presented 'Zollernadler' to the Bremen Flying Club and taken delivery of a more powerful Cessna 182, which was named 'Preussenadler' at a little ceremony held at the local airport. Like so many private owners, he has developed a liking for air rallies. These usually take the form of a leisurely tour around Europe and include stops in countries such as Greece and Bulgaria. His total pilot experience amounts to some 1,500 hours. Considering that he received his licence forty years ago this is not a lot of flying, but now that he has rediscovered the true enjoyment of aviation as a sport he is busy making up for the years when circumstances kept him on the ground.

To appreciate the Hohenzollern history which led to Prince Louis Ferdinand's flying achievement, we must go back to the era of the balloon, and the earlier days of the last Hohenzollern ruler, Kaiser Wilhelm II.

Much has been written about the Kaiser—generally he is portrayed as an autocrat, arrogant in manner and uncertain as to his day-to-day likes and dislikes. How much of this is true, and to what extent this image has been engendered by a rather fearsome moustache and the sinister pose he almost invariably adopted when facing the camera, is difficult to assess. Certainly those working close to the Kaiser were known to have lived with feelings of periodic insecurity, and he certainly was feared, even at times by his own mother. The Kaiser had a younger brother, however, Prince Henry of Prussia (born on 14 August 1862), who was of less fiery temperament and more kindly countenance. Prince Henry was a tall, imposing, good-natured man who generated great loyalty and affection in those who had dealings with him. He became a great patron of German sport, and was often described by his contemporaries as 'the protector of motoring and flying.' From his earliest schooldays, the Prince had been deeply interested in the possibility of flight. He was not alone in this interest. Several German rulers and princes had been active balloonists and patrons of all manner of flying experiments.

The distinction of being the first royalty in the world to ascend in an aeroplane went not to Prince Henry, but to his nephew, Crown Prince Wilhelm, eldest son of the Kaiser. This was the occasion in October 1909 (already related in Chapter I) when the heir to the throne of Germany flew with Orville Wright. At that time the hierarchy in Germany considered aeroplanes to be fit only for lunatics, and consequently the thought of his son, a prince of the blood royal, being so undignified as to fly was too much for the Kaiser. Because of this little adventure, the Crown Prince was placed under house arrest!

Like most Western nations Germany had its aviation pioneers and none was more highly regarded than August Euler. It was in November 1910 that Prince Henry stood watching the great aviator as he tested a flying machine of his own design. After he had landed, Euler explained the operation of his aeroplane to the Prince. The latter was much impressed. As he later wrote in an article for the *German Journal of Aeronautics* entitled 'Between Heaven and Earth; Reflections of a Student Pilot,'

> 'When I had been watching Euler's flights and landings with admiration and absorption and examining his machine in detail, I asked him somewhat shyly if he would teach me to fly. Euler looked me straight in the eye for a while and then said, shortly and succinctly: "Yes, but only on condition that you do exactly as I tell you."'

Prince Henry readily agreed and the pilot's course began, with a week of intense theoretical instruction followed by 'exercises at the stationary machine to learn the controls.' The Prince was later to admit that during this part of the course he could not sleep, so obsessed had he become at the thought of realising his schoolboy ambition to fly. From all accounts this pleased Euler, because 'he considered from his experience with former pupils that this passionate interest boded well for learning the art of flying.'

Euler was a very devoted believer in the need to teach emergency drills to his pupil pilots. They had to be thoroughly taught, so that an unforeseen incident would automatically produce a life-saving reflex, and enable the pilot to avoid unnecessary damage to his delicate flying machine. Euler would fly his pupils around the local area, pointing out the usual high obstructions, trees, church steeples, pylons and so forth.

His running commentary would always include an ominous reference to the staff-officers' cemetery lying just to the left of the take-off and landing path.

Ground instruction ended with an oral examination and a practical test on the use of controls, with the flying machine on the ground and its engine stopped. At this point Prince Henry was pronounced ready for solo. He remembered the moment in these words:

> 'Had I suspected at that moment, how many inner worries I would still have to overcome, (I was 48 and had a wife and children! This is drawn to the attention and kindly judgement of those who have the art of flying in their flesh and blood), I think I might well, at the eleventh hour, have given up my decision to learn to fly.'

His misgivings became so great that he implored Euler to accompany him on his first flight.

> 'I gripped the control lever. With a good deal of spluttering, the engine started. It rattled and crackled, I raised my left hand as a signal for the ground staff to let go, and the machine immediately started to move—I could still hardly remember if the lateral control was on the left and the altitude control on the right, or vice versa. With uncanny speed the machine dropped forward as if it wanted to burrow into the earth—then two powerful hands, not my own, gripped the elevators and the joystick, the engine stopped, the machine raised its head, and like an obedient instrument, followed its master, my instructor. The engine spluttered into life again and after a few more leaps of a hundred metres or so, this first flight came to an end.'

At this stage, Euler warned the Prince not to forget all he had been taught the moment his hands were on the controls, as indeed flying instructors have warned their pupils ever since. Another flight followed, and the Prince reported 'This time it had better results, and then it was good-bye to my instructor, good-bye to the earth.'

On 28 November 1910, after a final examination by Euler and two officials of the German Airship Federation, Prince Henry was awarded pilot's certificate No. 38 on an Euler-Zweidecker (biplane) flying machine. He was then, at 48, the oldest pilot in the world. No doubt his relative seniority tempered the Prince's great enthusiasm for flying because he later wrote:

> 'Anyone who is thinking of learning to fly needs to be told that an aeroplane is neither an open grave nor a child's toy, and that courage, composure, a strong will and calm of mind are basic conditions in which to master a subject which perhaps today has become an exact science!'

This was an opinion expressed several years before World War I, and written with a conviction born of experience: shortly after gaining his pilot's certificate, Prince Henry landed in a tree. The wings and tailplane of his machine broke away and fell off while the engine continued to run, thrashing the leaves and branches with its enormous slow-running propellers. Fortunately, he escaped with only superficial injuries.

In these years preceding World War I, the German High Command was strongly in favour of the airship, a policy that attracted the support of the Kaiser himself. Vigorous efforts were made by the service chiefs to ensure that all available funds were channelled into the Army and Marine Airship Service. Not even the considerable influence of Prince Henry and his nephew, the Crown Prince, could move the War Ministry from its stubborn beliefs. It was not until the Kaiser himself visited The Flying Machine Company operated by the Wright brothers at Tegeler and there discovered, to his pained surprise, that four of their machines had been ordered by the French War Office, that his country began to show a real interest in the aeroplane. As a result of this visit, German officers were sent for pilot training at the Wrights' school of flying.

Prince Henry was, of course, a prime mover in stimulating this interest. He even

Prince Henry of Prussia (left) watching the start of the Circuit of Britain at Brooklands, August 1911. *'Flight'* Photo.

sponsored a national fund for German aviation which by April 1912 had raised more than seven and a half million marks. He obtained the services of one Dr. Sablatnig, inviting him to leave France where he was training Italian pilots for the war in Tripolitania, so that he might run the 'Union Aircraft Works' at Teltow, Berlin. When Sablatnig succeeded in breaking eight height records a delighted Prince Henry persuaded him to become naturalised, so that the world records would be accredited to Germany. He attended many flying meetings, military and civil, encouraging the pilots to greater achievements while at the same time warning them against recklessness and the habit of indulging in aerobatics, at the time little understood and the cause of some avoidable accidents.

Despite his early flights with Orville Wright, the Crown Prince never became a pilot. However, when the Great War began in Europe there were several Princes of the Hohenzollern family deeply involved in aviation, two of them nephews of Prince Henry—Prince Friedrich Sigismund of Prussia, who practised as an aircraft designer, and his younger brother, Prince Friedrich Karl, a leading athlete in Germany. Prince Friedrich Sigismund was a horseman of international status but died after a fall while show-jumping in Lucerne. Prince Friedrich Karl of Prussia became Commanding Officer of a German Air Force Squadron during the war, and although primarily engaged on reconnaissance duties, his first love was for the Albatros fighter. He was considered to be something of an 'ace' in these beautiful little biplanes and his personal machine, kept for him at a neighbouring fighter squadron, had a skull painted on its sides. A significant but tragic emblem, for it was while flying this Albatros over France on 21 March 1917 that Prince Friedrich Karl was shot down and killed.

For some years before World War I, when Prince Henry of Prussia was engaged in his national aviation fund campaign, he consistently reminded the German people that the Zeppelin was not the only type of aircraft, that it had its limitations and that smaller machines of the faster, heavier-than-air type were urgently required. Within a few years he was to be proved correct. After its initial success as a bomber, the Zeppelin, operated by the Germans in naval-style flotillas, became more and more vulnerable to the defending fighters based in southern England and eventually losses were of such proportions that these very large and expensive lighter-than-air machines were withdrawn from operations.

With the signing of the Armistice, German air activity was restricted by the Allies to gliding, and it is hardly surprising that these politically imposed conditions had the effect of compelling the resourceful Germans to direct all their aviation talents in that direction. For this, more than any other reason, Germany began to excel in the building and flying of sailplanes. To the layman a sailplane is perhaps even more of a mystery than powered flight. 'Is it not a glider?' he will ask, and while this is

The Rhone sailplane competitions of August 1924.
Prince Henry of Prussia is examining a Messerschmitt S16 with particular interest as it was the first time powered aircraft had participated.
Messerschmitt Archives.

perfectly true, the sailplane is nevertheless as far removed from the simple glider as is the ocean-going racing yacht from the Mediterranean fishing boat. It is all a matter of efficiency—a good sailplane can remain in the air supported by the weakest of up-currents, so that flights over great distances may be accomplished without an engine. All over Germany gliding schools flourished and Prince Henry did much to encourage the activity, which became something of a national sport. He could always be relied upon to lend his name and support to a good cause so that his death in 1929 was a grievous loss to his country, not least to the air-minded men and women of Germany.

With the lifting of the light aviation embargo there emerged a number of accomplished aerobatic pilots. Prominent among these highly skilled flyers were Prince

Eugen zu Schamburg-Lippe and his cousin Tassilo. Apparently some rivalry developed between the two men and this came near to the point of hostility, until a mutual friend made the peaceful gesture of getting them together around the dinner table.

In a Germany where royalty no longer enjoys any legal standing, what are the feelings of Prince Louis Ferdinand? Are those events of modern history that have denied him the German Imperial Crown a source of resentment to him? Does he harbour ambitions for the return of the monarchy in Germany? In part the Prince answers these questions in the foreword he has written for a book on his family, entitled *Die Hohenzollern*.

> 'We, the living Hohenzollerns, are grateful to the founder of our family, and because our forefathers were allowed to take a leading part in the history of the German people for almost a thousand years.
>
> 'The achievements of the past cannot be wiped out, either by the revolution of 1918, or the total breakdown of Germany in 1945 with all its consequences, for the name of Hohenzollern remains closely bound up with the history of the Nation.
>
> 'Historical facts can be obscured by the stream of political events, but no one can say that they did not happen or were not so. They cannot be erased.'

Scholar, musician, author, pilot and above all, humanitarian, Prince Louis Ferdinand has clearly been recognised as such from his early days at university to the time when he became the first of his family to go out into the world and live as an ordinary working man. He said 'If your book helps to break down barriers and promote a better understanding among men then I am with you.' Then he added, 'If the world were run by pilots it would be a better place, free of trouble—except when they started arguing about flying!'

The Hashemite Kingdoms

The Hashemite Kings are descended directly from the Prophet Mohammed himself. A namesake of the present King of Jordan, Hussein, ruled over the Hejaz, a wild desert country that embraces the sacred Mohammedan shrines of Mecca and Medina. After him came three brothers who with the support of Lawrence of Arabia defeated the Turks during the first World War and later became King Ali of the Hejaz, King Abdullah of Jordan and King Feisal of Iraq. The Hejaz was lost to the followers of Ibn Saud and is now Saudi Arabia. Iraq remained under two generations of Hashemite Kings until the assassination of Feisal II, when it became a republic. Jordan's case was rather different. Until the end of the First World War it had been part of Syria. Then Britain and France divided the area into Syria, Lebanon, Palestine and Trans-Jordan. In 1921 Prince Abdullah Ibn Al-Hussein, one of the three Hashemite brothers, established an Emirate under British Mandate. During World War II Trans-Jordan supported the Allied cause and on 22 March 1946 Britain agreed to end her mandate and enter into a treaty of friendship with the new state which became known as the Hashemite Kingdom of Jordan. On 25 May of that year, a date now celebrated as Independence Day, Prince Abdullah was proclaimed King.

Almost immediately a parliament was constituted and Jordan continues to be a democracy with a House of Representatives and a House of Notables.

On Friday 20 July 1951 King Abdullah was attending El Aksa Mosque in the old city of Jerusalem. With him was his devoted fifteen-year-old grandson Hussein, only recently appointed an honorary aide to the King. An assassin's bullet rang out and the elderly monarch fell dead while most of those present ran for cover. The young Prince Hussein gave chase after the murderer who fired again, the bullet ricocheting from a medal he was wearing for the occasion and which undoubtedly saved his life.

Abdullah was succeeded by his son Talal and his consort Queen Zein but soon the new King's health began to decline and a Council of Regency was appointed until Crown Prince Hussein, their eldest son, came of age. In May 1953 he returned to Jordan from Sandhurst and at the age of eighteen became King Hussein. He is the third Hashemite King of Jordan.

RIGHT His Majesty King Hussein of Jordan.

CHAPTER 8

JORDAN

King in the Desert Sky

The troubles of the Middle East, rarely out of the newspaper headlines, have impinged harshly on Jordan. Few of the personalities involved in the Arab–Israeli conflict have escaped the television camera and in consequence King Hussein is instantly recognisable to the man in the street, or even the radio listener, for there can be no mistaking the deep, distinctive voice that comes as such a surprise from so compact a frame. For Jordan, disaster was to reach its zenith not at the hand of Israel but as a result of a conflict from within which developed into fighting of near civil war proportions between her regular forces and the Palestinian guerrillas. The months of pressure and anxiety, never knowing when the situation might become completely out of hand, coupled with the threatening posture adopted by some of the neighbouring Arab States (and indeed a short-lived invasion of Jordan by Syria) had its cumulative effect on the King and he began to suffer from exhaustion. It was to Britain that he turned for medical treatment and in fact it was at the Fitzroy-Nuffield Nursing Home that he talked of his flying, in January 1971. A uniformed policeman stood in the entrance, every inch a London 'Bobby.' Several Arabs were in deep conversation in the foyer. On the fourth floor, an English secretary opened the door to a small private room and spoke a few words of introduction to the King who was sitting up in bed, beaming at the visitor who had come to talk flying. He looks much younger than his thirty-five years and it is difficult to believe he has been King of his turbulent land for seventeen years. Tea was brought in and offered with an apologetic 'Perhaps you would prefer coffee?' His Majesty speaks fluently, the words pouring forth like a torrent checked at intervals by long, throaty sounds of hesitation while he carefully chooses the next phrase. Like most royalty, he has a talent for putting one at ease; the atmosphere is immediately friendly and informal, questions being received with a smile and answered with sincerity, often humility and always with the utmost courtesy. It is something of an experience to be called 'Sir' by a King!

To one side of the bed was a record player and an impressive collection of high-powered transmitters and receivers. For some twelve months past the King had been an ardent radio 'ham.'

'I found it not only a good hobby but a very nice way of making friends; in fact a very nice way of escaping from whatever is on one's mind at the time. I talk to people the world over.'

A way of escape—how often must the young King have wanted to escape from this crisis or that impossible situation. From time to time he referred to his pilot's log book, correcting a date or recalling an incident and as the story unfolded above all else there emerged an impression of supreme courage in the face of many set-backs and a determination to lead his people to happiness and prosperity. His were eventful years.

Hussein was born on 14 November 1935. He could well be described as a Prince in near poverty for, although the family lived happily enough in their Amman home, there was none of the wealth usually associated with royalty. Even the boy Hussein's pride and joy, a bicycle given to him by his wealthy cousin, King Feisal of Iraq, had to be sold to make ends meet. Not until his father became Crown Prince was their State allowance increased and then only to £1,000 per annum. Nevertheless, his parents (later King Talal and Queen Zein) made sacrifices so that young Hussein might receive an appropriate education, first in Amman, later in Alexandria where he learned English, then at Harrow. The influence of a British public school developed in him a liking for various team games and fencing. It was an enjoyable time, made the more lively by an early passion for fast cars and the inevitable near-misses that were a product of youth and his little previous experience of motoring.

It was while on holiday in Switzerland that Prince Hussein first learned of his father's rapidly declining health and inability to exercise constitutional powers. He must therefore prepare himself to become King. A Council of Regency would be appointed until His Royal Highness came of age, but meanwhile he was to spend one of the happiest years of his life at the British Royal Military Academy, Sandhurst. He returned to Jordan still only a boy of eighteen and on 2 May 1953 acceded to the throne.

The King's first interest in aviation was not the result of any particular incident; his awareness of the aeroplane and what it had to offer developed over a period of time. During the war years there was little excitement in Jordan, although periodically news would be received of the battles further West. Spitfire met Messerschmitt; Hurricane shot down Dornier; Halifax, Lancaster and Flying Fortress bombed Germany. Like boys all over the world the Arab youngsters became enthralled at the exploits of such legendary figures as Germany's Adolph Galland, South Africa's 'Sailor' Malan and 'Johnny' Johnson, Britain's highest scoring fighter pilot. The boy Hussein was as deeply interested in all this as his compatriots.

Then he was eighteen and on the throne of Jordan, acting as host to several R.A.F. squadrons. This was inconsistent with his plans to 'Arabise' the Armed Forces. The Army, hitherto trained and administered by a British General and staff, was soon officered by Jordanians, and whereas in the past no Air Force existed save for a few ageing transport 'planes, the young King expedited its development with the introduction of modern aircraft and up-to-date training methods. What was more, he would learn to fly! There was immediate opposition from the Palace and Parliament but he was insistent. The King had never flown in a light aeroplane and a trial flight was arranged in an Auster Aiglet, a robust, spartan and remarkably noisy fabric-covered aeroplane which, in the right hands, was capable of quite spectacular aerobatics. The pilot of the Auster was 'Jock' Dalgleish, Colonel in command of the Jordanian Air Force, who had snatched Hussein from an ugly situation in Jerusalem two years earlier, when his grandfather was assassinated at the mosque of El Aksa.

They took off into the unbelievable clarity of a Jordanian sky. It was 2 July 1953 and the Colonel must have been under some pressure to dissuade the King from learning to fly. He tied the Aiglet in knots, looping, rolling, flicking inverted and generally pulling a lot more 'g' than was comfortable. It developed into a pretty ghastly ride and on landing the King got out of the aircraft and was promptly sick. Then he turned around and said, 'It's no use, Colonel Dalgleish, I will fly again tomorrow!' And fly again he did, practically every day, coming up against all the usual problems that beset a student pilot; inability to keep straight during take-off, difficulty with his airspeed, trouble maintaining a steady height and above all else those impossible landings! But the breakthrough came and he progressed from the crotchety old Aiglet to a more refined Chipmunk. At this stage of training a pupil would expect to go solo but to those around the King it was unthinkable that he should fly without his instructor. Instead he was introduced to the de Havilland Dove and the luxury of two engines.

The transition from singles to twin-engined aircraft is not a particularly difficult one. In itself size is of little consequence and most pilots rapidly attune themselves to great areas of aeroplane spreading around them in all directions, even when the conversion is from a light aircraft to a multi-engined transport. Generally, the twin-engined aeroplane handles in much the same way as its single-engined cousin, so long as everything is in working order. But when for some reason an engine fails, docility may be replaced by capriciousness. Suddenly, it has a marked desire to turn sharply towards the dead engine, an unhealthy reaction which if left unchecked will rapidly develop into a spiral dive with rather final results. Dramatic as it may sound on paper, single-engine flying on a twin-engined aircraft does not in fact make particularly heavy demands on a properly trained pilot, but engine failure is a real enough emergency nevertheless, and very wisely 'Jock' Dalgleish was insistent that the King should know all about 'Asymmetric Flight,' to use its rather forbidding title. Part of the training included the deliberate stopping of an engine, its propeller feathered to prevent further rotation.

As was often the case on these training flights, an armed guard sat in the passenger cabin and, since the unexpected sight of a propeller coming to a decisive halt in the air can be rather disturbing, the King and Dalgleish were at pains to acquaint the guard with what to expect during the flight. 'Do you understand that we shall be stopping an engine?' they asked the Arab guard. Wishing to be polite, he said 'Yes' when he really didn't understand at all. They took off, practised one or two exercises, then Dalgleish pulled back a throttle and yelled 'engine failure' whereupon the King went through the emergency drills like a well-rehearsed actor, finally pulling back the pitch control and feathering the propeller. Scarcely had it ceased to rotate when the door to the flight deck burst open. The Arab guard appeared, suspicion frozen on his face, then pointed his gun at Dalgleish and said 'Hey—do you know that engine has stopped?' It was some minutes before the King could persuade him to go back to his seat in the cabin.

One summer afternoon 'Jock' Dalgleish left the little flight deck and went back

The Royal Dove, a defenceless target for Syrian jet fighters.

King Hussein with Colonel 'Jock' Dalgleish.

to the passenger cabin. The King was virtually on his own for the first time, entrusted with landing the twin without help from his instructor. It was as far as the authorities were prepared to go and he was expected to regard the gesture as his solo. But this was simply not good enough for a determined young man and one afternoon, finding the aircraft unattended, he climbed aboard, started the engines and before anyone could intervene was airborne, to the consternation of those left behind on the ground. Within a short while he had landed expertly and from that time all objections to his flying solo were gone for ever. Flying had become something more than a relaxation for the King:

> 'When I returned to Jordan at the age of eighteen I felt the necessity not only to encourage people to fly but also to escape from the responsibilities that were rather heavy at an early age. I found that the best answer was the empty sky and the aeroplane.'

The King of Jordan flying a Vampire jet fighter.

The King is very close to his people, sometimes travelling the countryside in a Land Rover perhaps for no other reason than to meet and talk with a few families living in some isolated settlement. He is particularly interested in the Bedouin and is saddened by their poverty—often they are too proud to ask for help. There have been times when in a display of fierce loyalty these tribesmen have almost manhandled the King in their eagerness to touch him or shake his hand. He tries to make himself available whenever an audience is requested. His office adjoins the Office of the Chief of Protocol. Anyone may enter the Palace and, provided he has reason, expect to meet the Sovereign unless his very full programme precludes an audience.

This proximity to a volatile people means that King Hussein is constantly at risk, for there has been no shortage of extremists trying to remove him from the throne. Attempts by bullet and poison too numerous to remember have often involved intrigue and plotting more akin to fiction than everyday life. They say that if one tries hard enough it is possible to get used to anything, and while King Hussein will often make light of these treacherous attempts on his life it was during an interview on B.B.C. television that the true courage of the man came through in the matter of fact reply he gave to the question 'Do these attempts worry you?'

> 'You live with yourself and when the time comes it does come. I have been through so much that I believe in that very much indeed. And I am certainly not going to run away from a bullet—I probably wouldn't be fast enough anyway.'

One attempt on his life was later described by the King as 'The narrowest escape from death I have ever had.'

There had been no secret of the fact that he was to take a short holiday in Rome. Before leaving Amman he had made a public speech telling the nation of his movements and the reason for his absence from Jordan. He would travel in the Royal Dove, flying as captain with Colonel Dalgleish in the second pilot's seat. An additional crew would come with them to Rome and return the aircraft to Amman after the King's arrival. It is, of course, the usual practice to obtain permission before overflying a foreign country and the Jordanian authorities took special care in this particular case because it meant crossing through Syrian airspace. Relations between the two countries were at that time not of the best.

They took off on 10 November 1958, the aircraft plainly marked with the Royal coat of arms. They reached the Syrian border and King Hussein called Damascus on the radio, giving his identity and intention which were exactly as flight-planned. The message was acknowledged and he was told to proceed. The Royal aircraft had been over Syrian territory for perhaps 15 minutes when Damascus airport radioed the King and said he had no right to be in Syrian airspace, whereupon His Majesty replied that the flight was pre-arranged with their authorities and he was proceeding to his first point of landing, Cyprus. Soon they were within sight of Damascus, convinced that an over-zealous controller had been indulging himself, when the radio burst into life again. 'You are violating Syrian airspace and must land immediately at Damascus.' Hurriedly the King changed radio frequency and advised Amman of this hostile and sinister development. Their advice was immediate and urgent: 'Fly on to Beirut in friendly Lebanon or return to Amman but on no account land at Damascus.'

By now the King had turned back towards the Jordanian border and was making for home. He was painfully aware of his defenceless position. There was no cloud cover and the Dove presented an easy target to any trigger-happy fighter pilot out for an easy kill. Furthermore, they were flying at nearly 10,000 ft., in an ideal position for the Syrian radar. King Hussein put the nose down and dived for the ground at maximum speed.

'I had a bit of a cold at the time and ruptured an eardrum but we got to the ground and were flying as fast as we could when one of the people at the back came and told us that he had just seen two jets crossing in the opposite direction.'

A few moments later two Syrian Mig 17 jet fighters swept past, overtaking to the right of the Dove. They turned, pulled up into a steep climb and started to dive towards the Royal aircraft.

'My first reaction was that this was it. I turned the aircraft towards them and wanted to land immediately, but then Colonel Dalgleish took over and said "No, let's try something else." He pulled harder and we found that with our slower speed we could turn in a much smaller circle. We kept this up for a number of minutes while I made a Mayday call [an emergency message which at that low altitude was never received in Amman].'

The two Migs flew together, making repeated passes at the Dove. Then for some reason their tactics changed and they came from both sides, nearly colliding with one another as they drew ahead of their violently twisting prey. It was a close thing and it seemed to have a sobering effect on the Syrian pilots because they suddenly broke off. King Hussein made the Jordanian border without further harassment. The explanation later given by the Syrians for this astonishing incident was that no proper clearance had been obtained. King Hussein described it as

'An attack on a Head of State as yet unparalleled in history and it will take me longer to forget it than it has taken me to forgive those responsible. One year later to the day, when relations were much improved, we flew with the same crew over the same route to Italy. It was a pleasant flight, nothing happened—but I had a very sore neck as a result of looking behind!'

Towards the end of 1959 British European Airways sold some of its obsolescent Airspeed Ambassador airliners to the Royal Jordanian Air Force. Although overtaken by the advent of the turbo-prop and jet, these fine aircraft were by no means at the end of their useful life. The Ambassador is a large, high-wing monoplane powered by two Bristol Centaurus engines and the version bought by Jordan offered comfortable accommodation for more than forty passengers. It so happened that a state visit to various African countries had been arranged for King Hussein and it presented him with a wonderful opportunity to fly himself on an interesting tour in one of his Air Force's new acquisitions. There was sufficient room on the aircraft for him to be accompanied by a large staff and so, with 'Jock' Dalgleish once again in the second pilot's seat, the King took off and aimed the retired B.E.A. airliner in the general direction of the African continent. The route was completely unknown to them, so this had the makings of an eventful trip, perhaps too eventful for some members of the royal staff watching the world go by from the passenger cabin. One of the first lessons to be learned was that in Africa what may appear on the landing charts as a major airport will often turn out to be a mud flat, baked hard in the all-consuming sun, where refuelling is often a tedious matter of handling countless tins, passing them through a human chain to the unfortunate soul pouring into a seemingly unfillable tank, his sweat mixing with the near-boiling petrol.

They flew to Lagos, then on to a Leopoldville in the throes of independence and torn by strife. It had been planned to make an overnight stop at Nairobi but refuelling delays at Luluabourg and prolonged hospitality at Usumbura upset their plans to arrive before dark. By nightfall they were in the vicinity of Mount Kilimanjaro, flying at 13,500 ft. and secure in the mistaken belief that the mountain was only 9,500 ft. high. Kilimanjaro is in fact 19,340 ft. above sea level and they had flown in close proximity to it in the dark, some 6,000 ft. below the summit!

They arrived over a fogbound Nairobi. The airport was closed and there was barely sufficient fuel to make for an alternative airport. It was no time for indecision. Dalgleish left the King to fly the aeroplane while he listened to the limited radio available and kept a sharp lookout. King Hussein concentrated hard on his instruments, calling out the height as he descended towards where they hoped the runway would be. 'I can give you another hundred feet but you must go no lower' said Dalgleish, then out of the fog appeared the yellow glare of the lead-in lights. A luminous green blur flashed below as the runway threshold came and disappeared in an instant. The King made a perfect landing and spent the next half-hour taxiing to the airport buildings, by now lost in the thickening fog. Such had been the tension that neither pilot could remember lowering the undercarriage before landing. Some months later the Royal Jordanian Air Force received a strongly-worded protest from the Kenyan Civil Aviation Authority, accusing them of risking the King's life at a time when the airport was closed because of fog. The letter found its way to King Hussein's desk, which under the circumstances seems in order, because he was the pilot involved.

The royal tour ended in Ethiopia, a memorable few days spent as guests of the Emperor Haile Selassie who presented King Hussein with two six-month-old lion cubs as a parting gift. By that age, a young lion is becoming large and inclined to be somewhat boisterous in a good-natured way. To the majority of people such a

RIGHT King Hussein at the controls of a Jordanian Army helicopter.

gift would amount to being offered a man-eating tiger because a lion at any age is imagined to be a savage, ill-tempered beast always ready to kill whatever is within reach. This of course is not true and when these animals are from early age raised as domestic pets they develop into the most delightful and trustworthy of creatures, full of personality that is neither cat nor dog, just unmistakable lion. On the flight around Africa the King and his party had collected many souvenirs, and with the aircraft's baggage-hold now full it was necessary to put the cubs in the rear of the passenger cabin. A special cage had been provided for the journey and a keeper was to accompany the cubs on the flight to Jordan. It was a hot day and the fully-loaded Ambassador lumbered into the air, climbing painfully slowly to its cruising level. In the hot, stuffy passenger cabin some members of the royal entourage were dozing and the lion keeper was fast asleep.

Up front on the flight deck, King Hussein and Colonel Dalgleish were settling into the cruise, when suddenly they became aware of an acute change in balance. The aircraft wanted to nose down and the pilots were experiencing some difficulty in preventing a steep dive. When everything appeared to be under control, someone came in from the passenger cabin and explained what had been going on. Apparently the lion cubs had got out of their cage and scared all the passengers forward. Then the lion tamer had woken up and chased the cubs back. When they arrived at Jidda to refuel, recalls the King, 'We opened the doors, the lions jumped out and I'm afraid everyone took off in different directions!'

Some years previously, on 19 April 1955, His Majesty had married Dina Abdul Hamed, a distant cousin and a member of the Hashemite dynasty. There was a child, Princess Alya, but the King was very young and difficulties arose which culminated in divorce. Certainly the pitfalls of marriage exist for Kings and Queens. For King Hussein the period following was one of misery, when the burden of responsibility could not be shared and loneliness alternated with anxiety. His temperament began to alter noticeably while those close to him looked on anxiously. They had reason for concern; he was in danger of becoming a recluse. The turning point came when he met Toni Gardner, the daughter of a British Colonel, living in Amman. There was no love at first sight, just a friendship that started as an escape from royal duties and enabled the King to relax and laugh for the first time in many months. He taught her to drive at the Amman Go-Kart Club and gradually their friendship turned into deep affection.

Marriage is a more difficult matter for a King than for one of his subjects. Not only is it a question of choosing a suitable partner but there are constitutional issues to be

RIGHT Preparing to visit the outlying settlements in his helicopter.
Peter Larson, Camera Press.

considered which involve Parliament and the people. Here was an Arab king wishing to marry a girl who was not of royal blood. And then there was the problem of religion. He sought the advice and wise counsel that a good son should expect from a devoted parent and his mother, Queen Zein, gave her unqualified blessing and approval. Of course there were obstacles and problems inherent in such a marriage, but none of these was insuperable and on 25 May 1961 the wedding day unleashed the exuberant joy of his subjects, which the Bedouin demonstrated in traditional style with rifles and pistols being fired into the air. Crowds overwhelmed the Royal car and from somewhere within the turmoil came a sound incongruous in an Arab world. Someone was playing the bagpipes! After the Moslem ceremony King Hussein named his wife Princess Muna al-Hussein.

King Hussein has flown most of the modern jet fighters as well as some of the earlier examples, but his first love has remained the de Havilland Vampire, one of the early British jets. It went into production before the advent of powered controls or most of the other complexities of present-day high-speed designs and it therefore retained an air of simplicity which, allied to a performance far in advance of its contemporaries, made it a delight to fly. So much did the King enjoy his Vampire that he developed a liking for low-level aerobatics. He would indulge in the pastime with considerable skill, which is as well because aerobatics at near-ground level leave no room for mishandling. It was while flying one of his spectacular routines over an airfield that he had a 'flame-out.' The term means exactly what it says—a jet engine is rather like a large blowlamp, propelling the aircraft by ejecting vast quantities of air which it heats by burning paraffin under pressure. When King Hussein's fire went out he was flying around on some manoeuvre at well over 400 m.p.h. Fortunately, with so much speed in hand he was able to glide around the airfield and position himself for a successful landing. It could well have ended differently.

The King is also a helicopter pilot. Soon after gaining his licence, he flew one to his home and kept it there so that he might teach himself night flying. He practised flying first at dusk, then later in the evening, gradually working up to total darkness. Sometimes he would fly around the hills on a jet-black night, the stars overhead and hardly a visible feature on the ground, thoroughly enjoying himself, until one day some experts arrived to service the helicopter. They were horrified to learn of the King's night flying because his machine had no landing lights or emergency flares. However, the helicopter was more to King Hussein than an expensive toy. Whenever he arranged a visit by road, people invariably knew in advance and made ready to receive their sovereign. The helicopter now enables him to arrive unexpectedly and see things as they really are.

RIGHT King Hussein, airline pilot.

By the beginning of 1971 King Hussein had flown approximately 1,800 hours in a great variety of aircraft. He is justifiably proud of his Airline Transport Pilot's Licence and no one should harbour illusions that because he is a king it was handed to him on a silver plate. He gained this highest of professional flying qualifications the hard way, like anyone else, by passing the stringent exams. King Hussein is a qualified Caravelle Captain, and his views on the part to be played by air transport in the future of Jordan are worth hearing:

> 'It is the land of history. Every civilisation has left its mark there. It is also a beautiful country and it has many resorts, such as Aqaba on the Gulf of Aqaba on the Red Sea. There is little humidity and it is very close to Europe. We are building a medium-sized airport at the moment and we are hoping it will be able to receive jets directly from Europe. We had 700,000 tourists up to June 1967 during that year only and it was increasing. Naturally it has suffered a great deal since. When things are normal again I am sure the tourists will come back.'

When things are normal again. On that day the Middle East will surely take its rightful place in the world; meanwhile mountains have to be moved and bridges must be built between the conflicting opinions in that area. But Jordan has a King and he is young, forward-thinking and determined to raise his people to better things. He has plans for the irrigation of the land and improvements in agriculture, the creation of hydro-electric power and of a mineral and chemical industry. The success or failure of these projects is in the hands of the people themselves and no one is more aware of the fact than King Hussein. He once wrote:

> 'A nation's ability to survive is not determined by size or population but by the will of its people, their faith in their country, their determination to make their lives worth while.'

At the end of the day King Hussein leaves his office in the Palace and returns to a modest villa some 10 miles outside Amman. It is called 'Darat al Khair' which means 'the house of goodness and happiness.' Here he lives with Princess Muna, their two sons Prince Abdullah and Prince Faisal and twin daughters the Princesses Zein and A'isheh. When he is able to relax the King has many interests; music, short-wave radio and photography. He is also a keen sportsman, enjoying scuba diving, water skiing, swimming and fishing, in fact anything to do with the sea. But when the strains of office mount and the safety valve must give it is to the aeroplane that he turns because 'The moment I climb into the cockpit I shake off my problems.'

The Kings of the Hellenes

The 1832 Treaty of London guaranteed the new state of Greece that emerged after the War of Independence had released her from four centuries of Turkish rule. It is therefore particularly sad that foreign domination was soon replaced by political strife. Otto of Bavaria, the first King of modern Greece, proved so unpopular that he was deposed.
In 1863 Prince William of Denmark, a boy of eighteen (whose sister Alexandra married King Edward VII of Britain) was nominated for the throne of Greece, accepted by the people and acclaimed King George I. As a gesture of goodwill towards the new Monarch, Britain returned the Ionian Islands to the Hellenes. King George led his people through a victorious war against the Turks only to be assassinated in Salonika during March 1913. He was succeeded by his son who became King Constantine I.

World War I was a source of conflicting loyalties to King Constantine. He had married Princess Sophia, sister of Kaiser Wilhelm II, and documents have since revealed that he was under considerable pressure from his brother-in-law to bring Greece into the conflict on Germany's side. Although Greece remained neutral the King's opposition to the Allied cause sent him into exile along with his eldest son, Crown Prince George. His second son Alexander then became puppet King but died within three years from blood poisoning following a monkey bite. Prince Paul, third son of King Constantine, was approached but declined the vacant throne on the grounds that his father was still the legal Sovereign, albeit in exile.

There was the difficulty of Venizelos, powerful premier and opponent of Constantine, but he was voted out of office and the old King returned. However, Venizelos had planned an ill-advised war against the Turks and King Constantine was unfairly held responsible for the subsequent defeat of Greece. In 1922 he left the throne for the second and last time, making way for his eldest son.

After only one year political intrigue forced the new King George II into exile and from 1924 until 1935 he remained in England with his younger brother, Prince Paul. Then the mood changed, the Greeks tired of the republic and the now popular King appointed Metaxas as virtual dictator.

In 1941 the Italians, and then the Germans invaded Greece and the Royal Family was evacuated by the British, first to Crete, then to Alexandria. King George II returned to his country in 1946 and died of a heart attack the following year; Paul the flying Crown Prince was acclaimed King. He died in 1964 and his son Constantine II is the present King in exile. Greece is now ruled by a military government.

RIGHT H.M. King Constantine II of the Hellenes.
Karsh of Ottawa.

CHAPTER 9

GREECE

In the Path of Daedalus

It is hardly surprising that the ancient Greeks should have yearned to enjoy the same freedom as the birds. Theirs was a sophisticated nation and like all mankind the Greeks pondered on their origins and the very beginnings of the Earth itself. They were quick to discover that, although the planets changed position week by week, groups of stars, when isolated into easily-recognisable patterns, remained in their relative positions year in, year out. These constellations assumed special significance to the ancient Greeks, just as they are important to the present-day astrologer.

Late in the last century, our knowledge of Ancient Greece was further extended by Sir Arthur Evans' remarkable discoveries in Crete. He showed that on that little island, centuries before the great days of Athens, there were magnificent palaces and fine cities, better in fact than those of the mainland. The Cretans had a navy, and while it would be stretching credulity beyond reasonable bounds to suggest they were aiming for an air force, King Minos did exist, and it will be remembered that Minos was the villain of the story about the flying Athenian Princes, Daedalus and Icarus. The flying princes, if only in fantasy, are behind a tradition that finds reality in modern Greece, a nation of ten million people.

When aviation had developed beyond experiment to practical reality, it was to Britain that Greece turned for technical advice and assistance. This approach was inspired by the failure in 1918 of the Naval Arsenal at Salonika to organise an effective aircraft repair and maintenance base. Towards the end of 1920 the Greek National Aircraft Factory was established at Old Phaleron, near Athens. Even in those days the manufacture of aircraft was a complex business and the Greeks, with little experience of this specialised branch of engineering, made so little progress that in 1924 the Blackburn Aeroplane and Motor Co. Ltd. (of Yorkshire, England) was invited to run the factory. This it did with notable success, until Greek technicians were able to assume control in 1938.

RIGHT H.M. King Paul of the Hellenes, the erstwhile 'flying Crown Prince' and father of the present King.
Paul Almasy, Camera Press.

Liaison with the British was not confined to the technical aspect of aeronautics and some of the military flying instructors in Greece learned their profession in England at the R.A.F. Central Flying School. One such was Wing Commander 'Babi' Potamianos (now a retired Air Marshal of the Greek Air Force) who managed to gain for himself an 'A1 category,' the highest instructor qualification in the R.A.F., one coveted by all flying instructors but attained only by the exceptional few. One day he was sent for by Prince Paul, who was 35, and apparently anxious to realise his boyhood ambition to become a pilot. As Crown Prince of Greece it was natural that Paul should be encumbered by all the protection usual for his important position, yet his father King Constantine I, a progressive monarch, had consented to his taking flying lessons. Training started with an Avro Tutor biplane based at Tatoi Airfield, and it soon emerged that the royal pupil had a natural gift for flying. Indeed Prince Paul's excellent progress was so widely publicised that Potamianos was astonished one morning to be confronted by Prime Minister Metaxas, who had made an early visit to the airfield so that he might arrive before the Prince. Under no circumstances was the Crown Prince to go solo, said the Prime Minister, who was a man of great power and more or less dictator of Greece. Moreover, threatened Metaxas, Potamianos would be held responsible for the Prince's safety. Now this of course was labouring the obvious, because to any flying instructor worthy of the name the safety of his pupil assumes first consideration. In any case, one of the most important decisions he has to make is when to send the pupil on his first solo. It may be thought that in the interest of safety a flying instructor should hold the hand of his pupil for as long as possible before letting him fly alone, but this is not so. Most experienced instructors agree that in the early stages of training there arrives a psychological moment when the pupil should be allowed to fly around the airfield on his own, for just one circuit and landing. To delay this important milestone can often cause a loss of confidence, followed by a marked deterioration in the pupil's flying, and several hours additional instruction may then be required before he is ready again.

At the time Metaxas no doubt appeared tiresome and interfering but he had real enough grounds for concern. Only recently the Prince had lost a brother and the possibility of another royal death must have been uppermost in the Prime Minister's mind. After only nine hours' tuition, Potamianos felt certain that his royal pupil was ready for solo but, after the Prime Minister's stern warning, he continued dual instruction for another two hours. The Prince made one or two untidy landings and it began to look as though a classic example of 'pupil deterioration' was about to begin. Metaxas or not, the time had come to 'unleash his fledgling' and Potamianos

LEFT The Royal Palace, Athens.
London Express Photo.

got out of his cockpit, carefully re-fastening his safety straps across the vacant seat to prevent any risk of their fouling the controls in the instructor's cockpit. 'I can see you are not very pleased with me to-day,' said the Prince. 'On the contrary, Sir' replied Potamianos, 'I would like you to do the next circuit on your own.' A delighted Prince Paul broke through the first barrier to becoming a pilot and there were no repercussions from the Prime Minister.

As training progressed on advanced exercises the Crown Prince became more and more fascinated by flying, frequently inviting Potamianos for weekends when they would ski between long discussions on every aspect of aviation. After one of these weekends there was a particularly memorable flight over Mt. Parnassus, one clear winter's afternoon. They landed back at the airfield so deeply moved by what they had seen that the Prince and his instructor agreed not to talk of their experience—no words could re-create the picture, a combination of awe-inspiring scenery and a light peculiar to the moment. And the story remained untold until one day in 1971 when it was related by 'Babi' Potamianos.

The time duly arrived for Prince Paul to qualify for his wings and an impressive board of examiners, most of them high in rank but somewhat short of flying background, attended the airfield to observe the Prince in an aeroplane and then present him with his wings. As this august body settled into their comfortable seats, an aircraft could be seen climbing high overhead. After a series of steep turns it went through an extensive repertoire of very polished aerobatics. No doubt this was the Prince's instructor putting on a show for their benefit, or so they all thought until a car drew up and out stepped—Potamianos. The Prince was on his own up aloft and flying like a professional!

The Crown Prince had become an ardent pilot but his wife had little affection for the aeroplane or flying. Prince Paul had married Princess Frederika Louise, a granddaughter of Kaiser Wilhelm II through her mother, Princess Victoria Louise. Although she was a Hohenzollern, the young Princess spent many of her early days in England. The complex relationship between the various royal houses and the fact that Her Royal Highness was a great-grandchild of Queen Victoria placed the young Princess rather remotely in line of succession to the British throne. After the war, on 1 April 1947, the Crown Prince and his Princess became King Paul and Queen Frederika of Greece.

King Paul's interest in flying continued during his life as Crown Prince. World War II was yet to start and freedom from the responsibilities of the throne allowed him to progress from small single-engined aircraft to the much-loved Avro Anson (a twin-engined design of splendid character in every way, except for the undercarriage which in the course of being manually retracted required the pilot to turn

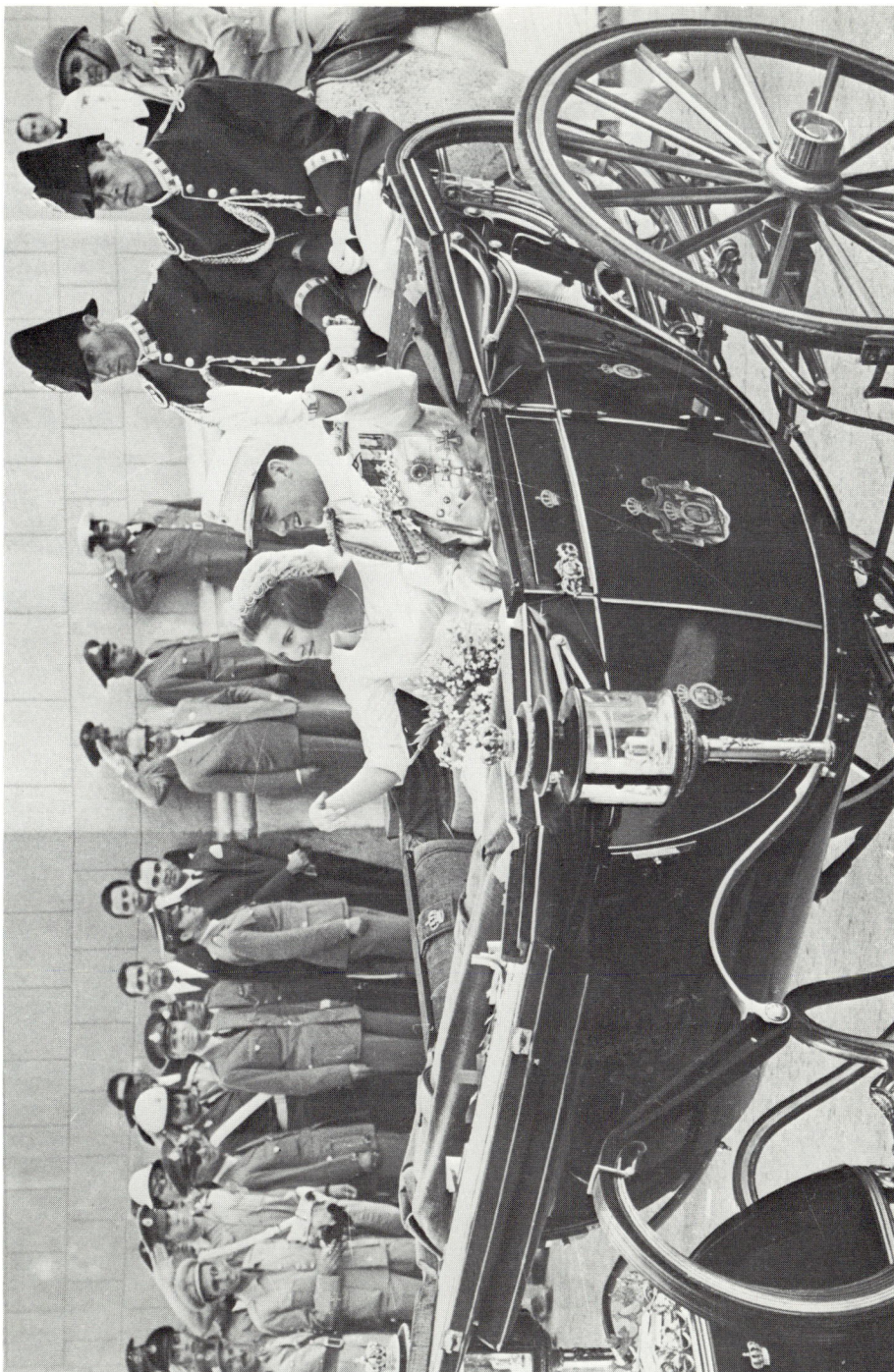

The King and Queen of Greece in their wedding carriage (September 1964). *London Express Photo.*

a handle 140 times, no less, each rotation feeling heavier than the last!). Many of his friends, particularly ex-colleagues from the Royal Hellenic Navy, would visit him and beg their first flight in an aeroplane. There was of course the added attraction of being piloted by no less a person than the Crown Prince.

Prince Paul had flown a total of some 300 hours as a pilot when war came, followed by the invasion of Greece, at first unsuccessfully by the Italians, then ruthlessly by the Germans. On 23 April 1941, King George II of Greece and ten members of his household, including the Crown Prince and his family, were flown to safety in a Sunderland flying boat of 228 Squadron (R.A.F.).

With the royal party in that Sunderland was a nine-month-old baby, the infant Constantine. Snatched from near disaster at the hand of invaders he grew up away from his homeland, began to learn English and soon developed a keen interest in music and athletics, particularly swimming. After the war he continued his education in Greece and in 1958 was sworn in as a Second Lieutenant in the Infantry, an Ensign in the Royal Hellenic Navy and a Pilot Officer in the Air Force. Training simultaneously in the three Services was only part of his daily task—he had also to prepare for the throne. His father, King Paul, was personally involved in this exacting training. Certainly there was plenty to occupy his time, yet the young Crown Prince managed to play squash, gain a third degree black belt in karate and also take part in show-jumping competitions. But it was as a yachtsman that he really excelled. In 1960, at the age of twenty, he returned to a hero's welcome in Athens wearing the gold medal he had won at the Olympic Games held that year.

Soon there was no time for competition jumping or sailing. King Paul died and on 6 March 1964 Constantine became King of Greece, the second of that name. That September he married the beautiful Princess Anne-Marie, daughter of King Frederik of Denmark, who had watched his Olympic success. The wedding was attended by international royalty and one of the incidents which helped to make it a most memorable occasion was a rock and roll demonstration given on the dance floor by Prince Bernhard of The Netherlands, ably partnered by one of his daughters, which won them the acclamation of the other royal guests.

This handsome athletic young King and his beautiful young Queen seemed to personify every romantic vision of Greece's glorious history, recalling the original Olympic Games and the magnificent figures of ancient sculpture. Such a King and Queen would surely be an inspiration to the people of Greece? But political unrest and the emergence of a military regime saw the development of a crisis which was intolerable to the royal house. King Constantine's attempt to control the situation

RIGHT King Constantine and Queen Anne-Marie of Greece during a private visit to London in 1971. *London Express Photo.*

failed, and he flew to Rome and exile in the Royal Gulfstream, perhaps recalling that other occasion when as an infant he left Greece in a Sunderland flying boat. Can history repeat itself in another way? His grandfather, King Constantine I, went into exile at one time, only to be recalled to the throne by the Greek people.

During a private visit to London, the King discussed his interests, particularly as they relate to flying. It was a grey November afternoon and the blue and white flag of Greece hung limply over Claridges Hotel, meeting place of the famous, and often temporary home of kings, princes and millionaires. Leading the way to the Royal Suite, the Marshal of the Court introduced the King, a tall, dark-haired young man with an almost military bearing, his navy blazer a reminder that here was a monarch whose love of sailing had earned him an Olympic Gold Medal.

The King revealed that his first interest in flying went back to early childhood, when he stood in awe and admiration at the exploits of his pilot father, the late King Paul. Sons do not always inherit the interests of their fathers but the young Constantine, commissioned in all three of his country's Armed Forces, soon found his aspirations towards flying the subject of Government opposition. His parents, however, had no objections to his learning to fly.

King Constantine flying the Royal Gulfstream.

Greece

As a pupil pilot he soon realised that although his rank and position ensured every consideration and courtesy from ministers and senior officials, flying instructors and check pilots were never less than frank with him at any time—'not once, thank God, otherwise I might not be here.'

Nevertheless, he has had his anxious moments as a pilot. A few years ago, when he lowered his undercarriage for a landing at an airfield in northern Greece, the nosewheel refused to come out of hiding with the main wheels. He flew back to Athens, radioed his plight to Control and as the lesser of two evils elected to 'belly-land' rather than attempt an arrival minus the nosewheel with its likely risk of the 'plane turning over and finishing upside down. The crash crew at the airport sprayed the runway with the special foam kept for such rare occasions. At the last second the nosewheel began to come down, but by then it was too late; the propeller struck the runway and shattered while the aircraft slithered gently to a halt on its bed of foam. Whether or not this incident is responsible, King Constantine freely admits that although Queen Anne-Marie thoroughly enjoys flying as a passenger, he does not:

'As a passenger, I always ask if I can come up front—I get a little bit hysterical in the back! If they are nice they ask me to fly. Once after leaving Rome I was just having a little shut-eye when the 'plane suddenly veered left and the nose dropped down steeply. Things were thrown across the cabin. I went up to the cockpit. The Captain's face was as white as a sheet. In broad daylight, having just come out of light scattered cloud, we had been on a collision course with another airliner which we missed by only 500 yards. Another time I was flying in a military aircraft in the U.S.A.—in '58, I think it was—in a DC6. It was virtually empty—about five or six people. I was relaxing. A man on the opposite side of me woke up, stretched and yawned, then walked up to the cockpit. There was a sudden explosion and the emergency door he had been sitting by suddenly burst open. The look on that man's face I will never forget! The captain flew as slowly as he could and we tried to get the door closed. Every time one tried to reach the door it swung higher and higher. I finally managed to reach it with four or five people hanging firmly on to my legs.'

On space travel, its value to mankind and the moral rights and wrongs of the idea, King Constantine expressed views similar to those of other Royalty in this book:

'I have very positive feelings on this. I could be completely wrong but I believe the fact that the U.S. and Russia have spent so much money on it is obviously right. We have come to the point where it would be quite possible to go to another planet—to create platforms in space. This is excellent and has created good feeling in the world so far. There is nothing to prevent man trying to explore, but one has come to the point when one should also give more thought to what money is spent on this. There must be more thought for the needs of people on earth, removal of poverty and so on. We should try to strike a balance, but certainly not cease progress.'

The King smoked incessantly as he talked of his other interests: 'I love music. I adore opera and ballet. My hobbies are basically in sporting activities—sailing and riding.' He added emphatically, 'I don't collect stamps or coins!' Recalling his schooldays he said:

'I was very conventional. I liked them. I got on well with my schoolmates. Every month or so I meet up with them, though perhaps not so much now. My parents were not very strict. I think they found a good balance.'

King Constantine the sailor would one day like to take up gliding—there are many similarities between the two sports. Among fixed-wing aircraft the veteran DC3 (Dakota) is perhaps his favourite, but for sheer enjoyment all fixed-wing aircraft must in his opinion take second place to flying the helicopter.

'In my country I used to use the helicopter all the time. Apart from the convenience, it is a relaxation for me. When you have business and other problems on your mind, flying a helicopter takes all your concentration and so you forget your worries. It is easier to fly this type of aircraft—a different feeling which I just adore. If a helicopter and an aircraft stood side by side I would choose the helicopter every time. It's much more exhilarating.'

The King's enthusiasm for helicopters is shared by his brother-in-law, Prince Don Juan Carlos, designated heir to the throne of Spain, grandson of King Alfonso XIII and another keen royal pilot. He learned to fly at the Spanish Air Force Academy in 1958 and has since put his hand to a variety of aircraft of many types, 500 hours on fixed-wing and 200 on helicopters. The Prince's attitude to flying is fairly typical of most pilots in so far as he regards it as a relaxation and not only quicker but infinitely safer than motoring, although he once had a close call flying in formation, when two

TOP RIGHT Prince Don Juan Carlos of Spain in close formation.
RIGHT And after flight.

of the other aircraft collided with one another. Then he had an engine stop while piloting a DC3 but this does not prevent him falling asleep within moments of take-off when flying as a passenger.

The marked preference for helicopter flying by the Greek King and his Spanish brother-in-law is interesting, because although helicopter pilots often regard fixed-wing flying as the poor relation, pilots regularly practising both kinds of aviation usually prefer an aeroplane with wings, particularly after the novelty of being able to rise and descend vertically and move sideways and backwards has worn off, giving way to the continuous vibration which is a feature of most helicopters.

The Greek throne is traditionally more deeply involved in everyday political matters than most other royal houses, since executive power has always been vested in the King and exercised by ministers appointed and dismissed by him. The Monarch has sanctioned and published laws passed by a Parliament which conducts its affairs within the royal palace. The King has had the right to pardon and commute or reduce sentences passed by the courts and according to the constitution is the supreme authority of State and Commander-in-Chief of the Armed Forces. His person has been inviolable. Greece, founder of so much we now regard as the Western way of life, suffered harshly during World War II and, in the opinion of many, fared badly when reparations were apportioned among the rebuilding nations. It is a sad thought that the cradle of democracy, whose armed forces not so long ago fought bravely against unprovoked invaders, should now be among the poorer nations of Europe. When this was written the King and Queen were still in exile, yet prayers for the Royal Family continue to be said in Greece and their pictures are in evidence everywhere. There have been other occasions in modern Greek history when the King and Queen have gone into exile. It is equally in the Greek tradition for them to be welcomed back by their people when differences have been resolved.

The House of Windsor

In 1042, when England was no more than a few thousand scattered villages, Edward the Confessor became the first English Monarch to be crowned at Westminster Abbey where Queen Elizabeth II had her Coronation forty-three monarchs and 910 years later. During this period of English and subsequently British Royalty the line went through a succession of Plantagenets, Tudors, Stuarts and Hanoverians.

The Hanoverian family name of Guelph continued until Queen Victoria's marriage to Albert, younger son of the Duke of Saxe-Coburg, when the style Saxe-Coburg-Gotha was adopted by the British Royal Family, passing to King Edward VII when the Queen died in 1901. The King survived his mother by only nine years, then his son came to the throne as King George V. It seems likely that but for the Great War the family name would have continued to this day but in 1917 an 'anti-foreign' campaign engineered by less responsible elements of the Press influenced King George to renounce Saxe-Coburg-Gotha and adopt the name Windsor.

The 'Sailor King,' as he became known, had six children. There was Edward, Prince of Wales, the eldest, born 23 June 1894; Albert, Duke of York; The Princess Royal; Henry, Duke of Gloucester; Prince John, who died in 1910; and George, Duke of Kent. Within the context of this book the Windsor family is of particular interest because the four surviving brothers all became pilots.

When King George V died in 1936 he was succeeded by the Prince of Wales who, as King Edward VIII, abdicated before his Coronation could take place. The throne passed to his brother, the Duke of York, who became King George VI and whose reign was dominated by the events of World War II. The King was never robust and after the war his health began to decline. The Palace doctors advised against a planned official visit to Montreal in 1951. Instead he was represented by his elder daughter Princess Elizabeth and Prince Philip whom she had married in 1947. The tour was an outstanding success and another was arranged, this time to Australia and New Zealand through Africa. As they departed from London Airport King George, only recently recovered from a serious operation, stood bareheaded in the January wind as he waved good-bye to his daughter and son-in-law. Eight days later, on 6 February 1952, he died and the young couple were recalled from Kenya. The Duke of Edinburgh brought home his wife, Queen Elizabeth II.

RIGHT King Edward VIII accompanied by his brother The Duke of York arriving at Mildenhall 16 July 1936 during a tour of R.A.F. stations. Behind the King's private Rapide may be seen the contemporary aircraft of the period; Hawker Hinds and Heyford bombers.

CHAPTER 10

BRITAIN

Flying Heirs of the Sailor King

'A nation of shopkeepers'—'A land of dog-lovers'—'A seafaring people'—these are some of the more printable attempts to describe the British, a people whose illogicalities have for centuries exasperated their allies and confounded their enemies. Aviation is a prime example: Britain at first was slow to recognise the potential of the 'flying machine' in peace and war, yet within a few years, when events forced the pace, her designers not only caught up with the leaders but went on to produce such masterpieces as the Sopwith Camel, the Bristol Fighter, the DH4 and the Handley Page bombers. During World War I, even the United States of America turned to Britain for its military aircraft—considerable numbers of de Havilland biplanes equipped parts of their Air Force, remaining in service well into the nineteen-twenties.

In the years between the two World Wars Britain slumbered on, resistant to change and opposing modernisation. While the emergent German aviation industry engaged itself in the design and mass production of such fine advanced aircraft as the Dornier 17, the Heinkel 111 and other high-performance monoplanes of all-metal construction, Britain clung with unswerving obstinacy to the fabric-covered biplane.

In the early 'twenties the attitude of the British people towards aviation was one of polite disinterest. Ships were 'in,' the tank was acceptable, horses much more fashionable, but aeroplanes—well, no-one of breeding would involve himself in that sort of nonsense. After all, the chaps who flew them had a screw loose, old man, and in any case aeroplanes were noisy, smelly things, likely to fall out of the sky in the most undignified manner.

One man more than any other had the vision, the planning ability and, above all, the tenacity, to create a separate military air arm in the face of continual, often bitter opposition from the Army and the Navy. Lord Trenchard, the 'Father of the Royal Air Force,' got his way; aircraft design leapt forward and the stick-and-wire biplane gave way to superb 'planes like the Spitfire, the Mosquito, the Lancaster. Even before this policy found triumphant vindication in the Battle of Britain, when a handful of pilots warded off the might of the Luftwaffe and forestalled Hitler's planned invasion, the popular view of flying had swung around. Perhaps the aeroplane was here to stay after all. Perhaps the characters who flew them were not all public menaces. After all, no less a person than the Prince of Wales had taken to flying and actually had his own 'plane.

How had the Prince of Wales become involved in aviation at a time when public opinion was biased strongly against the aeroplane? It was certainly not with the approval of his father. King George V had little interest in the aeroplane, and neither he nor Mary, his Queen, ever flew. His first love was the sea, and he was known affectionately to his people as 'The Sailor King.' In spite of his lack of interest, even active discouragement, the four of his five sons who grew to manhood were all pilots. Of them, the Prince of Wales was to have a profound influence on British aviation. As Duke of Windsor, he now spends much of the year at his Paris residence, with the Duchess.

Set in the Bois de Boulogne, the residence is approached through a black iron gate capped with gold, a style that recalls Balmoral or Sandringham. A long winding drive of well-raked, crushed gravel leads to a beautiful white mansion set amid lawns like green velvet. An old English lamp-post, bearing the cypher of King George IV, is a quaint object, yet in keeping with its surroundings. Wrought-iron doors backed with glass panels lead into a grand hall surrounded by an upper gallery from which hangs the Sovereign's Standard, from St. George's Chapel at Windsor. Ahead is the drawing room, a masterpiece of elegant decor, with its blue-grey walls panelled in gold and containing a mixture of Regency and other furnishings. Among the royal pictures are two which particularly hold the attention; one of H.M. Queen Mary, painted in 1919, and the other a recent portrait of the Duke himself.

To the right is a smaller ante-room filled with treasures collected over a lifetime, and it was here that the Duke spent several hours discussing his early flying activities and recalling his family and friends.

It seems that as a young man the Duke was particularly fond of his German uncle, Prince Henry of Prussia:

> 'He was at Buckingham Palace to see my father because he used to spend his holidays in Britain, and he was in my father's room the day before war was declared. He was very pro-British. The Kaiser was very jealous of him.'

The Duke of Windsor is now in his late seventies, yet when he smiles the effect is almost uncanny: in an instant he seems to become the young Prince of Wales; the clock spins back forty or fifty years and there before you is the personality so many remember. His memory is excellent and he describes the events of many years past in the voice of one perhaps thirty years younger. By an inflection here and a change there, he has a gift for conveying so much more than the actual words spoken. Here was a man once King of Britain and Emperor of India. As Prince of Wales he had been a leader of fashion. Suits tailored in 'Prince of Wales check' were to be found in the wardrobes of most smart men of the day. He had always been an excellent horseman, often pushing himself to the limit. Indeed, he had a bad fall during an Army point-to-point in 1924, and soon afterwards, yielding to pressure from many sources, but primarily in an effort to please Queen Mary, he reluctantly agreed to give up steeple-chasing and turned instead to golf. How then had he become involved in what was at the time widely regarded as the most hazardous of occupations—flying? The Duke had no particular recollection of his first flight, in 1916:

> 'It was before the Battle of the Somme. I don't think I was particularly scared. It was just a new experience.'

Later, while visiting the Italian front in April 1918, he was flown over enemy territory in a Bristol Fighter by Captain Barker, a Canadian pilot. Not long afterwards, Barker was badly shot up in a dog-fight, and this earned him the V.C. Back in postwar London, his arm still in a sling, he met the Prince of Wales at a party. 'Why don't you come and fly with me tomorrow morning?' he invited. 'Let us renew our acquaintance with the air.' The Prince, who was never known to refuse a little excitement, readily accepted the invitation. Of course the newspapers were on to the story and there were pictures of the Prince of Wales being flown by a one-handed pilot. The Duke remembers the subsequent painful interview all too well:

> 'My father saw this in the newspaper and he gave me absolute hell. He said "What were you doing flying with this man?" and I replied, "Well, you know, Father, he is a very gallant man and you gave him the Victoria Cross, so I supposed it was all right to fly with him."'

The flight with Barker undoubtedly angered the King, but it was another quite unrelated incident which put the final seal of disapproval on the Prince's flying activities. Edward's brother, Prince Albert (later King George VI), had taken part in the Battle of Jutland, and on his return from the war in 1919 he transferred from the Royal Navy to the Royal Air Force. He began taking flying lessons at Waddon, an airfield south of London (later incorporated into the old Croydon Airport), and from all accounts these were not progressing very well. He did not really enjoy his flying and

TOP RIGHT The Prince of Wales in a Bristol Fighter with Captain Barker. One of his first flying experiences during the first World War.
Crown Copyright.
RIGHT The Prince of Wales, wearing a parachute over an old overcoat, about to leave Marseilles aerodrome (April 1930).
Associated Newspapers Photo.

was in urgent need of moral support. His older brother, Edward, rallied to the family cause and began to take flying lessons himself. About this time several important personalities woke up to the glamour of becoming a pilot. Among them was the late Sir Winston Churchill, though he had so little natural talent for piloting that he very soon crashed; his flying instructor sustained two broken legs. On learning of the accident, King George V sent for the Prince of Wales and said, 'You see what has happened to Winston. Now this has got to stop.' And stop it did, for a time.

The Prince was not to set foot in an aeroplane again until May 1926, when he flew from London to Paris in an early airliner of Imperial Airways. At the controls was the legendary Captain O. P. Jones, the pilot with the white silk gloves and trim beard who did so much to raise the status of airline pilots throughout the world. The flight sparked off a renewal of interest in aviation for the Prince. Soon afterwards there were more flights, in Bristol Fighters, and in May 1928, the Communication Flight of No. 24 Squadron, based at Northolt, near London, took delivery of an additional Bristol Fighter which was to be used for 'special purposes.' It was a V.I.P. aircraft, the beginning of what later developed into the present-day Queen's Flight.

By now the Prince of Wales was using the aeroplane as a practical form of transport. On 3 April 1929, he flew to Bognor, where his father was recovering from a serious illness. In June of that year he flew to Manston for an R.A.F. athletics meeting, and the following month saw him landing in a field adjacent to Bass's Brewery, to attend the Jubilee of Burton-on-Trent.

An incident on 9 August that year probably impressed him more than any of his passenger flying up to that date. He was taken up in a Moth, a small biplane, which within a few years was to become a household name. It was the first really successful light aeroplane in the world, occupying a place in the air akin to that of the Model T Ford in the world of motoring.

Over the next few weeks the Prince, with Squadron Leader David Don, his personal pilot, spent much of his time in the open cockpits of the little biplane. Exactly when the heir to the throne decided to become a pilot is not certain, but his first dual instruction was recorded as being on 30 August 1929, when he flew with Don from the now defunct Stag Lane airfield to Windsor Park, in Moth G-AAKV. They had visited the de Havilland factory to see the Prince's new Moth, then being built to his order, the first of a not unimpressive line of private aircraft bought by him over

TOP LEFT The Duke of York (later King George VI) with his flying instructor, Lt. Coryton (left) at Waddon Aerodrome where he learned to fly during May 1919.
LEFT The Duke of York settling into the rear cockpit of an Avro 504 while Lt. Coryton (now Air Chief Marshal Sir Alec Coryton) gets into the flying instructor's seat (May 1919).

ABOVE The Prince of Wales with the 1929 British Schneider Trophy team, standing before the Gloster IV biplane.

RIGHT After flying over the Schneider Trophy course. The Prince of Wales during his visit to R.A.F. Calshot (3 September 1929).

the next seven years. He was to become the leading patron of aviation in Britain, and while people marvelled at the thought of a royal pilot, others considered his interest to be quite natural. Had not his grandfather, King Edward VII, championed the motor car when it was at a similar stage in its development?

It was only to be expected that the 'Flying Prince' was news, and typical of the reports of the day was one published shortly after he took delivery of the new Moth, which carried the registration letters G-AALG.

THE PRINCE AND THE MOTH

The Prince of Wales has travelled by aeroplane for so long now that it is not surprising he has bought his own machine. That he should have chosen a Moth is a further tribute to our leading light 'plane, which is now in regular use all over the world. The Royal machine carries the colours of the Brigade of Guards' Club, has a cowl of aluminium, and is upholstered in red leather. Dual controls and instruments are fitted so that the Prince can take over whenever he feels inclined. Landing grounds are being cleared near Windsor and at Sandringham, and it is

the Prince's intention to use the machine on all possible occasions other than for official visits.

Another report drew attention to certain modifications incorporated in the Royal Moth:

The usual space for luggage has been enlarged to accommodate several suitcases, a hat box, golf clubs and sticks.

Throughout the Autumn of 1929, flying lessons in the Moth alternated with passenger trips, usually in the military biplanes of the day with their open cockpits and vast, fabric-covered wings. He could often be seen alighting from their massive airframes, wearing a parachute over a shapeless old overcoat.

The Prince of Wales was known to hold strong views, often to the despair of the politicians, on unemployment, poor working conditions and exploitation of the working man, which were all too common at the time. In the depressed areas of Wales, his concern for their well-being endeared him to the people and made him something of a hero. The British public at all levels regarded the aerial exploits of the Prince with a mixture of admiration and genuine fear for the safety of the heir to the throne.

More than forty years later, in the elegance of that beautiful residence in the Bois de Boulogne, it was not difficult to imagine the Duke of Windsor as he then was, the 'trend-setting' Prince of Wales. Very early in the conversation he put right one mistaken belief which has persisted for many years. It has been supposed that he was never allowed to fly solo and that his instructor, David Don, sat in the aircraft with him on a certain day in late December 1929, pretending to be a passenger. 'Oh, no,' insisted the Duke. 'He climbed out, removed the second control stick and waved me off to do two landings. The second was a bad one!'

At the same time his younger brothers, Henry, later Duke of Gloucester, and George, Duke of Kent, were themselves taking flying lessons and a healthy rivalry developed between them all: 'I seem to remember we had a fiver on who went solo first—or was it just pride?' he added with a not-very-serious touch of self-reproach. Whatever the stakes, the first thing he did was to telephone them in turn and announce 'I've beaten you to it!'

Now the Prince of Wales was using his private Gipsy Moth regularly to attend hunts and golf tournaments, but it was not always possible for Squadron Leader Don, a serving officer, to be spared from duty on these occasions. The Prince needed a personal pilot, and help came from an eminent politician of the day:

'Freddy Guest was a great friend of Lloyd George and Winston. He had once been Minister for Air and he had a 'plane. He said, "I know you're interested in flying and I'm going to do something I wouldn't do for anyone else. I'm going to let you have my pilot."'

'Mouse' Fielden, as he was nicknamed, had flown Guest all over Europe, Africa and the Middle East. He had gained the most varied experience in the Royal Air Force and now he was to be personal pilot to the Prince of Wales. It was an association with the Royal Family which continued until his retirement in 1961. Today Air Vice-Marshal Sir Edward Fielden can look back on his life as a pilot caught up in royal history. There was the Prince of Wales to fly and his Gipsy Moth to look after. He also taught Prince George to fly and sent him solo on 22 June 1930. Not far behind was Prince Henry, sent off solo by Fielden on 12 October that year.

The two Princes eventually owned a Gipsy Moth (G-ABDB) between them and then the three Royal brothers joined that rare species in 'thirties Britain—the private owner-pilot. By now the Prince of Wales was buying and selling his aircraft as others change the family car. He was even buying them in pairs and it seemed natural to ask why? 'I don't know,' he answered, looking rather perplexed at the thought, 'I must have been very flush with money!'

The Duke of York took his initial training with Alec Coryton (now Air Chief Marshal Sir Alec Coryton, R.A.F. retd) and continued his association with the

Private transport de luxe. The Vickers Viastra, a large comfortable twin-engined aircraft owned privately by The Prince of Wales.

R.A.F. at Cranwell, while the Prince of Wales and the Dukes of Gloucester and Kent enjoyed their purely civil flying from Smith's Lawn, a private airfield in Windsor Park. As the Prince of Wales now owned three aircraft, Fielden had to find a more suitable home for them, with adequate facilities for maintenance. Hendon, within easy reach of Central London, was an obvious choice and there the aircraft could be seen, a much-admired trio in the red and blue colours of the Brigade of Guards. Inevitably Fielden's little air force became known as 'The Royal Flight,' although no such organisation existed until the Prince of Wales became King in 1936.

The duties of a Prince of Wales are many and the advent of modern transport has, if anything, added to the task. Even before the emergence of long-distance, high-speed air travel, the Prince had visited more than forty-five countries, covering some 150,000 miles, over a period of six years. He has always liked the company of businessmen and been profoundly interested in commerce—so much so that in 1925, on a tour of South America, he became, in fact, the first Royal salesman for Britain. It was primarily a trade visit and it was demanding work, but he also played hard, often going on to a night club after doing his stint as official guest at banquets.

There were other ways of relieving the tedium of Royal duty. An African safari recommended to him by his brother, the Duke of York, provided more than a little entertainment, especially when he was charged by an elephant on the shore of Lake Albert! He returned to East Africa in 1930, this time armed with nothing more lethal than a cine-camera, only to catch malaria. But the importance of his flying activities to Britain has never been fully recognised. Perhaps he did not gain a great deal of pilot experience himself, although he took every opportunity to fly something new. But he owned a variety of aircraft, from the little Gipsy Moth to the Vickers Viastra, which was almost as large as a Dakota, and these activities helped to make his country airminded at a time when awareness was lacking but desperately needed for the sake of future freedom. How valuable his lead would prove in years to come!

Then, early in 1936 on 20 January, came the death of King George V. He was surrounded by his family, and the last moment of an era came shortly before midnight. The Duke of Windsor took up the story from the moment when he became King:

> 'When my father died we were at Sandringham. I had to go to the Accession Council which must be held within twenty-four hours. The train service was very slow so I had Fielden come up to an airfield nearby and we [the new King and his brother the Duke of York] flew together. I was King then and they made the

RIGHT King Edward VIII inspecting Handley-Page Heyford bombers at R.A.F. Mildenhall. Next to him is Wing Commander 'Mouse' Fielden, later Air Vice Marshal Sir Edward Fielden, Captain of the Queen's Flight.

remark that if anything had happened there would have been two gone. I would have been killed and my brother who would have succeeded me would have been killed too.'

On this sad occasion the new King made additional history by becoming the first British Monarch to fly.

The body of King George V was moved to London, there to lie in state in Westminster Hall. A great crowd filed slowly past the catafalque, while at intervals the guard of officers changed. When the new King and his three brothers took their turn it was past midnight, and as they stood in full dress uniform, heads bowed over reversed swords, few if any of the public could have been aware of their presence.

Edward, Prince of Wales, had become King Edward VIII. His was to be a short and remarkable reign. In his book *A King's Story* he wrote, 'I had no desire to go down in history as Edward the Reformer. Edward the Innovator—that might have been more to the point.'

One such innovation developed naturally from his interest in aircraft: 'There was the Royal Yacht,' he explained, 'and as I was beginning to use aeroplanes as a means of getting around in my official job, I thought there should be a King's Flight.'

So for the first time an aircraft was provided especially for the sovereign, and Fielden became Captain of the King's Flight, an institution that continues to this day, now as the Queen's Flight. The unit occupies a hangar at R.A.F. Benson, in Oxfordshire. From the Captain down to the most junior mechanic it would be difficult to imagine a more dedicated team. There are three Andovers, two Wessex helicopters and a Basset light twin-engined aircraft, all kept in perfect condition. No airline has ever attained such standards of maintenance—indeed none could afford to—and it all originated from King Edward VIII.

But in those pre-war days the airminded King was not at peace with himself. Even before his accession to the throne, there had been moments of doubt when he felt an urge to step down from the line of succession in favour of his brother Albert, Duke of York.

Edward the Innovator was not to rule for long. The whole world knows the story of how the King abdicated, to become the present Duke of Windsor. The various moves—his attachment to Mrs Wallis Simpson, an American lady twice married and facing a second divorce; the restraint of the British press under the influence of Esmond Harmsworth (now Lord Rothermere) and the late Lord Beaverbrook; the battle behind the scenes with the Prime Minister, Mr. Baldwin; the open

RIGHT H.R.H. The Duke of Windsor in his Paris residence, standing before the painting that withstood a heavy landing.
Alan Bramson Photo.

criticism by an English bishop; the efforts of the King's friends, among them Walter Monckton and Winston Churchill, to rally support; the drawing up of the Instrument of Abdication; the final message to his people, broadcast by the B.B.C.: the title 'His Royal Highness the Prince Edward' which the late Lord Reith used to introduce him—these are all part of history. At 2 a.m. on 12 December 1936 the Duke of Windsor (the title suggested by his brother George), left England's shores on board H.M. destroyer *Fury*, bound for France and his Duchess. The curtain had come down.

Whatever suffering they endured in those troubled days is forgotten now in one of the happiest of marriages. The Duke's conversation contained many affectionate references to his wife—'I married a beautiful lady who doesn't like to fly too much.' Apparently the Duchess's concern about flying extends to the Duke, especially where helicopters are concerned:

> 'I've never been in a "chopper"—the Duchess won't let me! A friend of mine was going to take me to see something near New York the other day and we were going in a "chopper." I couldn't hide it from her. "Oh no," she said, "You're not going to go in that, you can go by car."'

The sight of his picture in Garter regalia in the next room brought to mind a bad landing:

> 'We flew in the pouring rain and I had with me James Gunn, the great portrait painter. There is the picture he painted and this picture was in the 'plane. We had a very good trip over, but when we landed at le Bourget the runway was very wet. As we came down, I noticed we were going to overshoot the runway, but instead of taking off again, going round and landing farther back, the pilot tried to turn, and we buckled the prop. A wheel went, and altogether it wasn't very good.'

The conversation turned to his brothers. What could he remember of the Duke of Gloucester?

> 'He and I were very different temperaments. He was mostly in the Army until I left, then I think he had to do one of the "Royal things." He was in the War, then he was the last "pommy" Governor of Australia. He was retiring—but he liked to ride and hunt.'

Closest to him in many respects was George, Duke of Kent, the youngest of the family and perhaps the most talented. He played the piano well and was something of an expert on antiques. The Abdication bore heavily on the Duke of Kent who wept unashamedly when the moment of exile came.

Prince George was a strikingly good-looking young man with an easy manner which endeared him to all, both in Britain and abroad. He and his older brother Henry, Duke of Gloucester, received their early education at St. Peter's Court School, Broadstairs. They were in fact the first sons of a British king to attend an ordinary preparatory school. He entered the Royal Navy in September 1916, first at the Royal Naval College, Osborne, then at Dartmouth, and although he became a midshipman on H.M.S. *Iron Duke* and later served on H.M.S. *Nelson* on the staff of the Commander-in-Chief, Atlantic Fleet, ill-health put an end to his Naval career. In 1934 he was created Duke of Kent and on 29 November that year he married the beautiful Princess Marina of Greece and Denmark, a cousin of King George of Greece and H.R.H. the Duke of Edinburgh. He recorded a number of 'firsts': the first British Prince to attend preparatory school; the first to enter the Civil Service (Foreign

H.R.H. The Duke of Gloucester with The Prince of the Netherlands.

Office, then Home Office). At a later date he became the first British Prince to cross the Atlantic by air, when he flew in a Liberator to Canada and inspected R.A.F. cadets under aircrew training. If the war had not intervened he would have become the first Royal Governor-General of Australia, but on 25 August 1942 fortune deserted the handsome Prince with so much to live for. On that day he became the first British Prince to die in an air crash.

Like his brother King George VI, the Duke of Kent had gained his R.A.F. wings. He was attached to the staff of the Inspector-General of the Royal Air Force. The King had sanctioned a visit to Iceland and shortly after mid-day Air Commodore H.R.H. the Duke of Kent boarded a Sunderland flying boat accompanied by his secretary, his equerry and his batman. The Duke's personal detective escorted him to the flying boat, but for some reason returned to London. There was a crew of ten and the unit Commanding Officer. Fuel for the long flight and depth charges carried in the hope of spotting an enemy 'U' boat made this a heavy Sunderland, and the ensuing take-off from Cromarty Firth in the north of Scotland was a drawn-out affair, prolonged by the smooth glassy water which seemed to cling tenaciously to the hull of the flying boat. They climbed slowly in a northerly direction, following the coast towards the north-eastern tip of Scotland, which had to be reached before they could head out to Iceland.

Far away from the other occupants, in the extreme rear of the hull, Sergeant Andrew Jack sat in his turret, checking first the guns and then the intercom. The pilot acknowledged receiving him 'loud and clear.' It was the last he would hear from anyone aboard that Sunderland. By now they had reached 1,500 ft. and the coast was clearly visible below. Suddenly they entered cloud and he was conscious of the aircraft descending. He thought little of it. The pilot was obviously intent on maintaining visual contact with the ground.

Down below the Sunderland, on the lonely moors, a farmer, David Morrison, heard the flying boat roar overhead:

'As the noise dwindled there was a sudden and tremendous crash followed by an equally sudden silence. My son called other people in the valley and we started to search.'

There was not a lot to be found. The Sunderland was in many small pieces, although the depth charges were still intact. Eleven bodies were found outside the main debris, including that of the Duke of Kent. He was lying quite naturally in the heather,

RIGHT The late Duke of Kent with his children Prince Edward (the present Duke) and Princess Alexandra visiting the Canadian Hospital, August 1940.

almost as though he had gone to sleep. It had been the oldest kind of flying accident in the book—the stuffed cloud, letting down on to high ground—call it what you will, the Sunderland had flown into the top of a cloud-engulfed hill, in the remoteness of Caithness. The Air Ministry communiqué was brief and not entirely accurate:

> The Air Ministry deeply regrets to announce that Air Commodore H.R.H. The Duke of Kent was killed on active service this afternoon when a Sunderland flying boat crashed in the north of Scotland.
>
> His Royal Highness, who was attached to the staff of the Inspector-General of the Royal Air Force, was proceeding to Iceland on duty.
>
> All the crew of the flying boat lost their lives.

All, that is, except Sergeant Andrew Jack. One second he was seated in his little glass-sided turret surrounded by cloud; the next he remembered was walking in the rain on the Scottish moors.

On receiving the news of his brother's death the King immediately sent other members of the Royal family to the Duchess of Kent. Only a month previously their youngest child, Michael Franklin, had been born. It was July 4th, American Independence Day and Franklin D. Roosevelt, the United States President, had been one of the godparents, the first U.S. citizen to give his name to a child of the British Royal Family.

So, after only thirty-nine years, ended the life of the flying Prince, killed on active service. The scene of the crash is marked with a simple cross.

Bereavements of this kind afflict royal families as severely as any others, but it is not a sadness without relief. Sometimes there are children to carry forward the talents, strengths and weaknesses of their forebears, often with an accuracy that is quite remarkable. The Duke of Kent left three children, Their Royal Highnesses Prince Edward, the present Duke of Kent, Princess Alexandra and Prince Michael. In 1962 the Duke of Kent and his younger brother learned to fly in a Chipmunk of the Queen's Flight. Prince Michael was a Sandhurst cadet at the time, intent on an Army career, and with examinations a first priority his flying has not continued. The Duke of Kent is also a professional soldier and in 1970, while stationed in Cyprus, he joined the local flying club and flew Cessnas.

Among the younger generation of the British Royal Family none is more active in aviation than H.R.H. Prince William, elder son of the Duke and Duchess of Gloucester. Prince William of Gloucester is a tall, good-looking young man with an engaging manner and a nice dry sense of humour. Not content with operating a

LEFT H.M. King George VI.

light aircraft from his private airstrip, he is President of the British Light Aviation Centre, an organisation which performs many important functions in aviation. It is responsible for the syllabus of flying training, the testing of flying instructors, safety standards, air racing, aerobatic competitions and a multitude of other activities too lengthy to mention here. In 1971 he also took on the Chairmanship of this busy organisation. In conversation there can be no doubting his genuine enthusiasm for flying and the sincerity of his desire to serve the cause of aviation. In many ways the Prince is performing a service for general aviation similar to that of his uncle, the pre-war Prince of Wales.

After schooling at Eton he went to Cambridge with thoughts of following the example of his soldier father, but at university he developed an interest in flying and applied to join the University Air Squadron, a unit operated by the Royal Air Force for the purpose of encouraging graduates to join the service.

Undergraduates normally spend two years in the U.A.S. Prince William joined in his third year and therefore had to cram one year's flying experience into a short space of time. He set aside three weeks to acquire the necessary fifteen hours' flying experience, including his first solo flight, and to start on the necessary ground training just before going up to Cambridge for his third year. This he achieved, with the help of the Queen's Flight and an instructor from the R.A.F.'s Central Flying School, in the same Chipmunk which had been flown by Prince Philip and was later to be flown by Prince Charles. He did most of this initial flying training at White Waltham, although the 'plane was based at R.A.F. Benson. There was no family opposition when Prince William became interested in flying, possibly because his father had been a pilot in the days before the war, yet surprisingly at that time he was unaware of this.

With university life at an end and a career in the diplomatic service newly started, the aeroplane suddenly assumed a new importance. The Prince was posted to Nigeria and what better method was there to cover great distances, badly linked by surface transport, than in a light aeroplane? He joined the Lagos Flying Club and made regular use of their Cessna 150 and Piper Cherokee aircraft, but there were times when the single engine up front seemed to protest at the vastness of the jungle or the desert below. The consequences of an engine failure were all too obvious—it was no place for a single-engined light 'plane. Prince William explained the situation to his trustees and asked them to buy him a Twin Comanche. This they agreed to do, 'Principally, I think, through a bit of blackmail—I said if they didn't buy me a new Twin Comanche I'd buy myself a second-hand Cherokee.'

Two engines would of course provide the additional safety he needed during his flights over the more remote and inhospitable areas of Africa and there was the added

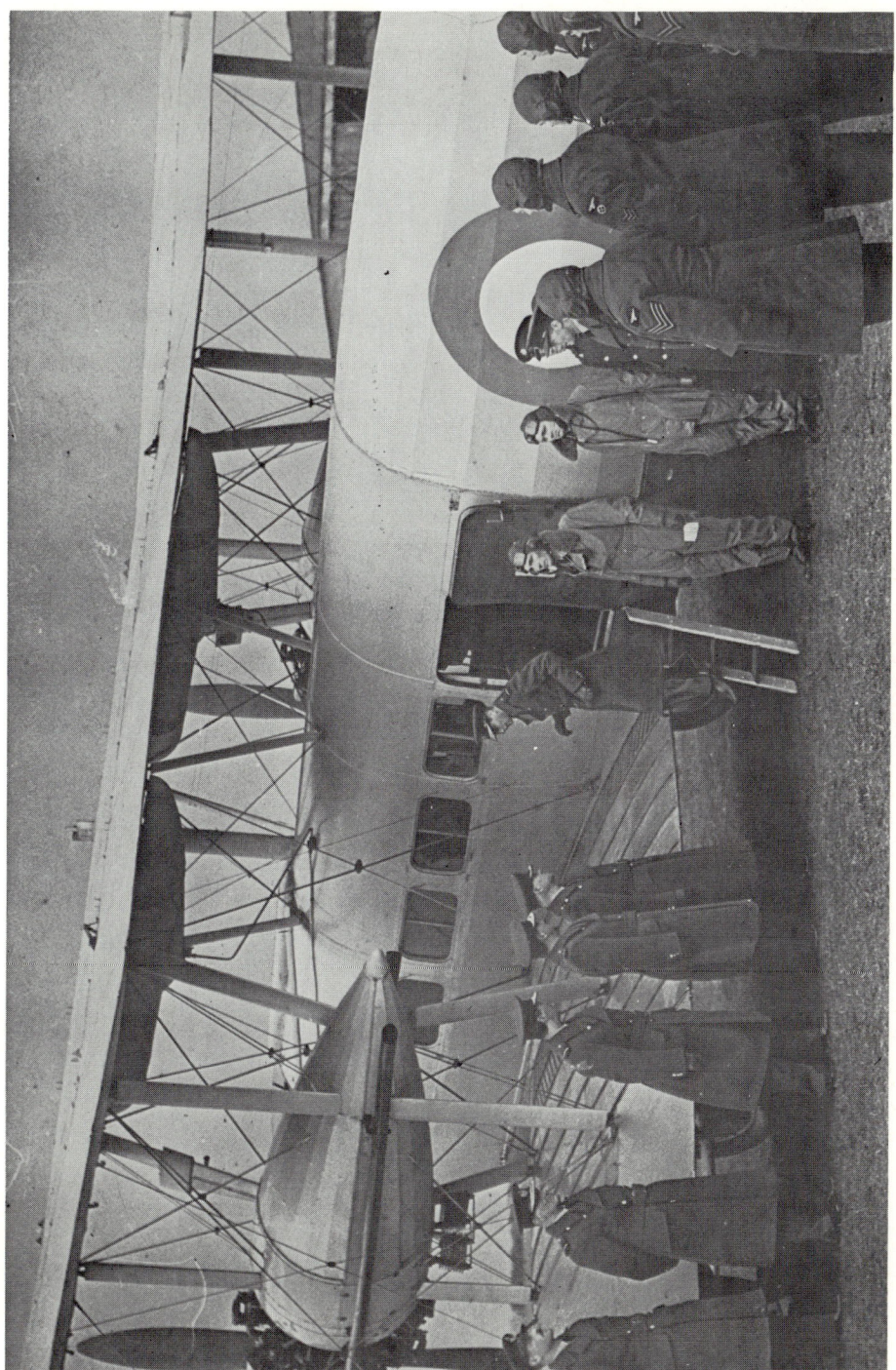

King George VI, visiting R.A.F. College Cranwell, 26 January 1938, seen leaving a Vickers Valentia troop carrier. Examples of these massive biplanes continued flying on communication duties as late as 1943.

charm of a comfortable quiet cabin, a longer range and a cruising speed of up to 190 m.p.h. This was 70–80 m.p.h. faster than the club aircraft.

Prince William's new aircraft was delivered, carrying its rather appropriate Nigerian registration 5N-APW. It was the most complex type he had flown and in a class quite different from the usual run of light aircraft, yet after only a few hours' conversion flying in England, and considerable help from members of the Queen's Flight, he took aboard an old friend, loaded his luggage and set off for Lagos. It was quite an undertaking for a young man with very little flying experience and hardly any at all on a twin-engined aircraft, particularly as there was no second pilot to help when the weather turned sour. At such times the basic task of flying the aircraft becomes swamped in the deluge of many others; radios to tune, instruments to watch, procedures to fly so that you arrive at the correct place at the proper time.

The route chosen for the flight was Malta—Tunis—Marrakesh (Morocco)—Dakar—Robertsfield (Liberia), and it went uneventfully until a line of thunder clouds running out across the sea from the Ivory Coast forced him to turn back. He landed at Tabou, a small airstrip normally used about once a week by a DC3, as torrential rain swept over the airfield and, simultaneously, the tropical night closed in. The value of instrument flying had been convincingly demonstrated by this incident and the lesson was not lost on the Prince. Soon afterwards arrangements were made in Lagos for suitable tuition. There are various ways in which a pilot may practise instrument flying, including the simulator, but sooner or later he is confronted by the real thing, an aircraft so equipped that he is effectively prevented from looking out of the windows. He must then devote all his concentration to the instruments, ignoring every instinct or sensation as it tells him with compelling urgency 'Look out! You are turning right' or 'We must be in a climbing turn.' Throughout the practice, a safety pilot keeps a good lookout for other aircraft and between times offers constructive criticism. For the pilot under training this form of flying is demanding and in the early stages, very tiring indeed.

Lagos had no simulator, so it was that Prince William had his head down, eyes glued to the twitching needles of his flight panel, while to his right sat the head of licensing at the Nigerian Department of Aviation, an Englishman with considerable experience of instrument flying. They had been practising radio approaches into Lagos airport for some 30 minutes when suddenly the privacy of their little world was invaded by a voice from without. It was the air traffic officer in the control tower at Lagos airport. 'What is your position?' he asked. Since Prince William was otherwise engaged, the safety pilot looked out of the window and recognised what was

LEFT H.R.H. Prince William of Gloucester at Bahrein, a refuelling point during his flight to Tokyo.

underneath. He pressed his transmit button and replied, 'We are over the Naval Headquarters,' whereupon Lagos Tower replied, 'We suggest that you leave that area—they have been firing at you for the last 15 minutes.' Prince William had been flying his 'holding pattern' over the guns! He told this story at Kensington Palace and as he spoke the insistent tick of a nearby clock faded in the gathering crescendo of an overflying jet, adding realism to his account of this astonishing incident. Had they really been shooting at him? 'Yes, they were,' insisted the Prince in a voice registering only the slightest trace of disapproval. 'But I didn't notice. I mean they're not very good shots—luckily.'

It should of course be remembered that at the time Nigeria was embroiled in the war with Biafra. Some DC3's were being used by the Biafrans to drop bombs on Lagos from time to time, consequently any unidentified aeroplane, however peaceful, was regarded as a likely raider. If the Nigerian anti-aircraft crews were inclined to shoot first and ask questions afterwards they were perhaps to be excused. On another occasion Prince William loaned his aircraft to a lady who was trying to add a 'twin-rating' to her pilot's licence. It so happened that on the very day she went flying, an aircraft had come over from Biafra and dropped some bombs, so that when the Twin Comanche appeared in the sky it was immediately identified as a 'bomber' and promptly shot at by the ground defence. Fortunately for the heroine of the story she was accompanied by an American pilot, who had flown in World War II and needed no reminding that the little puffs of smoke appearing around them were anti-aircraft shells. He took over the controls, went into a dive and rapidly disappeared behind some trees.

'I've often had difficulty with red tape when flying,' admitted Prince William somewhat plaintively. While many a sporting pilot the world over must have echoed the same complaint, he was thinking more of his experiences in those parts of Africa where anything could happen and very often did. Every possible clearance, diplomatic and military, did not prevent him from being arrested on his return from one flight in Nigeria, to a town called Warri. He was taxiing over to the passenger buildings when a small party of armed guards waved him down. While the propellers continued to turn one of the soldiers opened the door, poked in a loaded pistol and said 'I'm arresting you' in a voice unlikely to enquire if there were any reasons why he should not. There were two Africans sitting in the back of the aircraft, along with Prince William's black Labrador, which eyed the guards with some distaste. It was an incongruous situation and the exasperated Prince answered 'Well, what on earth do you expect me to do, first of all with the aeroplane and secondly with my dog?' The guard, poor chap, had been instructed to arrest the pilot. No-one had mentioned anything about parking aeroplanes or flying dogs and since he was at a loss to answer

Prince William with a Chipmunk of Cambridge U.A.S.

The Prince in the Jet. Prince William alighting from a Gnat advanced trainer.

the Prince took over. 'I suggest you put that gun away and I'll go and park the aeroplane then come back and see you in your office.' Of course it was eventually sorted out and Prince William now makes light of the affair with 'It makes life interesting.' After being at the wrong end of a loaded gun, his comment endows the word 'interesting' with a new richness of meaning.

The end of his engagement in Nigeria was seized upon by Prince William as an opportunity to see new places. He would return home the long way round, flying east to the Sudan, Egypt and the Lebanon, then north-west from the Middle East. There was a civil war in Chad at the time and, mindful of the recent Biafran troubles, he anticipated that the authorities might be more than a little sensitive about strange aircraft. He therefore gave six days' notice of his intention to land at Abeche after visiting a nearby game reserve. On arrival the airport was completely deserted. After an hour a policeman came, was curious about the Nigerian registration on the aircraft and detained Prince William and his passenger until their credentials could be verified. The novelty of being arrested was beginning to wear a little thin.

At Khartoum he picked up an old school friend who was to join him for the remainder of the journey, an act of innocence that spelt trouble farther along the route. They had landed at an airport that shall be nameless, with thoughts of staying the night, when an official noticed that the Prince's companion had no yellow fever certificate and said he must go into the isolation hospital. 'Steady on' said the Prince. 'In that case we'll have all the luggage back in the aeroplane and we'll fly on to Beirut.' He was becoming expert at dealing with red tape, a skill required by all pilots whether Royal or otherwise, and the remainder of the journey to England was fairly routine, apart from plug trouble in one engine shortly after taking off from Luxor.

Back in England, Prince William telephoned the registration office at the Department of Civil Aviation and explained that he wished to have the Twin Comanche transferred from the Nigerian to a British registration. The lady at the other end said she would look at the list and give him the next letters available. There was a brief pause, then she returned to the telephone and, in the most apologetic voice imaginable, gravely announced 'I really don't think your Royal Highness will like this but the next registration available is G-AWOG.' The lady was obviously conscious of Prince William's recent stay in Africa because AWOG was read over the telephone almost as though it was a four-letter word at a vicarage tea-party. 'That's fine' replied the Prince, 'it stands for William of Gloucester.'

It was not uncommon at one time for private owners to ask for a particular registration. With more and more aircraft coming on to the register the Civil Aviation Department has had to discourage this little idiosyncrasy, so that the appearance of WOG on Prince William's aircraft precipitated an indignant letter from another private owner who complained of Royal privilege to the editor of *Flight* magazine. There was of course no question at all of V.I.P. treatment—the chance availability of WOG was purely coincidental.

The Foreign Office decided to send Prince William to Tokyo for his next appointment. Naturally, he wanted to fly there himself. It is a long enough journey from England to Japan in a jet: to attempt it in a light 'plane is something quite different. There are vast barren areas where even the relatively long range of a Twin Comanche becomes stretched in the event of an unexpected headwind leaving insufficient fuel for a diversion. Then there is the Monsoon, a great, damp barrier hanging over the Calcutta area. This steaming grey cloud-mass is not in itself too unpleasant and indeed flying conditions may at times be quite smooth, but here and there, buried in the murk, lies a cumulo-nimbus cloud larger than anything of the kind to be seen in the skies of Europe. Without weather radar it is impossible to avoid flying through them, a really unpleasant experience. The aircraft is thrown around in a most alarming manner and the rain, already heavy, turns into a seemingly impregnable cascade of water. Over sixty-five hours of flying would be involved, much of it over water.

Very wisely, the Prince was persuaded to take with him a professional pilot, although the only time he flew the aircraft was over Syria when, because of the turbulent political situation in that country, it was thought prudent that the Prince should fly by scheduled airline and rejoin his own aircraft at Amman in Jordan. Except for this leg of the journey Prince William did all the flying, including the 250 miles of Monsoon which were well up to expectations!

The flying 'man from the Foreign Office' was certainly unusual in Tokyo. Other than Prince William's Twin Comanche, there were only fourteen privately owned aircraft in the whole of Japan. G-AWOG was also the only non-Japanese registered aircraft to be flown regularly in Japan on internal, as opposed to international, flights at that time. When the time came for his return to England he had ambitious plans to fly home across the Pacific, a venture which would have put the Twin Comanche at the very limit of its range, so it is perhaps as well for the Prince that the project rapidly went off the rails. At the last minute, in the Philippines, his co-pilot was indisposed. Then, at the very time he wanted to fly back, his cousin, Her Majesty the Queen, wanted him to visit Tonga. At this point he decided the fates were against his Pacific flight and resigned himself to being a passenger in a high-flying jet. Now there was the problem of having the aircraft ferried back to England. There was also the serious decline in his father's health, which meant giving up the diplomatic service so that he could manage the family estates. He could probably find room for an airstrip but it would be too small for the Twin Comanche, so all in all it made sense to dispose of it in Japan. Now he has a single-engined Piper Arrow which provides reasonable speed with a comfortable cabin and the ability to fly in and out of the private airfield at Barnwell Manor.

A few moments of conversation with the Prince are enough to confirm his deep interest in flying, not just as President of B.L.A.C. but as a practical pilot with more than 600 hours in his log-book. In his own words:

> 'I think I have been fortunate, perhaps more so than some other members of my family, in that on the whole I have been left alone to do my flying as and when I felt like it. I certainly wouldn't have been able to do what I have done if anyone had been sitting watching over my shoulder.'

For a pilot of his experience the Prince has a lot of long-distance flying behind him and this is an aspect of aviation that continues to fascinate:

> 'I think the greatest kick I get out of flying is going to a new place—and finding it! I remember one occasion when I flew up with some friends to Timbuktu. We'd flown over a tremendous amount of desert without any [radio] aids and we did in fact get to Timbuktu—it's exactly where the map said it was. You know, this can be very satisfactory.'

Certainly it is much more satisfactory than getting lost over the desert, yet no-one should harbour illusions that Prince William is one of those 'press on and damn the consequences' pilots. He described finding a small airfield in the middle of nowhere with a 'sense of relief—I couldn't believe it was actually going to appear.'

As Chairman of the British Light Aviation Centre, Prince William felt he should gain experience in aspects of aviation other than his well-practised long-distance flying. He attended the International Aerobatic Championship meeting when Britain was host to the visiting teams. He flew to Malta and took part in the island's annual Air Rally in 1971. With the 1971 King's Cup he became the first British Prince to fly in an air race. His 'plane came seventh out of the twenty-seven aircraft participating. He has now been elected Chairman of the newly-constituted Aviation Council of the Royal Aero and United Service Club, which deals with all aspects of light aviation, including gliding and ballooning.

Recently he tried his hand at a vintage aeroplane, flying with one of the authors in a Tiger Moth. It was his first flight in a biplane and his introduction to the charms of an open cockpit. He arrived at the airfield without a flying helmet and the only spare one available was a rather grubby-looking affair which he nevertheless accepted

And vintage flying too! Prince William with Alan Bramson after flying a Tiger Moth.

with commendable composure and put on without hesitation. Most pilots used to flying modern aircraft are in for the humiliation of a lifetime when they try a Tiger Moth for the first time. It handles like nothing conceived since the mid-thirties; at first, the Tiger flies the pilot and it is only when pilot masters Tiger that it becomes a delightful little vintage sports car of the air, on a hot summer's day a source of endless fun and enjoyment. Prince William climbed aboard and strapped himself in. The flight that followed is now described by his check pilot:

I had loaned Prince William my old wartime leather flying jacket because he had arrived in his own modern aircraft lightly clothed and would undoubtedly freeze in the open Tiger Moth. As I taxied out for the take-off I acquainted the Prince with one or two of the Tiger's more unpredictable habits. We positioned ourselves at the end of the runway and I asked if he would like me to demonstrate the first take-off but the Prince said he would try one himself, adding that he hoped I would be ready to lend a hand should the old biplane become capricious. I expected the worst. Most pilots used to modern aircraft fly off the airfield in a quite unexpected direction which bears little resemblance to the one intended. This one was straight down the runway. We climbed to a safe height and I asked him to go into a spin. It must have been some years since he had tried one. Unlike the rather insipid spiral that an American trainer will produce, the Tiger Moth enters into the spirit of things with some gusto. I think he was rather taken aback by the sudden dramatic nose-dive lunge, yet when I shouted 'recover' we were back in level flight without fuss. I was impressed. At this point I rolled the Tiger upside down, executed a few other aerobatics, then closed the throttle over the airfield and yelled 'Forced landing—see if you can get it on the ground without using the engine'—and he did. We taxied back to the clubhouse and went in for lunch. Prince William sat at the table looking a little bewildered, wiped his hands over his eyes and burst out 'All that fresh air—I just cannot think clearly.' Fresh air and inverted flying in an open aeroplane seems to agree with him, however, because that afternoon he flew to an important polo match and scored for his team.

Of his other interests the Prince is a keen photographer and in addition to polo, enjoys shooting, skiing and scuba diving, but his deep interest in aviation is important because not content with being a pilot he is at the centre of General Aviation in Britain, giving that neglected and often misunderstood activity Royal support— shades of the pre-war Prince of Wales.

The Duke of Edinburgh

The Infante Don Alfonso, Prince of Spain, jokingly said, 'My Greek relations are not Greek at all. They're Danes—and that really means Germans.' The remark could almost have come from the Duke of Edinburgh. His great-grandfather, King Christian IX of Denmark (1818–1906), married the German Princess Louise of Hesse-Cassel and their son William became King George I of the Hellenes. He married Grand Duchess Olga of Russia who bore him seven children, the eldest destined to be King Constantine I of Greece. Of more immediate interest is the youngest member of the family, Prince Andrew. His wife was Princess Alice of Battenberg, whose family had Polish-German connections.

The disastrous outcome of the 1922 war with Turkey had its repercussions. Five ministers along with the Commander-in-Chief of the Greek Army were tried and shot by a revolutionary council. Lieutenant General Prince Andrew, returned from the campaign and enjoying the peace of Mon Repos, his Corfu home, was summoned to give evidence on the mainland. It was an act of deception, an excuse to get him off the island. He was arrested and held in prison for many weeks before Princess Alice became aware of the situation. Letters sent by her to heads of state appealing for help were in most cases met with polite indifference. King George V of Britain despatched a warship. The events that followed would do justice to any spy thriller. Prince Andrew and Princess Alice were spirited out of Greece along with their youngest child (and only son) Philip. For him, exile meant schooling in Paris followed by a brief period of education in Germany which ended when his headmaster opposed the Hitler regime. The school moved to Gordonstoun in Scotland where Prince Philip became head boy before going on to Royal Naval College Dartmouth. During summer 1939 he was detailed to entertain the young daughters of King George VI, Princess Elizabeth and Princess Margaret.

World War II was a source of particular anguish for Princess Alice. Her brother, Lord Louis Mountbatten (now Earl Mountbatten of Burma), and her son Philip were on active service in the British Navy while three of her daughters were married to German officers.

Prince Philip remained a Greek Prince until after the war when he became engaged to Princess Elizabeth. He then used the surname Mountbatten until his marriage in 1947 when he was created Duke of Edinburgh. His son Charles, Prince of Wales (the heir to the throne) retains the name of Windsor, together with Princess Anne, Prince Andrew and Prince Edward.

RIGHT Marshal of the Royal Air Force H.R.H. The Duke of Edinburgh.

CHAPTER 11

BRITAIN

Like Father, Like Son

As Consort to the Queen, the Duke of Edinburgh cannot choose his own destiny. He has no job as such, yet so many jobs to do. That he is forthright is universally known; that he has little patience with institutional inefficiency is likewise common knowledge; that old institutions are rarely receptive to change is no secret to him, so that these opposing human forces could well have generated something of a constitutional explosion. Yet the Duke has avoided the danger by knowing when to be persistent in his demands. He has refused to become a mere opener of boys' clubs or an inactive patron of this or that good cause. Any charity successful in getting the prestige of his name on its letterhead gets the Duke of Edinburgh as well, not as a sleeping partner, but in the role of Managing Director and an enquiring one at that. He will argue a point to its limit yet never fail to withdraw when proved wrong. His job is what he has made it. Not all of his work is interesting, and while there is no reason why he should involve himself in many of the dull activities that come his way, if the need is there and the cause is worthwhile, all his considerable energy is directed towards its success.

Early in this project, the Duke granted an interview for some twelve months ahead. By that time most of the other interviews had been completed, usually with the utmost punctuality. The one nearest home, unfortunately, made a late start; there was an electric power dispute in progress and trains into London were disrupted. The arrival at Buckingham Palace ten minutes later than arranged did not pass unnoticed. At the Privy Purse entrance a uniformed footman hastily produced the visitors' book, then led the way along the corridors and upstairs, past one or two antiquated passenger lifts with ornate, openwork cages. Inside, the Palace is a light and cheerful place, and the white-painted corridors are covered in red carpet with a simple pale blue design. Buckingham Palace used to be known as Buckingham House and it was not until the reign of George IV that Nash transformed it to its present grandeur. Now it is perhaps as much an administrative centre as the home of the Sovereign—the Duke of Edinburgh was once heard to say that he 'lived over the shop.'

A walk which seemed never-ending terminated in the library ante-room where the footman handed over to a member of the Palace staff who advised the Duke his visitors had arrived, albeit fifteen minutes late. The Duke led the way into the library, lined with books from floor to ceiling. A lower shelf was devoted to painted figurines of Lord Attlee, Field-Marshal Viscount Montgomery and other famous personalities.

From the beginning this was to be a precise, businesslike discussion. Had there been any opposition to his learning to fly, either by the Royal Family or Parliament?

'No. I don't think so. There was no obvious opposition. I think there was a certain amount of misgiving once it was decided, in the sense that every phase of the programme more or less had to be checked over by the Air Council and whenever it came to "Ooh, you couldn't possibly do that!" it had to be argued that this was really part of the course and everybody did it, and so on. There were, I suppose one might say, anxieties, as opposed to opposition.'

Why had he started to fly? The Duke said at once:

'I don't think I really needed any encouragement. I had started flying even before the war, in trainer aircraft, when I was staying with my cousin who was then Crown Prince of Greece—the present King of Greece's father. He was learning to fly—I think in an Avro or something—and I used to go with him occasionally to the place where he was being taught by the Greek Air Force. While he was going with one chap, I'd go with somebody else.'

He revealed that, given a free choice, he would have served in the R.A.F. rather than the Navy. In 1952 he was able to take to the air again, and flying lessons in a Chipmunk started on 12 November at White Waltham, west of London. From the beginning of the exercise Flight Lieutenant Caryl Gordon, his flying instructor, must have doubted whether the honour of training his Royal pupil was compensation for all he had to endure from the authorities above. 'Of course, you know the consequences if any harm comes to Prince Philip,' he was warned on at least three occasions, by those who ought to have known better. No flying instructor needs reminding of the obvious, whether or not his pupil is of Royal descent. On 20 December of that year, Gordon left the aircraft and sent the Duke of Edinburgh on his first solo flight after ten hours dual, which is good by any standards and particularly so, considering the many other topics on Philip's mind. Instructor was never slow to criticise pupil when the occasion arose, even on the day Prince Philip arrived resplendent in the uniform of a Marshal of the Royal Air Force.

Although he now makes light of it, at every stage of his training some authority would refuse to sanction the next step. These constant interruptions, which would have proved tiresome enough to a less vitalistic spirit, were insufferable to the Royal pupil. It had to stop, he demanded, and stop it did after discussions with the Chief of the Air Staff where he is said to have expressed himself in 'forthright terms.'

Of the various rumours that found currency among the flying fraternity, none proved more acceptable than the one about hospitals being alerted whenever he flew. Could there be any truth in the story? The Duke's answer was characteristic:

'It's no good asking me. I haven't a clue. It's just the sort of idiotic thing that some busybody might easily do. Frankly, I don't believe it.'

In a private ceremony at Buckingham Palace on 4 May 1953, Prince Philip was presented with his R.A.F. wings in the presence of the Queen, Sir Edward Fielden, a small group of senior R.A.F. Officers, and Flight Lieutenant Caryl Gordon. Flying is treated by Prince Philip like any of his other activities, with enthusiastic energy and a determination to become expert. He will describe himself as an amateur but few would agree that he is anything less than professional in his approach to the skill.

The Duke of Edinburgh in a Harvard aircraft shortly before receiving his R.A.F. wings (May 1953).

H.M. The Queen with The Duke of Edinburgh watching an R.A.F. fly-past at Odiham (24 July 1953). Next to the Queen in Royal Air Force uniform are The Duke and Duchess of Gloucester. On the extreme right of the picture are The Duchess of Kent and her daughter Princess Alexandra.

He flew whatever came his way, from the little single-seater Turbulent with its Volkswagen engine to the biggest and fastest aircraft. When he felt himself below standard, he was the one to suggest further training, as happened once some years ago, during his tour of South America. Two Herald turbo-propeller aircraft were provided, one for the Prince and his immediate staff, the other as a baggage and supply carrier. Although Prince Philip did most of the flying he was accompanied by Captain 'Bill' Johnson, a very experienced airline pilot who is Flight Manager, Training, with British European Airways. The Prince was dissatisfied with his landings, so taking advantage of a temporary lull in the official programme he arranged for Johnson to give him a short training session at Lima airport. The press saw his aircraft being prepared. 'What's going on?' they enquired. 'Nothing of any consequence' was the evasive reply. Next day the newspaper headlines read CAPTAIN JOHNSON DISSATISFIED WITH PRINCE PHILIP'S LANDINGS. No-one was more amused than the Prince himself.

Included in his 2,000-odd hours as a pilot are over 300 in helicopters. This is a branch of flying he took up with the active disapproval of Winston Churchill. He became something of a trend-setter with helicopters because, despite their ability to land and take-off from a space the size of a tennis court, in Britain at any rate it was

LEFT Looking over a VC10 airliner, The Duke of Edinburgh is accompanied by Sir George Edwards (left) of British Aircraft Corporation.

RIGHT 'Contact'. Prince Philip in a Turbulent single seat light aeroplane being started by his equerry.

a long time before they were operated from anywhere other than airports. How long it would have continued that way before the true (and perhaps only) advantage of the machine was exploited is anyone's guess, but the rule, 'choppers at airports only' was demolished by Prince Philip in 1952. He put it this way:

'Although the Queen's Flight had used helicopters since 1947, six or even five—I can't remember—they weren't for carrying passengers. They were used for mail and things of that sort. In 1953, just before the Coronation, I realised there was a big contingent of Commonwealth troops at Pirbright and a big contingent of Colonial detachments at Woolwich, and no-one had been to see them. I felt that these were quite important people and I reckoned someone ought to show an interest in them. I looked at the thing, and I simply physically couldn't fit it in by normal transport. Then I had a bright idea and asked "What about a helicopter?" We rang up the—well, I won't go into that! What happened ultimately was that the only helicopter available was a Naval Whirlwind and this arrived here and I did the thing, whereupon all hell broke loose, because everybody said "It's against the rules." Well, of course, there weren't any rules; nobody had thought of landing in the Palace garden before. But there was no clearance; we hadn't covered it with everybody who thought they ought to have approved it;

and so on. Eventually some rules were written round it, but that's how it started, and we've been using them ever since.'

Prince Philip obviously enjoys his helicopter flying—'Of course it's an amusing business sort of wriggling your way in, and plonking down where you want to plonk down.' As if to illustrate the point an unmistakable 'chop-chop-chop' was heard in the room. It grew louder, swamping the conversation as a Wessex helicopter 'let down' past the library window and settled on the lawn outside. 'Really idiotic' commented the Duke, obviously amused by it all. 'This is the Wessex coming in—the Prince of Wales going out. I suspect that's what's happening.' Now that he has set the fashion, helicopters are regularly used by most members of the Royal Family. From time to time one may be seen, gleaming in its red paint, on the lawn at Barnwell Manor, with an eleventh-century castle as background. The slight figure of the Duchess of Gloucester will be seen to enter the helicopter and depart on one of her many official engagements.

RIGHT Introduction to a new type of aircraft. Prince Philip entering a Condor at R.A.F. Benson. *Jack Piercy Photo.*
BELOW A Prince and his helicopter.
B.O.A.C. Photo.

The Duke of Edinburgh's enquiring mind has almost become a British institution. The cynics will claim that he has a genius for learning a little about a lot of subjects and that he will discuss these as though he knows it all. Even if it were true, this in itself would be something of an achievement, but in his own right he has set the pace in a great number of activities. Not all of these are of a technical nature, although he was preaching the urgency in a modern world of better scientific education long before most politicians thought of the idea. He was in at the beginning of Wild Life Conservation and this is an activity he shares with Prince Bernhard. With this and the problems of disease and poverty in the world, what did he think of all the money being spent on the moon project?

'Well, I think this is a very difficult line of thought, to say that if you didn't spend money on that you'd spend it on something else. It hardly ever happens this way— that you can suddenly translate an allocation of money from one purpose to another. All allocations of money depend on people's philosophy, what is tolerable in itself, and what is required in itself. I don't think you spend more money on something than you need to, and equally you may spend less than you need to. I wouldn't like to pass judgement on this; this is a thing for the people doing it to judge, and it is so easy if you are not doing it yourself to say, "Well, of course it's all a lot of wasted money." I suppose almost every scientific, technical, adventurous achievement is a waste of money. What possible purpose can there have been in going to the South Pole and spending vast sums of money getting there, or all the money spent getting to the top of Mount Everest—or of all the useless things, if you come to think of it in terms of social progress—if that is your criterion? This applies to masses of other things. In terms of scientific discovery, it is very difficult to argue that if you *can* get to the moon, you *shouldn't* get to the moon. This seems to be wholly reasonable. But, if people are prepared to foot the bill, I think it is a marvellous discovery, in the same way that climbing Mount Everest was a marvellous discovery—not only that you can do it, but that somebody has actually been there.'

Had he experienced any memorable sights while flying? He answered with a feeling born of first-hand knowledge. To him the most beautiful sight in aviation was when the runway lights appear at night after descending through driving rain and low cloud. It seemed appropriate at that moment to enquire if Her Majesty the Queen enjoyed flying. The Duke's answer was brief:

'She doesn't dislike it. For her, it's just a means of getting from A to B. I don't think it gives her any particular pleasure.'

RIGHT In Army uniform at the controls. *B.O.A.C. Photo.*

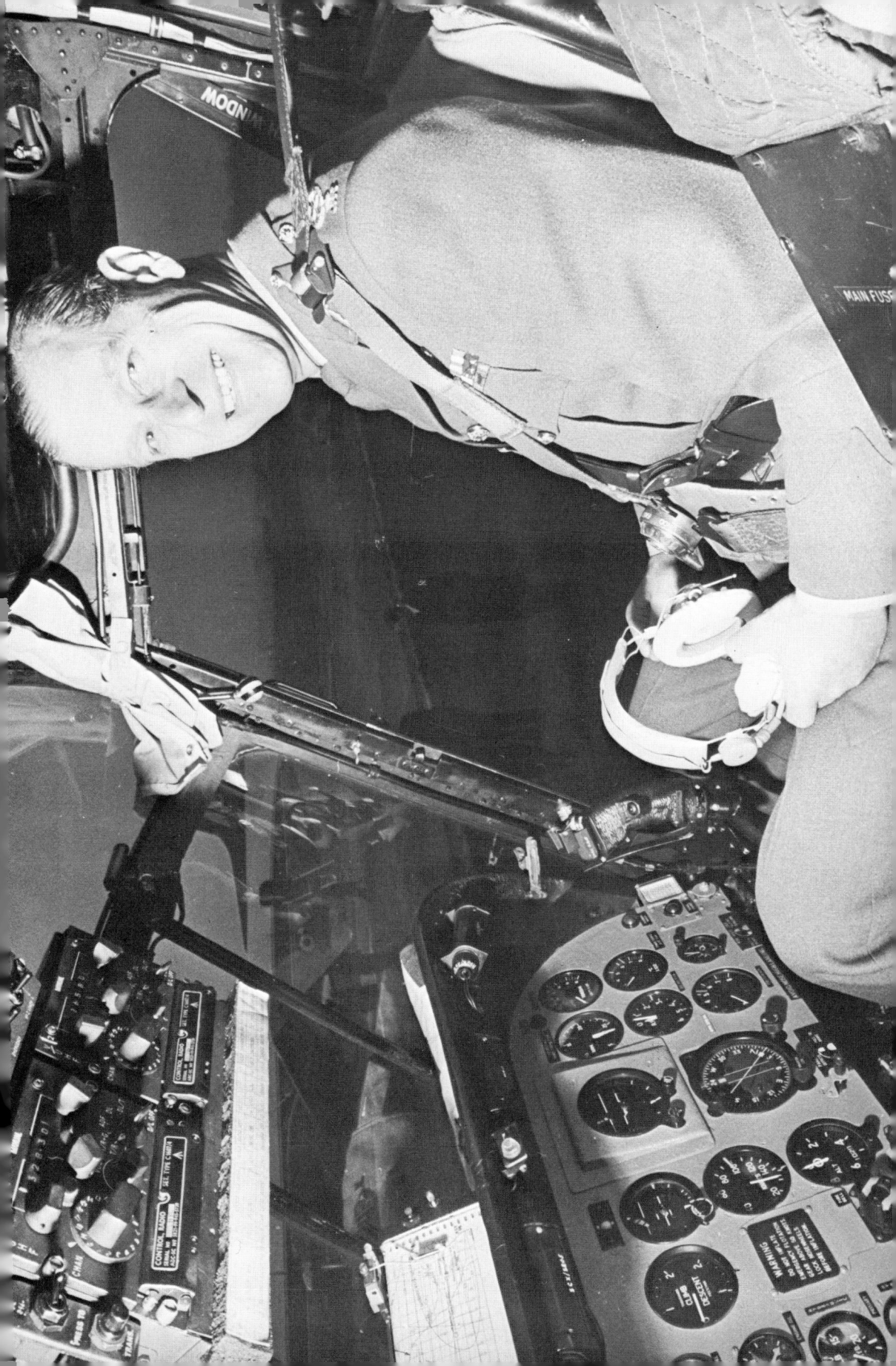

He does a lot of flying in varying conditions, sometimes over remote parts of the world. Did the Queen worry about this? 'I would imagine the anxiety has worn off a bit,' he replied. 'Frankly, I am really much more anxious about my children driving about the roads than flying.'

He is easy to talk to, but hypothetical questions are simply 'not on.' Ask him if he would like to go to the moon, and he will brush it aside. Ask him if he would like to be a King and he will answer 'Well, I'm not—that's a hypothetical question.'

It is hard to imagine any situation where he might display the slightest trace of shyness, but he came nearest to it when reminded of the remark he once made on television about sharing with Prince Bernhard membership of the smallest union in the world. Who was the shop steward? The Prince of the Netherlands had left the answer to Prince Philip. With a grin which betrayed the faintest suggestion of self-consciousness he replied 'We run it on a committee basis!'

The Duke's energy is positively staggering; polo, shooting, flying, sailing, perhaps 300 engagements a year, foreign visits and more than 80 speeches a year, which are never dull and often brilliant. Yet with it all he remains a family man. The Queen and Prince Philip have always devoted time to their children and on no account may these periods be interrupted by anyone. He is particularly good with young people and alert to the peculiar problems that must face his son, the Prince of Wales. 'You can't train a boy to be a King,' he once said, 'but if you train him to be a man, then he can be anything.'

It will come as no surprise that the 'training' mapped out for Prince Charles should have included a strenuous course at the R.A.F. College, Cranwell. The authors met the Prince on his last day as a Flight Lieutenant in the R.A.F. Only a few days previously the newspapers of the world had been full of his parachute descent, the first by a British prince.

A visit to R.A.F. Cranwell is in itself something of an experience. It is set in beautiful Lincolnshire countryside and the grandeur of the historic College building contrasts most vividly with its rural surroundings. To the right of the main entrance is a foundation stone bearing this inscription:

This building was opened by H.R.H. The Prince of Wales, K.G. on 11th October 1934.

The present holder of that title is a tall young man, every inch his father's son. Charles, Prince of Wales, has his father's temperament, his father's voice and indeed many of the Duke of Edinburgh's mannerisms. Superficially he could be the product of any good school, but it requires little time to recognise that here is an exceptional

RIGHT Charles, Prince of Wales.

young man, full of personality, brimming with enthusiasm, while at times revealing a perception and philosophy of life that is quite extraordinary in one so young.

When the infant Charles was born to Princess Elizabeth on the evening of 14 November 1948 public acclaim outside Buckingham Palace was by British standards at the point of near hysteria. The cheering and general noise reached such proportions that an appeal for quiet had to be made through the Palace railings so that Princess Elizabeth could sleep. Progression from infancy to boyhood brought with it the problem of schooling, for this was modern Britain and the more usual royal private tuition gave way to normal schooling. And so to Cheam, where the young Charles acquitted himself by behaving like other little boys and remaining quite untarnished by the blaze of publicity that followed his every move. In his entertaining biography *Philip* Basil Boothroyd explains these pressures as they impinged upon the boy Prince in this day of instant and far reaching communications:

> 'It was hard on an eight year old, and with a more self-important child could have been disastrous to find what you had for breakfast sharing the front page with Suez, Ike's re-election or the Hungarian Rising.'

From Cheam to Gordonstoun (his father's old school), to school in Australia, then on to Cambridge and a spell at Aberystwyth University—the story was always the same; a well liked, well balanced young man of character and a determination to set himself high standards which had to be attained. He was and still is game for anything.

In his office overlooking the airfield the Prince talked of his flying; outside, a long line of immaculate Jet Provost aircraft gleamed red and silver in the hot morning sun, which was now rapidly burning away the early morning mist. Why had he taken up flying?

> 'My father has been flying ever since I can remember, and then I'd always wanted to fly. It was a natural thing to do. I like doing things myself, this is really what it amounts to—I'd much rather fly than be flown, or drive than be driven. I'm not a nervous passenger but it's like anything—I'd rather do it than watch it. I'm always game to try things—that's why I tried parachuting the other day. I wanted to see what it was like.'

He had initially learned to fly in a Chipmunk of the Queen's Flight, then continued with the University Air Squadron while reading history at Cambridge. First solo, that milestone in a pilot's progress, was recalled by the Prince of Wales with some animation:

> 'It was all right until he [the flying instructor] suddenly said "Right, I'm getting out—you're on your own" and then I thought, "God, can I do it? Will I be able

to land the damn thing again?" In fact, the moment he got out it was marvellous. I think the adrenalin going around makes you much more on the ball. Anyhow I went round quite happily, and to my amazement landed first go.'

Though restricted by other duties, the Prince of Wales enjoyed active encouragement while pursuing his interest in flying. Not for him the officialdom that afflicted his father, the Duke of Edinburgh, when he was learning to fly, or the restriction suffered by his great-uncles, the four flying Princes. Was Her Majesty the Queen worried about her pilot son? A personal question, but it was answered with characteristic candour: 'Well, possibly, but she's never said so if she has. I think women do tend to worry perhaps a little bit more,' he said, adding with some pride, 'My parents have never put anything in the way of things I've wanted to do.'

Wednesday, 28 July 1971, must without doubt have put parental trust to the Royal test, for on that day the heir to the throne hooked on two parachutes (one for use

21st Birthday portrait at the controls of a twin-engined Basset aircraft.

on the way down, the other an emergency reserve) then jumped from an R.A.F. Andover flying at 1,200 feet, to land in the sea off the Dorset coast. He had no need to do it; parachuting is not part of an R.A.F. pilot's training, but it was the taskmaster within that urged him on:

> 'I purposely didn't think very much about the whole operation until I got into the aeroplane. Then I did get slightly apprehensive before getting out—they say you should have butterflies. It makes you sharp, I discovered, because out I went, after this hairy Flight Sergeant had shouted into my ear and given me a tap on the shoulder.'

Had he been given a push? The Prince laughed and then described the conversation he had had shortly before entering the aircraft:

'I said, "You're the chap who pushes me out" and he said, "Oh no, sir, no, no, no, we don't do that, we just help." The slipstream is terrific, particularly getting out of the side of an Andover. You appear to be flipped on your back, and of course the next thing I knew my feet were up above my head caught in the rigging lines, which was very odd. Either I've got hollow legs or something, it doesn't often happen. The first thing I thought was, "They didn't tell me anything about this." Fortunately they weren't twisted round the lines and they came out very quickly.'

On the way down there were things to do: the reserve parachute had to be unhooked and lowered on a cord, so that it would hit the sea first and not encumber him; then various straps had to be released in readiness for divesting the parachute on entering the water, which by now was coming up to meet him, relatively speaking. 'The

LEFT Prince Charles in animated conversation, discussing the Phantom jet fighter.
Crown Copyright, 1971.

RIGHT After flying the Nimrod at R.A.F. Kinloss, 21 July 1971.
Crown Copyright, 1971.

Royal Marines were roaring around in little rubber boats underneath and I was out of the water within ten seconds.'

Of course, plenty of people go in for parachute descents. There are clubs for like-minded people who make a sport of it, but this is hardly the point and it is not easy to decide who was the more courageous, the Queen for sanctioning the drop, or the Prince of Wales for making it. He dismissed the episode with

> 'I'm stupid enough to like trying things. I tend to be "Jack of all Trades" and not really master of very much. But in the last five months I've become as near a professional as I will ever get to be on those [he gestured at the Provosts]. This is what has given me such intense pleasure.'

Cranwell had made it possible for Prince Charles to stick at his flying, rather than snatch the odd hour of instruction when circumstances allowed. The staff of the

LEFT Preparing for his parachute jump.
Crown Copyright, 1971.
BELOW Moment of departure. The Prince of Wales has just left the Andover and his feet may be seen caught in the lines of the parachute (29 July 1971).
Crown Copyright, 1971.

college were very much aware that in teaching the Prince of Wales to fly the R.A.F. had a Naval tradition to compete with. Father had seen action in the Navy, while the Mountbatten side of the family had reached the pinnacle of the Admiralty, so that when the Junior Service took Prince Charles into its care things had to be just right. He would go through substantially the same course as his fellows, but special arrangements clearly had to be made. Two of the latest Jet Provost trainers were set aside in a closely guarded hangar, and these were maintained to Queen's Flight standards, even higher than the impeccable servicing achieved at Cranwell. Golden Eagle Flight was the name chosen for the enterprise, and the key figure, Squadron Leader R. E. Johns, instructed the Prince of Wales throughout. He was, of course, acutely aware of the fact that a future King had been entrusted to his care. It was an odd arrangement, with Dick Johns, senior in R.A.F. rank, calling his pupil 'Sir' while the Prince referred to his instructor as 'Dick,' but it worked well, not only because 'Dick' would lose no time taking 'Sir' to task when the need arose but also because the Prince is what he is. Had the Squadron Leader been daunted by his responsibilities?

> 'When he was in the aeroplane he was a pupil. On the ground I was always conscious of the fact that he was heir to the throne and the Queen's son. He said to me his aim was to wear R.A.F. wings and I made clear there would be no short cuts, even prolonged spinning which made him feel ill, but I had to be certain that if he got himself in a fix he could get out of it. Prince Charles has an absolute, complete and utter determination to do his best. I've never had a pupil like it.'

He went solo on the Jet Provost in eight hours compared with the usual ten or twelve, but this does not mean to say that it all came easily. The Royal history graduate from Cambridge did not take readily to the intricacies of jet engines, flight instruments and aerodynamics. Indeed, the best report Cranwell's Chief Flying Instructor could muster was, 'He has a polite interest in technical subjects.' The flying was another matter. He rapidly developed a taste for aerobatics and formation flying, although this very demanding skill created its own problems. He could master difficult formation positions, but the easier 'line astern' troubled the Prince.

> 'My flying instructor said, "Even my most idiotic students manage line astern. You're unique." "I know," I said.'

It was all a question of relaxing; in time the Prince of Wales would slot in behind the leading aircraft and sing 'Mad Dogs and Englishmen' in a convincing Noël Coward

RIGHT Wings Parade at R.A.F. College Cranwell. The Prince of Wales receiving his brevet on 20 August 1971.
Crown Copyright, 1971

voice while his instructor shook with laughter. 'He can mimic anyone,' said Johns. 'You want to watch him—it can be positively frightening at times.'

Other than the special arrangements already mentioned, the Prince of Wales lived like most of his fellow officers under training at Cranwell. Most of the pitfalls of mixing freely in a closely-knit society of this kind were avoided, because the Prince was already prepared for them by his education in Britain and Australia. Nevertheless, when a member of the Royal Family meets the people, the burden of establishing a convivial atmosphere is unequally shared. Witness the way Her Majesty the Queen or the Duke of Edinburgh will put at ease the most reserved of persons. To the casual onlooker it may appear simple. In reality it is nothing of the kind and no-one is more aware of it than the Prince of Wales. How had he coped with the situation when he became a member of the Officers' Mess at Cranwell?

> 'It's always inevitably a slight effort to begin with, you know, to get other people accustomed to someone like myself, because you have to break down a certain amount of prejudice. And I think it has been a strange mixture; I mean, one's life is a paradox, with people expecting you to be as ordinary as everybody else one minute, and yet not; and I hope and like to think I can cope in this particular sense. But it is quite a strain sometimes.'

Can he be the same as anyone else? There was the widely publicised 'April Fool' episode, when Prince Charles 'arranged' an announcement over the loudspeaker system. This invited officers residing in the Mess to deposit their shoes for inspection at some conspicuous place in the care of the porter. Sure enough, an impressive heap of footwear arrived. Unfortunately the Prince had not kept to the rules of All Fools Day, the announcement having been made after the twelve noon deadline for such pranks, and it was a case of beer all round at the Prince's expense. He is not much of a drinker himself but he nevertheless met the fifteen non-commissioned airmen who had maintained his aircraft for a farewell drink at a pub in the local village. His ability to be the Prince of Wales, while at the same time remaining a good mixer, is acknowledged by all who have been fortunate enough to meet him. It cannot be easy to retain these qualities when one is so often in the public glare, but as with everything else he expresses himself with forthright charm on the subject:

> 'Damn it, I'm only twenty-two for a start. I'm not particularly autocratic. If I was autocratic perhaps people would be more frightened, but I don't think it is becoming in someone who is only twenty-two.'

He was leaving a deep impression on his fellow-officers at Cranwell. That evening there was to be a farewell dinner for him. In an unguarded moment, his instructor

Flight Lieutenant H.R.H. The Prince of Wales, qualified R.A.F. pilot.
Crown Copyright, 1971.

admitted that he was going to miss him, 'Not because he is who he is but because he's such a bloody nice bloke!'

The love-hate relationship between the aeroplane and the Press is one that over the years has baffled all pilots, Royal or otherwise. Several dozen aviators may race from England to Canada or Australia and earn no more for their endeavours than a brief paragraph on an inside page. But the aeroplane in trouble is another matter. Any incident, however trivial, will reach the headlines. When that incident involves a Royal pilot, it is news in the best 'man-bites-dog' tradition. There was a lot of fuss on television, and even in the more responsible press, over a quite unimportant event that occurred before the Prince of Wales went into the R.A.F. He was with his instructor, flying a light twin-engined aircraft of the Queen's Flight, and it so happened the Duke of Edinburgh was sitting in the cabin, being flown by his son for the first time. It was while climbing out of R.A.F. Tangmere that another aircraft was seen landing at an adjacent airfield. In effect it seemed to conflict with the general traffic direction, and although there was no potential 'near miss' or any other danger,

Like father, like son. Prince Charles with H.R.H. The Duke of Edinburgh after the wings ceremony. *Crown Copyright*, 1971

the Prince's instructor saw fit to report the matter. The news leaked and the 'other pilot' involved, not unnaturally, made the point that *he* was a professional and well aware of what he should or should not do. Newspaper headlines, radio reports and indeed fact became fantastic, attributing to the poor 'other pilot' every manner of uncomplimentary remark about the 'non-professionals' in the Royal aircraft. It left Prince Charles a little breathless: 'This man annoyed me because he said "Oh, Prince Charles is just a week-end flyer!" That really got my goat.' Then, glancing out of the window in mock anger he added, 'And it happened to be a Wednesday, anyway!'

In discussing his brief stay at Cranwell one cannot but detect that somewhere at the back of his mind is a nagging doubt. Has he really done well or were they just being kind because he is who he is? The best graduates from Cranwell progress to fighters and the Prince of Wales would certainly have gone with them had he not been transferring to the Navy. Yet even this does not seem to have convinced him; he will tell you 'I hope and pray they have been frank.'

Space travel, which he describes as 'A necessary part of man's endless search for the unknown,' presented an opportunity to ask a hypothetical question (his father has no time for these at all) which perhaps more than any other revealed the true character of this remarkable young Prince. If he had the opportunity, would he go to the moon? There was a short silence, then with a grin of resignation he admitted:

'I think I might, not now perhaps but later. If it actually came to the crunch I don't know whether I wouldn't have another think, but if I say these things that I want to do I feel constrained to carry them out. I don't know—I always feel it's worth challenging yourself and this is what I do most of the time—perhaps to too great an extent sometimes—I mean to push yourself too much. But this is my outlook on life and I can't help it—I like doing it.'

* * * * * *

This has been a story of Royal contrasts: between the very young and the very old, the happy and the desperately sad. Some of those interviewed were among the truly great, some have yet to achieve greatness, while others will never be makers of history. Yet in every case it would be a pleasure to meet them as ordinary citizens. And meeting these Royal persons has confirmed that they are subject to the same hopes and fears as the rest of humanity. Linking them all is their enthusiasm for flight, their participation in the brotherhood of the air.

Captains and Kings—pilots all.

Index

Abalshea the Sassarian, 67
Abdullah, Prince of Jordan, 160, 176
Aberystwyth University, 240
A'isheh, Princess of Jordan, 176
Albert, Duke of York, see George VI
Albert, King of the Belgians, 40, 42, 48, 51–62
Albert, Prince of the Belgians, 42
Alexander, Prince of Yugoslavia, 122
Alexandra, Princess, 213, 215, 231
Alfonso XIII of Spain, 9, 12, 17, 21, 22, 24, 28, 29, 33, 190
Alfonso of Orleans and Bourbon, Infante of Spain, 12–39, 226
Alice, Princess of Greece, 226
Alonso, Prince of Spain, 34, 36
Alya, Princess of Jordan, 172
Ambiorix, 45
Ananda Mahidol, King of Thailand, 114, 133
Andrew, Prince of Greece, 226
Anne-Marie, Queen of Greece, 186, 187, 189
Antonescu, General, 151
Aosta, Duke of, 27
Arfa, Madame, 69
Argand, Aimé, 7
Argyll, Duke of, 8
Aryamehr, 84
Arlandes, the Marquis d', 6
Arthur, Wing Commander Cyril, 102
Astrid, Princess of Sweden, 42
Atcherley, Air Marshal, 99
Avicenna, 67

B.E.A., 169
Bacon, Roger, 4
Balbo, General, 31
Baldwin, Stanley, 208
Banks, Sir Joseph, 7
Barker, Captain, 198, 199
Baudouin, King of the Belgians, 40–47
Beatrice, Infanta of Spain, 15, 17, 25, 26
Beaumont College, 16
Beauvechain, air base, 45
Beaverbrook, Lord, 206
Bedouin, 167, 174
Benson, R.A.F. station, 129, 130, 208, 216, 234
Berlin University, 141–143
Bernhard, Prince of Lippe-Biesterfeld, 91
Bernhard, Prince of the Netherlands, 76, 80, 88–113, 186, 211, 236, 238
Bettington, Major Vere, 56
Bhumibol, King of Thailand, 114, 126, 133

Biggin Hill, R.A.F. station, 96
Birabongse, Bhanudeg Bhanubandh, Prince of Thailand, 115–125
Birch, Neville, 50
Black, Dr, 5
Blackburn Aeroplane and Motor Co. Ltd, 180
Bladud, King of England, 2, 3
Bleriot, L., 10, 51
Boin, Victor, 56
Boothroyd, Basil, 240
Brabant, Duc de, see Baudouin, King of the Belgians
Bramson, Alan, 36, 224
British Light Aviation Centre, 216, 223, 224
Busteed, 22

Cambridge University, 126, 137, 216, 240
Carol, King of Rumania, 151
Cartagena, 34
Cavallo, Tiberius, 5
Cavendish, Lord, 7
Chakrabongse, Crown Prince of Thailand, 120
Chakrabongse, Prince Chula, 116, 117, 118, 120, 121, 123, 125, 129
Chakrabongse, Princess Chula, 116, 121, 123
Chakri Dynasty, The, 114, 133
Chanute, Octave, 9
Charles, Prince of Wales, 216, 226, 234, 238–251
Charles, Professor J. A., 6
Chartres, Duc de, 6
Chirasakti, Prince of Thailand, 120
Chulalongkorn, King of Thailand, 114, 116, 118, 126
Churchill, Sir Winston, 12, 70, 90, 201, 205, 210, 232
Cicognes squadron, 56
Claridges Hotel, 188
Congress of Civil Aviation 1921, 24
Constantine I of Greece, 178, 183, 188
Constantine II of Greece, 178, 179, 186–192
Coppens, Willy, 52, 54, 60
Coryton, Sir Alec, 200, 205
Cranwell, R.A.F. College, 25, 206, 217, 238, 246–251
Crombez, Henri, 58, 59, 60
Cuatros Vientos aerodrome, Madrid, 20, 22
Curtiss, Glenn, 10
Curzon, Lord, 58

Daedalus, 1, 81, 180
Dalgleish, Colonel 'Jock', 164, 165, 166, 168, 169, 170, 172
Damian, John, 4
Dartmouth, Royal Naval College, 211, 226
Department of Civil Aviation, 222

Index

Dina Abdul Hamed, 172
Don, David, 201, 204
Don Muang airport, Bangkok, 120, 133
Doolittle, General Jimmy, 102
Douglas, Air Chief Marshal Sir Sholto, 104

EDINBURGH, Duke of, 107, 113, 194, 211, 216, 226–238, 248–250
Edward VII of England, 194, 201
Edward VIII of England, *see* Windsor, Duke of
Edward, Duke of Kent, 213, 215
Edward, Prince of Wales, *see* Windsor, Duke of
Edwards Air Force Base, California, 107
Edwards, Sir George, 232
Elizabeth II of England, 90, 151, 194, 223, 226, 231, 236, 238, 240, 241, 245, 248
Elizabeth, Queen of the Belgians, 52–60
Eton College, 48, 116, 216
Eugen zu Schaumburg-Lippe, Prince, 158
Eulalia of Bourbon and Bourbon, Infanta of Spain, 30
Euler, August, 153, 154
Evans, Sir Arthur, 180

FABIOLA of Mora and Aragon, Queen of the Belgians, 46, 57, 59
Fabyan, 3
Fairoaks aerodrome, 102
Faisal, Prince of Jordan, 176
Farah Diba, Queen of Iran, 77, 78, 79, 84–86
Farman, Henry, 17, 51
Feisal, King of Iraq, 124, 160, 163
Fielden, Sir Edward, 205–208, 230
Filton aerodrome, 76
Fitzroy-Nuffield nursing home, 162
Ford, Henry, 30, 32, 142
Franco, General, 12, 27, 32, 33, 34
Franco, Ramon, 27
Frederik, King of Denmark, 186
Frederika, Queen of Greece, 184
Friedrich Karl, Prince of Prussia, 156
Friedrich Sigismund, Prince of Prussia, 156
Fury, H.M. destroyer, 210

GALLAND, Adolph, 163
Galyani, Princess of Thailand, 133, 135, 136
Gardner, Toni, *see* Muna al-Hussein
Gatwick Airport, 124
Geoffrey of Monmouth, 3
George, Duke of Kent, 194, 204, 205, 206, 210–213, 215
George III of England, 7
George IV of England, 7, 197, 228
George V of England, 56, 194, 197, 198, 201, 206, 226
George VI of England, 60, 61, 94, 105, 194, 195, 198, 201, 205, 208, 212, 216
George II of Greece, 96, 178, 186, 211
Gestapo, 148
Gifford, 8
Gladstone, 15
Gloucester, Duke of, 194, 204, 205, 206, 210, 211, 231
Gloucester, Duchess of, 234
Godard, 7
Gordon, Caryl, 229, 230
Gordonstoun School, 226, 240
Grandi, Count, 31
Greek National Aircraft Factory, 180
Gregory, Ivor, 137
Grimble, Miss, 141

Guest, Freddy, 205
Gunn, James, 210

HAILE SELASSIE, Emperor of Ethiopia, 170
Harrow School, 163
Hashemite Kings, the, 160
Hatfield, No. 1 E.F.T.S., 93, 94, 96, 97
Heidelberg University, 16
Hendon aerodrome, 206
Henry, Duke of Gloucester, *see* Gloucester, Duke of
Henry, Prince of Prussia, 152–157, 197
Hitler, 42, 144, 145, 146, 148, 196
Hoare, Sir Samuel, 25
Hohenzollern, House of, 138
Holkar, Maharaja of, 124
Hussein, King of Jordan, 160–176

ICARUS, 1, 81, 180
Iran, Shah of, 64–86, 108

JACK, Andrew, 212, 215
Jacquet, Colonel, 52, 53, 54
James IV of Scotland, 4
Jeffries, Dr, 7
Jerez, Base Aerea, 14, 37, 39
John, Prince of England, 194
Johns, Squadron Leader R. E., 246
Johnson, Captain Bill, 232
Johnson, 'Johnny', 163
Jones, Captain O. P., 201
Josephine-Charlotte, Princess of the Belgians, 42
Juan, Prince Don, 33
Juan Carlos, Prince Don, 190, 191
Juliana, Queen of the Netherlands, 80, 88, 90, 110
Jusmão, Friar, 6

K.L.M. Royal Dutch Airlines, 92
Kai Kaoos, King of Persia, 67, 68
Kaiser, *see* Wilhelm II
Kao Yang, Emperor of China, 2
Kent, Duchess of, *see* Marina, Princess
Kent, Duke of, *see* Edward, Duke of Kent; George, Duke of Kent
Keyes, Admiral Sir Roger, 56
Kindelan, General, 21, 22
King's Flight, *see* Queen's Flight
Kira, Grand Duchess of Russia, Princess of Germany, 144, 151
Kitty Hawk, North Carolina, 8
Koniev, Marshal, 32
Kurnika, Otto, 145
Kuwait, Sheikh of, 124

LAFFONT, 20
Lagos Airport, 219
Lagos Flying Club, 216
Latham, 19
La Vaulx, Comte de, 51, 52
Leffrinckoucke airfield, 56
Leopold I of the Belgians, 40, 48
Leopold II of the Belgians, 40, 51, 52
Leopold III of the Belgians, 40, 42, 44, 47–51, 61
Lesley, John, Bishop of Ross, 4
Levavasseur, Leon, 18
Liliane, Princess, 42
Lindbergh, Charles, 51
Louis XVI of France, 5

Louis XVIII of France, 8
Louis Ferdinand, Prince of Germany, 139–158
Louis Ferdinand Junior, Prince, 147, 149, 152
Lufthansa, 143
Lunardi, Vincent, 7
Lympne airport, 121

MAGDALENE College, Cambridge, 126
Malan, 'Sailor', 163
Malinovski, Marshal, 32
Maria Christina, Queen of Spain, 12
Marie Antoinette, 5
Marina, Princess, 211, 212, 231
Marlborough College, 126
Marshall's flying school, 120
Mary, Queen of England, 56, 197, 198
Mauvais, 22
Mayne, Lieutenant, 24
Meeus, Jacques de, 54
Metaxas, 178, 183
Michael, King of Rumania, 150, 151
Michael, Prince of Kent, 213, 215
Milton, 4
Minos of Crete, 1, 180
Moëres airfield, 52, 54
Mohammed Reza Shah Pahlavi, *see* Iran, Shah of
Mola, General, 33
Monckton, Walter, 210
Montgolfier, Stephen and Joseph, 5
Montgomery, Viscount, 95, 96, 229
Moore-Brabazon, L., 10
Morrison, David, 212
Mossadegh, 84
Mountbatten, Earl, 226
Mourmelon, flying school, 15, 17, 18, 20
Muna al-Hussein, Princess of Jordan, 172, 176

NAIROBI, airport, 170
Nakhjevan, General Ahmud, 70

OLIESLAGERS, 51
Oliver of Malmesbury, 4
Olympic Games, 186
Orange-Nassau, House of, 88
Orleans, Lieutenant, *see* Alfonso of Orleans
Orta, Tony, 56

PAUL, King of Greece, 178, 181, 183–186, 188, 229
Payne brothers, 101
Perry, Sir Percival, 31, 32
Persia, the Shahs of, 64–86
Peter, King of Yugoslavia, 101, 186
Philip, Duke of Edinburgh, *see* Edinburgh, Duke of
Philippe, Count of Flanders, 40
Pierce, Wing Commander R. J. B., 122
Pike, Wing Commander 'Clem.', 94
Pilâtre de Rozier, Jean François, 6
Pixton, Howard, 22
Potamianos, Wing Commander 'Babi', 183, 184
Prestwick airport, 95
Purachatra, Prince of Thailand, 120

QUEEN'S FLIGHT, 201, 208, 216, 219, 233, 240, 246, 249

R.A.F. Central Flying Schoool, 25, 102, 183, 216
Rama VI of Thailand, 114, 116
Rambai, Queen of Thailand, 122

Reith, Lord, 210
Reza Cyrus, Crown Prince of Iran, 79, 85, 86
Reza Shah of Persia, 64, 69, 70
Richthofen, Baron von, 53
Rickenbacker, 143
Rio Tinto Mines, 35
Roberts brothers, 6
Roosevelt, Franklin D., 143, 148, 215
Rota airbase, 38
Rothermere, Lord, 208
Royal Aeronautical Society, 8

SABENA, 61
Sablatnig, Dr, 156
Salmond, Air Marshal, 25
Sandhurst, Royal Military Academy, 160, 163
Sanghvi, Ramesh, 70
Sanlucar, 15, 36, 39
Saowabha, Queen of Thailand, 118
Schamburg-Lippe, Prince Eugen zu, 158
Schiphol airport, Amsterdam, 88, 112, 113
Seeley, Colonel, 22
Seible, 143
Sheldon, Dr John, 7
Shield, Major, 56, 60
Shun, Emperor of China, 2
Simpson, Mrs Wallis, *see* Windsor, Duchess of
Smith, Sir Roland, 30
Smiths Lawn airfield, 101, 102, 206
Spanish Royal Aero Club, 36
Stampe, Jean, 49, 60, 61, 62

TALAL, King of Jordan, 160, 163
Tassilo, 158
Tatoi airfield, 183
Taylor, 3
Tempelhof airport, Berlin, 143, 145
Toledo Military Academy, 17
Trenchard, Sir Hugh, 25, 60, 196
Truelove, 22

VARANAND, Prince of Thailand, 114, 126–137
Victoria Eugénie, Princess, 12
Villette, Giroud de, 5
Voisin, 51

Walker, H.M. destroyer, 60
Walton, Rev. Edward, 108, 109
Wang Mang, Emperor of China, 2
Waterton, Bill, 76
Wheeler, Sir Charles, 118
Wilhelm, Crown Prince of Germany, 10, 140, 141, 145, 152
Wilhelm II of Germany, 9, 138, 140, 142, 144, 146, 148, 152, 184, 197
Wilhelmina, Queen of the Netherlands, 88, 93, 105
Wilkie, Wendell, 71
Wilkins, John, Bishop of Chester, 4
Willem Ruys, liner, 121
William, Prince of Gloucester, 215–225
William IV of England, 8
Windisch-Graetz, Princess of Austria, 122
Windsor, Duchess of, 197, 208, 210
Windsor, Duke of, 32, 194, 195, 197–210, 238
Windsor, House of, 194
Woodvale, R.A.F. station, 105
Wright brothers, 8, 9, 17, 51, 155

256 Index

Wright, Orville, 8, 10, 152, 156
Wright, Wilbur, 8, 9, 17

YEAGER, Chuck, 35
York, Duke of, *see* George VI of England

ZAHEDI, General, 84
Zein, Queen of Jordan, 160, 163, 174
Zein, Princess of Jordan, 176

Index of Aircraft Types

Aero Commander, 46
Airspeed Ambassador, 169, 172
Aisa I-IIB, 36, 37
Albatros, 156
Andover, 208, 241, 242, 245
Antoinette, 14, 15, 18, 19, 20
Auster, 120, 121, 164
Avro Anson, 184
Avro 504 biplane, 200
Avro Tutor, 183, 229
Basset, 208, 241
Beechcraft, 72, 151
Bristol Boxkite, 22
Bristol Fighter, 56, 60, 61, 196, 198, 201
Bristol-Prier, 22
Bucker Jungmeister, 35
Caproni CA 42 triplane, 57
Caravelle, 134, 176
Cessna, 44, 125, 151, 152, 216
Chipmunk, 134, 135, 164, 215, 216, 221, 229, 240
Condor, 233
Curtiss Jenny biplane, 142
DC3 (Dakota), 108, 128, 129, 145, 19, 192, 206, 219, 220
DC6, 46, 189
DC9, 113
DH4, 62, 196
Dornier 17 bomber, 163, 196
Dornier Super Wal flying boat, 27
España, airship, 17, 20, 21
Euler-Zweidecker, 154
F86 Sabre, 107
F104 Starfighter, 44, 45, 46, 106, 109
Fairey Fox, 49
Farman F40, 52, 53, 117
Flying Fortress, 102, 163
Fokker Friendship, 108, 112, 113
Gloster IV biplane, 202
Gnat, 221
Graf Zeppelin, airship, 34
Gulfstream, 188
Halifax, 163
Handley-Page Bomber 24, 54, 196
Handley-Page Heyford, 195, 207

Harvard 102, 230
de Havilland Dove, 164, 165, 168, 169
de Havilland Mosquito, 102, 129, 130, 196
de Havilland Rapide, 195
Hawker Hind, 195
Hawker Hurricane, 74, 100, 103, 163
Heinkel III, 196
Herald, 232
Javelin, 131, 133
Jet Provost, 240, 246
Junkers, 69, 145
Klemm monoplane, 92, 143
Lancaster, 163, 196
Liberator, 94, 102, 212
Lightning, 80
Link trainer, 108
Lockheed 12 transport, 100
Lockheed Jetstar, 79, 80, 108
Lockheed Starfighter, 45, 46, 106, 107
Lohner, 21, 22, 23
McDonnell Phantom, 75, 80, 242
Maurice Farman, 22
Messerschmitt, 128, 157, 163
Meteor, 74, 131
Mig 17 fighter, 169
Miles Gemini, 122, 123–125
Miles Master, 100
Miles Messenger, 121
Morane-Saulnier, 76
Moth, 31, 201, 202, 204, 205, 206
Nieuport, 22, 52
Nimrod, 243
P47 fighter, 102
Piper Arrow, 223
Piper Cherokee, 216
Piper Cub, 134
Piper Twin Comanche, 216, 220, 222, 223
Savoia 79 bomber, 33, 34
Sikorsky helicopter, 44
Sopwith Camel, 54, 196
Spad biplane, 55, 58, 60
Spitfire, 94, 96, 100, 105, 126, 129, 163, 196
Stearman, 35
Sunderland, 186, 188, 212, 215
SV4 Stampe biplane, 62
T-33 trainer, 134
Tiger Moth, 35, 71, 76, 93, 94, 96, 97, 107, 133, 135, 224, 225
Turbulent, 232
Vampire, 94, 129, 131, 167, 174
Venom, 131
Vickers Valentia, 217
Vickers Viastra, 205, 206
Vickers Viscount, 79
Vickers VC10, 79, 134, 136, 137, 232
Vigilant, 106
Wessex helicopter, 208, 234
Whirlwind helicopter, 233
Wright Flier, 8, 9
Zeppelin, 156
Zodiac, airship, 51